About the Author

Born 1942. Early life in Norfolk, where his father and grandfather helped found the Horsford Cricket Club in the 1940s, which is now the home of Norfolk County Cricket Club. Played for Norfolk at sixteen. At seventeen, played for England Schools at Lords. A year later, disaster struck, when through over-coaching, lost the ability to bowl fast. Fellow of the Institution of Civil Engineers and successful management and involvement of large construction projects in the UK and around the world. Now lives in Holt, Norfolk.

The Second Youngest Wicket Taker for Norfolk Cricket Club

Derek Godfrey

The Second Youngest Wicket Taker for Norfolk Cricket Club

Olympia Publishers
London

www.olympiapublishers.com
OLYMPIA PAPERBACK EDITION

Copyright © Derek Godfrey 2022

The right of Derek Godfrey to be identified as author of
this work has been asserted in accordance with sections 77 and 78
of the Copyright, Designs and Patents Act 1988.

All Rights Reserved

No reproduction, copy or transmission of this publication
may be made without written permission.
No paragraph of this publication may be reproduced,
copied or transmitted save with the written permission of the
publisher, or in accordance with the provisions
of the Copyright Act 1956 (as amended).

Any person who commits any unauthorised act in relation to
this publication may be liable to criminal
prosecution and civil claims for damage.

A CIP catalogue record for this title is
available from the British Library.

ISBN: 978-1-80074-112-6

First Published in 2022

Olympia Publishers
Tallis House
2 Tallis Street
London
EC4Y 0AB

Printed in Great Britain

Dedication

James Godfrey 1972–2020
A fine sportsman, an all-rounder who enjoyed hitting sixes.
He was the kindest of men.

Acknowledgements

I would like to acknowledge the inheritance of the love of cricket encouraged by my grandfather, Ernest Overall, and my father, Gordon Godfrey

Introduction

This story tells the history of the life of a good olde boy who was raised in Norfolk and after many years of living away from the county he loved has finally returned to his roots. This story tells of his upbringing in Horsford, about six miles from Norwich, the developing of his love of cricket through his father and grandfather, leading to his being selected to play for the full county team in 1958 at the age of sixteen and then, a few weeks later, being selected as a last-minute replacement to play for Norfolk at the famous Test Match ground of Trent Bridge where, in clean bowling two Notts 2nd team players he became 'the youngest wicket-taker for Norfolk'.

Since commencing the writing of this book, he has had to change the title to 'the second youngest wicket taker for Norfolk' as a result of 15-year-old Ben Panter, the son of his nephew, Rob Panter, playing for the full Norfolk XI against a strong Nottinghamshire 2nd XI in a 20/20 match on Thursday 10th September 2020 taking his 1st wicket. Ben is a very fine young man who bowls quickly with a superb action and all the attributes needed to bowl well at the highest level. He is currently on Nottinghamshire's Academy, and to be selected at the age of fifteen to represent the full Norfolk XI shows his potential.

The story goes on to tell of the happy time at Loughborough College, now Loughborough University, studying to become a Civil Engineer. The main reason for choosing Loughborough being the excellent facilities for playing cricket and hockey. The happy time at Loughborough was enhanced by the meeting of his future wife, whom he eventually married on July 30th 1966, the day that England defeated Germany at Wembley to win the World Cup.

Having qualified as a Civil Engineer, this required his move initially to Anglesey, then with wife and children to London, North Lancashire, Cape Province, KwaZulu/Natal, Kentucky, Buckinghamshire and finally Norfolk. During all these years of enjoying family life and a challenging career, his interest and love of cricket never waned.

It is hoped that this book will be enjoyed by cricket lovers and all who can appreciate the challenges of raising a family in various parts of the UK and South Africa where it was necessary for the family to be apart for long periods because of the requirements of his chosen profession.

CHAPTER 1

EARLY DAYS 1947–1953

In 1947, our family, the Godfrey family moved from the lovely little Hertfordshire village of Little Munden about five miles from Ware into our new home in Horsford, some six miles from Norwich. At the time I was 5 and my sister Linda was 3. Our family at the time consisted of mum and dad, maternal grandparents and my Uncle Ron.

Our new home was a converted army hut which had been owned and lived in by an elderly and intelligent and slightly eccentric gentleman who we always referred to as Mr Dare. The land that belonged to the home consisted of seven acres of woodland with large oak trees throughout. Mr Dare sold the home and land to my parents on the condition that they would continue to look after him. This was not easy for my mother, who in addition to looking after myself and my sister, and helping my father on the small-holding, was also required to look after this elderly gentleman, who over time became incontinent. The purchase price for the whole was £500, quite a sum in those days.

These early days were memorable for many reasons. I started school in September 1947, at the local junior school in Horsford, where the infant teacher was Miss Roberts, the middle-class teacher was Mrs France and the top class was taught by the head teacher, Mrs Barnell, a lovely Christian lady, very strict but kind and a very good teacher. There were about eighty children in the school at the time.

My parents had decided to start raising chickens and our address became Pinelands Poultry Farm, Holt Road, Horsford. They worked very hard in clearing the land, felling trees where necessary, putting up wire-netting fences and building wooden houses for the chickens. During these early days my grandfather established the most superb garden containing every vegetable and soft fruit. At the same time, he established a lovely little orchard where apples, pears, plums and damsons grew prolifically.

I can recall my dad and granddad talking about the feats of those great cricketers, Denis Compton and Bill Edrich in scoring well over 7,000 runs and thirty centuries between them in 1947. Denis Compton was my dad's favourite cricketer. I never even considered at the time that in a dozen more years Bill Edrich would be giving me the new ball against Cambridgeshire at Fenners in Cambridge. I do not remember any discussions taking place in 1948 when Don Bradman's wonderful team crushed England by 4 wins to none including the debacle at Headingly when Australia chased over 400 for victory and at the Oval where Ray Lindwall bowled England out for 52!

Those early schooldays were happy and memorable, although I shall always remember the terrible afternoon, in 1947, when I was 5, on the way home from school, my good friend, Ivan Keeler, ran across the road straight into the side of a 40-tonne lorry. We were not messing around and Ivan just did not look out for oncoming traffic. The driver of the lorry had little chance to avoid the dreadful accident. I ran home as fast as I could to tell my mother and father what had just happened. The whole village was in such a state of shock at the loss of this grand little boy.

I can recall Mrs Barnell at the morning prayer time the following morning, praying for Ivan and his family. This was such a terribly sad time. The school bought a beautiful commemorative print for Ivan showing Jesus Christ calling "Suffer little children to come unto Me". I can see this beautiful illustration of God's love to this very day.

We had a moment of worship every morning and a final prayer before we left to go home at a quarter to four each evening. We were mostly Anglicans at the time and the few children from Roman Catholic families were allowed to be excused from the time of worship. Visits from the local rector, the Revd. Roberts were regular happenings and with the school being a Church of England School, Christian ideals were the norm. Every Ascension Day, the whole school would trek through the village to the church about half a mile away. These early days helped to form the ethics and principles which were so important throughout the rest of my life, even though I failed so many times to live up to these early teachings.

Life at Horsford School was not difficult and I was keen to learn and being good at mental arithmetic and determined to be at the top of the class stood me in good stead for the challenges encountered in later life. There was intense rivalry with a young lady called Suzanne Bowman, whose father was the local Baker. We competed to be top of the class over the latter years and Mrs Barnell, on two separate occasions offered 20 marks for the first person who could recite the lovely poem "The Owl and the Pussycat" by Edward Lear. There was also another challenge when 20 marks were awarded to the first person who could recite Matthew 4 verse 1-11 when Jesus was tempted by Satan. Again those 20 marks provided the necessary incentive to finish above Suzanne at the top of the class. What excitement when Suzanne became my first ever girlfriend at 13 and I had my first teenage kiss! Suzanne and I managed to pass our 11 plus exams and she went to the Notre Dame School for Girls and I went to the City of Norwich School (referred to as the CNS).

Mrs Barnell, the Headteacher at Horsford, was well respected within the village, by parents and pupils alike. She was a strict teacher who was not afraid to use the cane when necessary. I was the recipient one morning after an incident had been reported to her of stones being lobbed at the roofs of passing cars the previous evening. Mrs Barnell, in front of the whole school called for the culprit to own up. I then received six strokes of the cane with the whole school looking on. To this day I do not consider this punishment had any detrimental effect or caused permanent psychological damage. Others may disagree!

School lunches were not memorable, to say the least, and I can remember being served a horrible piece of fatty meat. When the teacher's back was turned, this was thrown over the back of a tall cupboard. How long this piece of meat stayed there never ceases to cause amazement. There was also another incident which brings back vivid memories. The teachers held a meeting one afternoon in an adjacent room and being one of the oldest in the school I was more or less left to keep some degree of control in the classroom. I took the opportunity of moving the hands of the clock forward by some 10 minutes! This was not noted at the time and so we got out of school a little bit early. Mrs Barnell said nothing that evening but casually mentioned the following morning that the clock had been fixed!

Junior School was a happy experience and on one particular day when I was about 11 years old, all the pupils were invited to bring their pet to school. There was a real collection of mice, rats, hamsters and the like. I did not have a small pet but did own a pony called Blackie which I rode to school, hitched him to the railings around the playground and made a small charge for those who wanted a ride! The journey home was not quite straightforward as Blackie was frightened by a passing car and I had difficulty keeping him under control. Fortunately, a passer-by saw the problem and grabbed the reins and in so doing prevented what could have been a serious accident.

Sports days were always fun and being competitive, a characteristic that remains to this present day, I managed to win several events, including the high jump. The real star of the school was Barry Bridges who was so much quicker than anybody else that we really competed for second place. Barry went on to compete at the All-England Schools Athletics and did exceptionally well in the 100 yards. Barry was a brilliant footballer, combining his speed, ball control and heading ability and after playing for Norfolk Schoolboys was spotted by Chelsea and signed by the club when he was 15 and made his First Division debut when 17 against West Ham scoring his first goal in a 3-2 win.

Barry's superb career saw him play for Chelsea for 8 seasons playing 176 games and scoring 80 goals. On leaving Chelsea, Barry played for Birmingham City, Queens Park Rangers, Millwall and Brighton. His goal-scoring ability was recognised by Alf Ramsey in 1965 winning four caps and scoring his single international goal against Yugoslavia. Barry was selected in the 40-man squad for the 1966 World Cup, and who knows, had it not been for a certain Sir Geoff Hurst he may have been the subject of the famous statement "they think it's all over — it is now" as Sir Geoff's third goal crashed into the German goal!

Those early days at Horsford Primary School were good times, as were those spent on the smallholding, now firmly established as Pinelands Poultry Farm. There were always jobs to do on the farm; collecting eggs and helping with the feeding and watering and cleaning out of the chicken houses. Despite all the things that needed doing on the farm, my love for and enthusiasm for cricket was kindled by the talk about cricket between my father and grandfather. Every year we would go up for a day to one of the Test Matches, either at The Oval or Lords. The first Test Match I saw was the third day of the Oval Test against New Zealand in 1949. Test Matches in those days were played over three days and New Zealand and England were evenly matched and each of the four matches were drawn.

CHAPTER 2

Early memories of Cricket
1949 England v New Zealand. The Oval August 16th. 3rd day.

We would leave Norfolk, in my father's van, at around 4 o'clock in the morning, arriving at the Oval at about seven thirty a.m., find a parking spot, generally on a site that had been cleared from bomb damage and get in the queue. The van was not the most comfortable but was reliable with a top speed of around 50 mph. Dad would go and get something to eat and drink and we were happy as Larry. With other cricket enthusiasts around us the time quickly moved round to the eleven thirty start. The journey home was not quite so exciting and usually finished with my falling asleep in the back of the van.

We managed to see the end of the England innings. Unfortunately, Len Hutton had been dismissed for 206 and Bill Edrich for 100 the previous evening. We were fortunate to see Denis Compton bat for a short time and then Trevor Bailey playing a typical obdurate innings before Freddie Brown and Godfrey Evans enjoying themselves with some lusty blows to bring England to a total of 482. We then saw some very solid batting from Bert Sutcliffe, John Reid and Mervyn Wallace with New Zealand declaring just before the scheduled close of play at 308–9. The English bowling was variable although I was impressed at how fast I thought Trevor Bailey bowled at the time. Although he went for 6 runs an over, he looked, to a seven-year-old, to be lightning quick. Looking back to a few years later in seeing Ray Lindwall and Fred Trueman bowling in 1953, Trevor was almost pedestrian but what a superb servant he was to English cricket.

Looking back through Wisden, it was noticeable that over the three days a total of 1,135 runs were scored and 326 overs bowled. A far-cry from the pedestrian over rate that we are subjected to these days. The over rate throughout the four-match series averaged well over 20 per hour. The New Zealand side was excellent with world-class players of the calibre of Bert Sutcliffe, John Reid, Mervyn Wallace and Martin Donnelly doing the batting and John Cowie, Henry Cave, Geoff Cresswell and Tom Burtt performing admirably with the ball. In this series, New Zealand, as their team has over the years performed so well as they have continued against much larger cricketing nations and lost only a single game during the 1949 tour, against Oxford University. Just think how close New Zealand was to winning the 2019 World Cup and had it not been for a player, by the name of Ben Stokes, born in New Zealand but playing for England, the result would have been so different. The way in which New Zealand reacted after losing that magnificent final at Lords was a real testimony to the sportsmanship and character of this fine nation.

Aug 16th 1949 The Oval 3rd Day England v New Zealand
New Zealand   Match Drawn

First Innings			Second Innings	
B. Sutcliffe c Bedser b Hollies		88	c Brown b Bedser	54
V.J. Scott c Edrich b Bedser		60	c Evans b Bedser	6
J.R. Reid lbw b Wright		5	c Wright b Laker	93
W.M. Wallace c Edrich b Bedser		55	st. Evans b Hollies	58
M.P. Donnelly c Edrich b Bailey		27	c Brown b Bailey	10
W.A. Hadlee c Evans b Bedser		25	c Edrich b Hollies	22
G.O. Rabone c Evans b Bailey		18	lbw b Laker	20
T.B. Burtt c Evans b Bailey		36	c Compton b Laker	6
H.B Cave b Compton		10	not out	10
J. Cowie c Hutton b Bedser		1	c Wright b Laker	4
G.F. Cresswell not out		12	not out	0
L-b 1, w 1, n-b 6		8	B 10, l-b 5, n-b 6	21
		345	**Nine wkts., dec.**	**308**

England First Innings

L. Hutton c Rabone b |Cresswell	206
R.T. Simpson c Donnelly b Cresswell	68
W.J. Edrich c Cowie b Cresswell	100
D. C. S. Compton c Scott b Cresswell	13
T. E. Bailey c Hadlee b Cowie	36
F.R. Brown c Hadlee b Cresswell	21
T.G Evans c Donnely b Cowie	17
J.C. Laker c Scott b Cowie	0
A.V Bedser c Reid b Cowie	0
W.E. Hollies not out	1
D.V.P. Wright lbw Cresswell	0
B 6, l-b 11, n-b 3	20
	482

England Bowling

	O.	M.	R.	W.	O.	M.	R.	W.
Bailey	26.1	7	72	3	11	1	67	0
Bedser	31	6	74	4	23	4	59	3
Edrich	3	0	16	0				
Wright	22	1	93	1	6	0	21	0
Laker	3	0	11	0	29	6	78	4
Hollies	20	7	51	1	17	6	30	2
Brown	5	1	14	0	10	0	29	0
Compton	2	0	6	1	1	0	3	0

New Zealand Bowling

	O.	M.	R.	W.
Cowie	28	1	123	4
Cresswell	41.2	6	168	6
Cave	24	4	78	0
Burtt	24	2	93	0

1950 England v West Indies. The Oval August 14th. 2nd day.

The following year 1950 we did the same journey to the Oval on the 2nd day against the West Indies. This was the famous series when the West Indies showed their strength through the brilliant batting of Weekes, Worrell and Walcott, the superb opening partnership of Rae and Stollmeyer, and of course the brilliance of "those two little friends of mine — Ramadhin and Valentine". John Goddard the only white man in the team captained the side superbly. The West Indies won the series by 3 wins to 1, a most comprehensive result for this team which played glorious cricket throughout the Summer.

August 12-16th 1950 England v West Indies. The Oval
West Indies won by an innings and 56 runs.

West Indies

A.F.Rae b Bedser	109
J.B.Stolmeyer lbw Bailey	36
F.M.Worrell lbw Wright	138
E.Weekes b Wright	30
C.L.Walcott b Wright	17
G.E.Gomez c McIntyre b Brown	74
R.J.Christiani c McIntyre b Bedser	11
J.D.Goddard not out	58
P.E.Jones b Wright	1
S.Ramadhin c McIntyre b Wright	3
A.L.Valentine b Bailey	9
B 5, l-b 11, n b 1	17
	503

England Bowling

	O	M	R	W
Bailey	34.2	9	84	2
Bedser	38	9	75	2
Brown	21	4	74	1
Wright	53	16	141	5
Hilton	41	12	91	0
Compton	7	2	21	0

England 1st Innings

L.Hutton not out	202
R.T Simpson c Jones b Valentine	30
D.S.Sheppard b Ramadhin	11
D.C.S.Compton run out	44
J.G.Dewes c Worrell b Valentine	17
T.E.Bailey c Weekes b Goddard	18
F.R.Brown c Weekes b Valentine	0
A.J.McIntyre c and b Valentine	4
A.V.Bedser lbw b Goddard	0
M.J.Hilton b Goddard	3
D.V.P Wright lbw b Goddard	4
B 5, l-b 6	11
	344

England 2nd Innings

L.Hutton c Christiani b Goddard	2
R.T Simpson b Ramadhin	16
D.S.Sheppard c Weekes b Valentine	29
D.C.S.Compton c Weekes b Valentine	11
J.G.Dewes c Christiani b Valentine	3
T.E.Bailey lbw b Ramadhin	12
F.R.Brown c Stollmeyer b Valentine	15
A.J.McIntyre c sub b Ramadhin	0
A.V.Bedser c Weekes b Valentine	0
M.J.Hilton c sub b Valentine	0
D.V.P Wright not out	6
B 6, l-b 3	9
	103

West Indies Bowling

	O	M	R	W	O	M	R	W
Jones	23	4	70	0				
Worrell	20	9	30	0				
Ramadhin	45	23	63	1	26	11	38	3
Valentine	64	21	121	4	26.3	10	39	6
Gomez	10	3	24	0	8	4	6	0
Goddard	17.4	6	25	4	9	4	11	1

Our day at the Oval saw a fine century from Frank Worrell making 138 in over five hours. This fine cricketer, and gentleman, was subsequently knighted for his service to cricket. West Indies scored 503 in their first innings and we managed to see Len Hutton and Reg Simpson play out the day. Len Hutton the following day went on to score a superb 202 not out from a total of 344. Len continued batting at the start of England's 2nd innings and was quickly out for 2 with England being bowled out for 103 to lose by an innings and 56 runs. Those wonderful bowlers "those little twins of mine" Sonny Ramadhin with 3–38 from 26 overs and Alf Valentine 6–39 from 26 overs were simply too good for the English batting. The West Indians in the crowd were very happy with their team and cheered every good piece of cricket played by both teams. Apart from the brilliance of Len Hutton there was little for the English spectators to cheer for during this Test match. I saw little if any racial prejudice throughout the whole day. This West Indies team were made of such brilliant players, superbly led by John Goddard, with the game played in the right spirit.

It would be wrong not to mention that very special

cricketer and statesman, Sir Frank Worrell. He was born in Barbados in 1924 and made his Test debut against the England team that toured the West Indies in 1947–48. Taking up residence in Lancashire he studied Economics at Manchester University and played for Ratcliffe in the Central Lancashire League. Besides scoring the century at the Oval he made his highest score, 261, in the Test match at Trent Bridge during the same series. He was one of the Wisden Cricketers of the Year in 1951. The following tribute to Sir Frank Worrell is taken, with thanks from Wikipedia.

"Frank Worrell, in 1960, became the first black cricketer to captain the West Indies cricket team for an entire series, thus breaking the colour barriers then found in West Indian cricket. He led the side on two particularly notable tours. The first was to Australia in 1960-61. Both Frank Worrell and his opposing captain, Richie Benaud, encouraged their teams to play attacking cricket. The first Test of the series ended in a dramatic tie. Though West Indies lost the series 2–1, with one draw in addition to the tie, they took much credit for contributing to the series. Such was their performance and conduct on Australian soil that they were given a large ticker-tape parade in Australia at the end of their tour.

On 3 February 1962, Nari Contractor, the captain of the touring Indian team, received a career-ending head injury from a bouncer bowled by West Indies fast bowler Charlie Griffith. Worrell was the first player from both sides to donate blood to the injured Contractor, which saved his life. In 1963, West Indies toured England. They were again popular, and this time they also won the series 3–1, and it was West Indies' second series victory in England after their 3–1 win in 1950.

This wonderful man, Frank Worrell, retired after the 1963

West Indies-England series. When he left professional cricket, he became Warden of Irvine Hall at the University of the West Indies, and was appointed to the Jamaican Senate by Sir Alexander Bustamante. He strongly supported a closer political union between the nations of the Caribbean. He was knighted for his services to cricket in 1964.

Worrell managed the West Indies during the 1964–65 visit by Australia, and accompanied the team to India in the winter of 1966–67. It was while in India that he was diagnosed with leukaemia. He died at the age of 42, a month after returning to Jamaica. A memorial service was held in his honour in Westminster Abbey, the first time such an honour was granted to a sportsman.

A truly great cricketer and a fine gentleman and Statesman."

1950-51 Australia v England. In Australia Radio broadcast

My father and grandfather used to get up early to tune into the end of play summaries each day of this disappointing Test series from an English point of view. Through the crackling and difficult to comprehend transmission, it seemed inevitable that England had a bad day every day. The storm at Brisbane during the 1st Test, produced the nightmare of a sticky wicket with medium paced bowlers making one ball bounce at the batsmen's head and the next shooting along the ground. Despite Len Hutton's brilliant innings of 62 not out in the 2nd innings out of a total of 122, England lost by 70 runs. The Australian bowling attack of Lindwall, Johnston, Miller and Iverson was good enough to bowl the best teams out on a good wicket. On an Australian 'sticky' they were just about unplayable.

The 2nd Test at Melbourne was close with Australia winning by just 28 runs. This was the one Test match that Len Hutton was unable to produce his very best form but thanks to fine bowling by Bailey, Bedser and Brown and a superb innings of 62 by Freddie Brown, England were able to fight nobly. In recognition of Freddie Brown's heroics in this match coupled with his captaincy throughout the series led to a fruit and vegetable vendor in the Melbourne market to shout "Lovely cabbages, with hearts as big as Freddie Brown's" — quite a compliment from an Australian!

In the 3rd Test in Sydney, Australia showed their superiority in winning by an innings and 13 runs. Keith Miller showed his brilliance in scoring 145 not out after having taken 4–37 in England's first innings. England struggled to 290 in their first innings with Len Hutton scoring 62 and Freddie Brown excelling again, batting with superb defiance against a class bowling attack scoring 79. England was bowled out by Jack Iverson, the "mystery spinner" in the 2nd innings for 123. Iverson taking 6–27 in 20 overs.

Although being just 8 at the time I could appreciate the disappointment felt by my father and grandfather as the news came in from the other side of the World. Perhaps this was good preparation for the disappointments that would lie ahead whilst supporting England! As the saying goes "Hope springs eternal".

The 4th Test at Adelaide was won by Australia by a small matter of 274 runs. Australia's first innings was dominated by Arthur Morris who scored a superb 206 out of 371. England responded with 272 of which Len Hutton scored a superb 156 not out, against the awesome speed and skill of Lindwall and Miller and the guile of Johnson, Iverson and Bill Johnston. Australia's 2nd innings of 403-8 declared was dominated by Harvey, that man Miller again and a maiden century for Jimmy Burke. Despite useful scores by Hutton, Simpson and David Sheppard, the future Bishop of Liverpool, England was bowled out for 228.

At last! A victory for England at Melbourne in the 5th Test in February 1951.

There was such joy around Pinelands and throughout the cricketing enthusiasts around the country as England fought nobly against the fine Australian team. Despite fine batting by Arthur Morris and Lindsay Hassett, England limited Australia to scoring just 217 in the 1st innings. Bedser with 5-46 and Brown with 5-49 bowled superbly. What a series these fine cricketers were having.

England then batted heroically after Len Hutton had scored 79 with his usual brilliance, Reg Simpson of Nottinghamshire then played the innings of his life. After seeing England collapse to 213-6, with Simpson then on 80. The following morning England lost Bedser, Bailey and Wright quickly and with Roy Tattersall coming in at 246-9. Tattersall hung on gamely and with determined Lancashire spirit helped Simpson to put on 74 priceless runs and by so doing enabled him to score 156 not out. Australia was bowled out for 197 in their 2nd innings despite good batting by Hassett, Hole and Harvey with the brilliant Alec Bedser taking 5-59 and Doug Wright 3-56.

With Hutton showing his customary brilliance in scoring 60 not out England was able to score the 95 needed for the loss of just 2 wickets. What a celebration in Melbourne and back in England, the first victory over Australia since Len Hutton's 364 at the Oval in 1938. From all accounts this series was contested in the true spirit of this wonderful game. Lindsay Hassett and Freddie Brown were fine captains and good friends, this friendship was extended through both teams. Hutton was the outstanding batsman of the series, scoring 553 runs for an average of 88.83. This was nearly 200 runs more than any other batsman from either side. Alec Bedser toiled gallantly in taking 30 wickets, the highest from either side. Australia deservedly won the series because they had the greater depth in both bowling and batting. Perhaps if Denis Compton had been in the same form as he had been in the previous 1946–47 series the results would have been much closer.

February 23-28 1951. England v Australia. 5ᵗʰ Test. Melbourne. England won by 8 wickets.

Australia

J.Burke c Tattersall b Bedser	11	c Hutton b Bedser	1
A.R.Morris lbw b Brown	50	lbw b Bedser	4
A.L.Hassett c Hutton b Brown	92	b Wright	45
R.N.Harvey c Evans b Brown	1	lbw b Wright	52
K.R.Miller c and b Brown	7	c and b Brown	0
G.Hole b Bedser	18	b Bailey	63
I.W.Johnson lbw b Bedser	1	c Brown b Wright	0
R.R.Lindwall c Compton b Bedser	21	b Bedser	14
D.Tallon c Hutton b Bedser	1	not out	2
W.A.Johnston not out	12	b Bedser	1
J.Iverson c Washbrook b Brown	0	c Compton b Bedser	0
B 2, l-b 2	3	B 2, l-b 8, n-b1, w 1	12
	217		**197**

England

L.Hutton b Hole	79	not out	60
C.Washbrook c Tallon b Miller	27	c Lindwall b Johnston	7
R.T. Simpson not out	156	run out	15
D.C.S.Compton c Tallon b Lindwall	11	not out	11
D.S Sheppard c Tallon b Miller	1		
F.R.Brown b Lindwall	6		
T.G.Evans b Miller	1		
A.V. Bedser b Lindwall	11		
T.E.Bailey c Johnson b Iverson	5		
D.V.P. Wright lbw b Iverson	3		
R.Tattersall b Miller	10		
B 9, l-b 1	10	L-b 2	2
	320	**2 wkts**	**95**

England Bowling

	O	M	R	W	O	M	R	W
Bedser	22	5	46	5	20.3	4	59	5
Bailey	9	1	29	0	15	3	32	1
Brown	18	4	49	5	9	1	32	1
Wright	9	1	50	0	15	2	56	3
Tattersall	11	3	40	0	5	2	6	0

Australia Bowling

	O	M	R	W	O	M	R	W
Lindwall	21	1	77	3	2	0	12	0
Miller	21.7	5	76	4	2	0	5	0
Johnston	12	1	55	0	11	3	36	1
Iverson	20	4	52	2	12	2	32	0
Johnson	11	1	40	0	1	0	1	0
Hole	5	0	10	1	1	0	3	0
Hassett					0.6	0	4	0

A victory at last for England against this fine Australian team. Prior to this victory the last time that England had beaten Australia was in 1938 at the famous "Hutton" match at the Oval when England won by an innings and 579 runs.

It is perhaps fair to say that over the history of England-Australia Test matches, Australia has generally been able to produce cricketers with that "something extra" in skill and determination. Whilst England has produced many magnificent players, Australia has been able to produce great cricketers of the ilk of Spofforth, Trumper, Bradman, Grimmett, O'Reilly, Lindwall, Miller, Warne, McGrath, Border and more recently, Smith, Johnson and Starc, all capable of winning matches by their own skill.

Test cricket is tough and especially so between Australia and England. There is however always a place for the game to be played in the right spirit and examples of this will always be remembered far more than the awful examples of bad taste that have crept into the game over recent years. The picture of Don Bradman and his team warmly congratulating Len Hutton at the Oval in 1938, the English team at the Oval in 1948 giving three cheers for Don Bradman on his final appearance, Rodney Marsh's recall of an English batsman in the Centenary Test and Adam Gilchrist's decision to walk reflects the true spirit of cricket.

My father and grandfather were so encouraged at last by England's victory at Melbourne and could perhaps look forward to the Ashes series of 1953! My experience of supporting England had certainly been whetted.

Minor Counties v South Africans at Norwich, September 5th–6th, 1951

As a family we did not manage a visit to Lords or the Oval to see South Africa play England in the Test matches. We did however manage to see the 1st day of the match between the Minor Counties and South Africans played at the famous old ground owned by Colman's at Lakenham in Norwich. There was added interest insomuch that Nigel Moore of Norfolk was representing the Minor Counties. Nigel Moore had first played for the county at the age of 17 in 1947 and went on to play for Cambridge University in 1952. The Cambridge University team in 1952 was possibly one of the strongest ever and with the likes of David Sheppard, Peter May, Ramon Subba Row and Gerry Alexander providing the batting strength and John Warr, Cuan McCarthy and Robin Marler the bowling strength, Nigel Moore could nor secure his place in the team. He did however gain his Blue for golf. He continued to bat superbly for Norfolk until 1964. Scoring 7 centuries with great style and also took 74 wickets. His top score was 163 v Buckinghamshire and best bowling v Hertfordshire in taking 5–27 at Croxley Green. When he let himself go, he was able to bowl very quickly.

Getting back to the game on 5th/6th September 1951 I will always remember the speed at which Cuan McCarthy bowled that day. Whilst Michael Melle, also bowling very quickly in taking 6–51, it was McCarthy who really made the impression that day. Nigel Moore was dismissed for 17 in the 1st innings and 11 in the 2nd innings.

The South Africans had a fine team out for this match, with the superb world-class players such as Eric Rowan, Jackie McGlew, Roy McLean, Jack Cheetham, John Waite, Russell Endean, Hugh Tayfield and Michael Melle and Cuan McCarthy. Despite losing the Test series 3–1 to a very good English team, South Africa played with style and went onto compete against the very strong Australian team in 1952–53 in Australia drawing the series 2–2 and establishing themselves as perhaps the best fielding side ever. Missing from the South African team at Norwich was "Tufty" Mann the slow left arm spin bowler who had Frank Mann, the England captain in the 1948–49 tour of South Africa, tied up in knots with his superb bowling in one of the Test matches. This prompted John Arlott, the Prince of all radio commentators to make the classic statement that this was a perfect example of "Mann's inhumanity to Mann!"

September 5, 1952 South Africans v Minor Counties Norwich South Africans win by innings and 23 runs

Minor Counties

T.W.Tyrwhitt-Drake (Hertfordshire) c Waite b McCarthy	4	b McGlew	12
J.F.Mendl (Oxfordshire) c Tayfield b Melle	6	b Tayfield	39
B.H.Belle (Suffolk) b Melle	48	c Tayfield b Mansell	17
B.A.Barnett (Buckinghamshire) c Waite b Melle	1	c Rowan b Tayfield	7
J.A.R.Oliver (Bedfordshire) c Cheetham b Melle	5	c Waite b Mansell	12
N.H.Moore (Norfolk) c Rowan b Melle	18	c Fullerton b Mansell	11
J.H.Hastie (Buckinghamshire) c Tayfield b Mansell	29	c McCarthy b Mansell	0
A. Coxon (Durham) c McLean b Melle 22 b Tayfield	0	b Tayfield	0
A. G. Coomb (Durham) b Mansell	23	b Tayfield	5
B.Shardlow (Staffordshire) not out	4	not out	4
S.M. Norcup (Staffordshire) c McLean b Tayfield	7	c Endean b Mansell	2
B 10, l-b 5	15	B 4	4
	182		**113**

South Africans

E.A.B.Rowan st. Barnett b Hastie	73
D.J.McGlew st. Barnett b Shardlow	40
R.A.McLean st. Barnett b Shardlow	3
J.E.Cheetham not out	114
J.H.B.Waite c and b Shardlow	18
G.M. Fullerton c Moore b Coxon	19
P.N.F.Mansell c Norcup b Coxon	0
W.R.Endean c Moore b Coxon	7
H.Tayfield st. Barnett b Hastie	36
M.G.Melle did not bat	
C.N.McCarthy did not bat	
B 3, l-b 2, n-b 3	8
8 wickets declared	**318**

South African Bowling

	O	M	R	W		O	M	R	W
McCarthy	15	5	31	1		4	0	10	0
Melle	24	6	51	6		9	0	32	0
Tayfield	10	2	36	1		14	6	26	4
Mansell	22	5	47	2		12.1	1	24	5
McGlew						3	0	16	1
McLean						1	0	1	0

Minor Counties Bowling

	O	M	R	W
Coxon	24	2	102	3
Norcup	17	1	67	0
Coomb	13	3	29	0
Shardlow	21	4	80	3
Hastie	5.3	1	12	2
Oliver	4	0	20	0

England v India at The Oval August 15, 1952

As usual, with my father and grandfather we arrived at The Oval at around seven thirty on the morning of the 2nd day. We saw some rather tedious batting from England in advancing their score from 264–2 to 326–6 in a full morning's play. Sir Geoffrey Boycott would have revelled in such frolicking at this pedestrian run rate! As lunch was being taken the heavens opened, perhaps to relieve the crowd of the tedium experienced in the morning. The ground was awash with water running through the ground and the streets adjoining. We were absolutely drenched, and my father decided that there would be no more cricket that day and we set off back to Norfolk. It was then decided that we would call into some relations in Little Munden near Ware. The TV was on and we were amazed to see that the Test Match had restarted at five o'clock. England had declared with their score at lunch, and by five thirty India's score was 5 wickets for 6 runs. Fred Trueman had taken 2 wickets and Alec Bedser had taken 3 wickets. India "recovered" to 98 all out with Trueman finishing with 5–41 and Bedser 5–48. The game ended with no cricket on the Saturday and only sixty-five minutes on the Monday, before finally being abandoned on the Tuesday.

August 14-19 1952 England v India. The Oval Drawn
England
L. Hutton	c Phadkar b Ramchand	86
D.S.Sheppard	lbw b Divecha	119
J.T.Ikin	c Sen b Phadkar	51
P.B.H.May	c Manjrekar b Mankad	17
T.W.Graveney	c Divecha b Ghulam Ahmed	13
W.Watson	not out	18
T.G.Evans	c Phadkar b Mankad	1
J.C.Laker	not out	6
A.V.Bedser	did not bat	
G.A.R Lock	did not bat	
F.S.Trueman	did not bat	
	B 10, l-b 2, n-b 1	13
	6 wickets declared	**326**

India
V.Mankad	c Evans b Trueman	5
P.Roy	c Lock b Trueman	0
H.R.Adhikari	c Trueman b Bedser	0
V.S.Hazare	c May b Trueman	38
V.L.Manjrekar	c Ikin b Bedser	1
P.R.Umrigar	b Bedser	0
D.G.Phadkar	b Trueman	17
R.V.Divecha	b Bedser	16
G.S.Ramchand	c Hutton b Bedser	5
P.Sen	b Trueman	9
Ghulam Ahmed	not out	2
	L-b 3, n-b 2	5
		98

India Bowling					**England Bowling**				
	O	M	R	W		O	M	R	W
Divecha	33	9	60	1	Bedser	14.5	4	41	5
Phadkar	32	8	61	1	Trueman	16	4	48	5
Ramchand	14	2	50	1	Lock	6	5	1	0
Mankad	48	23	88	2	Laker	2	0	3	0
Ghulam Ahmed	24	1	54	1					
Hazare	3	3	0	0					

Fred Trueman bowled beautifully in this, his first series. In the 4 Tests he took a total of 29 wickets at 13.31 apiece. Alec Bedser managed 20 wickets at 13.95 apiece. The Indian team did not seem able to compete against the skill and hostility of these fine bowlers. Fred Trueman had taken 8–31 in the 3rd Test at Old Trafford. With his beautiful action combined with natural aggression and fearsome pace England had unearthed a bowler who would compete with the very best over many years and serve this country with such skill and passion. More will be said of this great bowler later. Fred Trueman was the real inspiration behind my wanting to bowl quickly and many was the time in later years did I imagine during my running into bowl that I was indeed the great man himself!

This series of Test matches against India was made memorable also for the calling up of Vinoo Mankad from the Lancashire League where he was playing for Haslingden. Whilst he had not been originally selected for this series, he was picked for the 2nd Test at Lords and produced the most magnificent performance imaginable. He scored 72 in the Indian 1st innings and 184 in the 2nd innings and bowled 73 overs taking 5–196 in England's 1st innings and a further 24 overs in the 2nd innings conceding just 35 runs. Over 250 runs and bowling close to 100 overs was remarkable and has not been improved on by any other cricketer in the history of the game. Despite the heroics of Vinoo Mankad, England won by 8 wickets after a superb 150 by Len Hutton and a swashbuckling century by Godfrey Evans before lunch on the 3rd day.

1953 The Ashes Year

Having heard my father and grandfather getting excited and encouraged at England's final Test victory at Melbourne in the 1950–51 series where Len Hutton, Reg Simpson and Alec Bedser had performed so heroically, and with new exciting talent in Fred Trueman, Tom Graveney, Brian Statham and Tony Lock, there was a fair degree of optimism in the Godfrey family for England to regain the Ashes after such a long time. What a superb Test series this turned out to be! England and Australia both had players who could truly be regarded as great. For England, Len Hutton, Denis Compton, Alec Bedser, Trevor Bailey, Jim Laker and Johnny Wardle all stood out whilst several others performed so well at various stages during this wonderful series. Brian Statham, Fred Trueman, Tom Graveney and Willie Watson all played notable parts during the series.

There has never been a poor Australian team, and over the years the pulling on of the famous "Baggy" cap has inspired so many wonderful Australian cricketers. The 1953 team was out of the top drawer. The batting of Arthur Morris, Lindsay Hassett, Neil Harvey and Keith Miller was truly excellent. The batting was well supported by the brilliance of possibly the finest set of all-rounders ever to have played Test cricket, namely Richie Benaud, Alan Davidson and Ron Archer. The fielding by Australia throughout the series was brilliant with several miraculous catches being taken.

The bowling was led by possibly the finest new ball attack up to that time in Ray Lindwall and Keith Miller, both of whom were fast, accurate and with the ability to bowl bouncers, yorkers and slower balls at will, all combined with movement in the air and off the seam. What a fearsome challenge for any batsman at the time. This superb opening pair was well supported by Bill Johnston who was able to bowl left arm quickly or slow orthodox dependent on the needs of the team and conditions of the wicket. These fine bowlers were supported by Alan Davidson, Ron Archer and Richie Benaud. This bowling attack would have challenged any team over the years and the English batsmen during this series had to perform heroically on several occasions to survive and eventually to win the series at The Oval at the final Test.

1953 England v Australia at Lords 26th June 2nd Test. 2nd Day

It was with great excitement that my father, grandfather and I set off from Horsford at around four o'clock on the morning of 26th June to see the 2nd day of the Test match at Lords. The 1st Test of the series had been played at Trent Bridge where England was left with needing a further 130 runs to win with nine 2nd innings wickets left and Len Hutton and Reg Simpson having put on 94 in an undefeated partnership. Some could say this was a moral victory for England, but who knows? England had scored 120–1 in 58 overs and bearing in mind they had been bowled out for 144 in the 1st innings, nothing could be guaranteed. Alec Bedser had bowled magnificently at Trent Bridge in taking 14 wickets for 99 runs over the two innings.

We arrived near to Lords at around seven o'clock and as usual found a parking space not far away. Long queues were already forming, and we had a bit of an anxious wait until the gates were opened at around ten o'clock. Having gone through the turnstiles we discovered that there were no seats left! An absolute potential disaster, but lo and behold, the authorities decided that we could, with several hundred others, sit on the grass at the Nursery End of the ground. Being eleven years old at the time, this was not a hardship, but thinking back this could not have been too comfortable for my grandfather, who was well into his sixties at the time. With our being allowed to sit on the grass at this famous ground this meant bringing in the boundary ropes thereby slightly reducing the playing surface and rounding off the corners of this famous old ground. Health and Safety did not exert too much control in those days and there was little need to worry about crowd control!

There was a real buzz around the ground as Australia resumed their 1st innings at 263 for 5. They lost wickets regularly during the morning's play adding just 83 runs for the last 5 wickets, including Lindsay Hassett who after scoring a century on the 1st day had to retire through cramp. The morning's play was made memorable by a beautiful innings from Alan Davidson who finished with 76 before being superbly caught by Brian Statham off Alec Bedser. Davidson hit one 6 and thirteen 4s. Alec Bedser again, as he was to do so through the whole series, bowled superbly to finish with 5–105 off 42 overs and was well supported by Johnny Wardle taking 4–77 off 29 overs.

The England innings did not start too well with Don Kenyon being well caught by Alan Davidson off the superb Ray Lindwall for 3 with the score at 9–1. What followed was possibly the finest batting seen for many a year at this lovely old ground. Len Hutton, surely the best batsman in the World at the time, and Tom Graveney withstood the fine bowling of Messrs Lindwall, Miller, Johnston, Ring, Benaud and Davidson to add 168 to take England to 177–1 at the close. Whilst being only 11 years old at the time I will always remember the speed of Ray Lindwall and the cover driving of both Len Hutton and Tom Graveney. As Wisden quoted "The sight of England batsmen giving free rein to their strokes brought undisguised delight to many who had bemoaned the lack of aggression in so much Test cricket. The spectacle was glorious to behold"

We had enjoyed the most wonderful day. The weather was perfect, and the cricket matched the occasion for a day at Lords. The bars were all heaving and being 'good olde Norfolk boys' we did not want to get into long queues for highly priced drinks and being thrifty we found a groundsman's tap round the back of the Mound Stand and survived on Adam's Ale for the day. We set off back to Norfolk after close of play knowing that we had seen a very special day of cricket.

Whilst not being at Lords on the following days we followed avidly the progress on the wireless. The cricket that followed on the 3rd and subsequent days was quite memorable. In the first over of the 3rd day, that great fast bowler, Ray Lindwall bowled Tom Graveney for a superbly made 78, thereby bringing in Denis Compton to partner Len Hutton. These two premier batsmen of England had to withstand the superb and spirited attack led by Lindwall and

Miller. What a battle this was! On this instance the England champions prevailed and added 102 runs. Hutton took his score to a magnificent 145, thereby reaching 2000 runs against Australia and Compton scoring 57. The latter English batting struggled against the brilliance of Lindwall who finished with 5–66 and the innings finished at 372. From 279–2 this was disappointing.

The Australian 2nd innings was memorable for a fine century from Keith Miller and 89 from Arthur Morris and a belligerent 50 from Lindwall in forty-five minutes. What a great cricketer this man was? Bedser with 3–77 and Brown with 4–82 kept Australia in check, although they still managed to score 368 leaving England to get 343 to win with one hour remaining on the 4th day and the whole of the final day. What followed was memorable as part of the wonderful history of cricket played between England and Australia. In that fateful hour before close of play Ray Lindwall dismissed Len Hutton for 5, Don Kenyon for 2 and Bill Johnston dismissed Tom Graveney, leaving England at 12 for 3. This could easily have been 12–4 when Watson, the new batsman was missed in the leg trap shortly after.

The final day was one of great drama and will go down as witnessing one of the great survivals of Test cricket. Compton, with Watson, batted for 90 minutes on that final morning to score 33, before he was dismissed by Bill Johnston, with the score at 73 for 4. At this stage the situation still looked desperate for England. However, "cometh the hour cometh the man" as George Hirst once may have said to Wilfred Rhodes some decades before, or was it Alec Bedser to Cliff Gladwin in the famous match against South Africa at Durban in 1948 when a single was needed off the last ball with just two wickets left? The final ball struck Gladwin on the pad and Bedser ran for all his worth to ensure an English victory.

Getting back to the Lord's Test of 1953, when Trevor Bailey joined Willie Watson England still had to withstand the full might of this superb Australian bowling attack to draw the match. What heroics took place over the next four and a half hours. Bailey and Watson combined Yorkshire grit with southern determination and high degree of skill and courage and withstood the Australian attack whilst adding 163 runs. Whilst the scoring rate was slow the excitement never wavered for a minute and when Bailey was dismissed England was still faced with thirty-five minutes to see out time. This was achieved by trenchant batting from Brown and Evans with England needing a mere 60 runs to achieve a most unlikely victory! Australia needing just 3 wickets and the ball turning square would probably have been the likely victors. Who can tell what would have happened in this wonderful game called cricket? Certainly, in this 1953 Lords Test neither side deserved to lose. This game had everything, superb batting, brilliant bowling, batting collapses, fighting recovery, brilliant fielding and above all wonderful sportsmanship from all involved.

1953 Second Test Lords June 25th–30th ENGLAND v AUSTRALIA match drawn

Australia

A.L.Hassett c Bailey b Bedser	104	c Evans b Statham	3
A.R. Morris st Evans b Bedser	30	c Statham b Compton	89
R.N.Harvey lbw b Bedser	59	b Bedser	21
K.R.Miller b Wardle	25	b Wardle	109
G.B.Hole c Compton b Wardle	13	lbw b Brown	47
R.Benaud lbw b Wardle	0	c Graveney b Bedser	5
A.K. Davidson c Statham b Bedser	76	c and b Brown	15
D.Ring lbw b Wardle	18	lbw b Brown	7
R.R.Lindwall b Statham	9	b Bedser	50
G.A.Langley c Watson b Bedser	1	b Brown	9
W.A.Johnston not out	3	not out	0
B 4, l-b 4	8	B 8, l-b 5	13
	346		**368**

England Bowling

	O	M	R	W	O	M	R	W
Bedser	42.4	8	105	5	31.5	8	77	3
Statham	28	7	48	1	15	3	40	1
Brown	25	7	53	0	27	4	82	4
Bailey	16	2	55	0	10	4	24	0
Wardle	29	8	77	4	46	18	111	1
Compton					3	0	21	1

England

L.Hutton c Hole b Johnston	145	c Hole b Lindwall	5
D.Kenyon c Davidson b Lindwall	3	c Hassett b Lindwall	2
T.W.Graveney b Lindwall	78	c Langley b Johnston	2
D.C.S.Compton c Hole b Lindwall	57	lbw b Johnston	33
W.Watson st Langley b Johnston	4	c Hole b Ring	109
T.E.Bailey c and b Miller	2	c Benaud b Ring	71
F.R.Brown c Langley b Lindwall	22	c Hole b Benaud	28
T.G.Evans b Lindwall	0	not out	11
J.H.Wardle b Davidson	23	not out	0
A.V.Bedser b Lindwall	1		
J.B.Statham not out	17		
B 11, l-b 1, w 1, n-b 7	20	B 7, l-b 6, w 2, n-b 6	21
	372		**7 wickets 282**

Australia Bowling

	O	M	R	W	O	M	R	W
Lindwall	23	4	66	5	19	3	26	2
Miller	25	6	57	1	17	8	17	0
Johnston	35	11	91	2	29	10	70	2
Ring	14	2	43	0	29	5	84	2
Benaud	19	4	70	0	17	6	51	1
Davidson	10.5	2	25	1	14	5	13	0
Hole					1	1	0	0

The Test at Manchester was badly affected by the weather, although that Prince of Left handers, Neil Harvey scored a beautiful 122 out of 318 and Alex Bedser again taking 5 wickets, this time for 115 runs in 45 overs. England responded with 276 of which Len Hutton scored 66 and Denis Compton 45 and Godfrey Evans 44. In their 2nd innings Australia was caught on a treacherous wicket and lost 8 wickets for 35, shades of a "sticky" at the Gabba some years before, Wardle 4 wickets for 7 runs and Laker, 2 wickets for 11, and Bedser with 2 wickets for 14 were superb and England again emerged with a further honourable draw.

The 4th Test at Leeds ended with Australia being in the driving seat, needing a mere 30 runs with 6 wickets standing. Len Hutton was bowled second ball by the brilliant Lindwall in front of the Yorkshire crowd of 30,000. Stunned silence around the ground. England struggled to 167 with only Tom Graveney batting well in scoring 55. The brilliance of Lindwall in taking 5–54 in 35 overs kept the scoring rate to around one and a half runs an over. Australia responded with 266 and Neil Harvey with 71 and Graeme Hole scoring 53 being the main contributors. The lion-hearted Alec Bedser taking 6–95 never for one instance letting Australia off the hook, thereby restricting Australia's lead to 99. What a great series this wonderful bowler was having! England's 2nd innings was again a struggle against the fine Australian attack. Lindwall and Miller bowled 100 overs between them conceding 167 runs whilst taking jointly 7 wickets. With Edrich scoring 64 and Compton 61 and fine efforts from Laker and Bailey England was bowled out for 275 in an innings of 168 overs, thereby leaving Australia to get 177 in one hour and fifty-five minutes. Australia went for the runs with great boldness and much skill and with 45 minutes remaining only 66 runs were needed for victory with 7 wickets in hand. Enter Trevor Bailey, who had performed so nobly throughout this series. Bowling off his long run and directing his attack outside the leg stump he conceded a mere 9 runs in 6 overs during the final forty-five minutes, to leave Australia a mere 30 runs short of their target. Trevor Bailey had been instrumental in preventing Australia from being two up in this series, thereby retaining the Ashes which they had held from 1934. Thanks to Bailey's efforts England had survived and were able to go into the final Test at The Oval all square.

1953 England v Australia at The Oval 18th August 5th Test. 3rd Day

There was much excitement as we managed to get into this famous old ground at around 10 o'clock. We were seated at the Vauxhall End near to the entrance opposite Harleyford Road, in what appeared to be a full ground. Australia had scored 275 on the 1st day with Hassett scoring 53 and Lindwall 62, against an English bowling attack which included Freddie Trueman for the first time in the series. How nobly Trueman had bowled in dismissing Harvey, Hole, DeCourcy and Lindwall for a cost of 86 runs. England responded with 237–7 at the end of the 3rd day against an Australian attack that was determined to hold on to the Ashes. Len Hutton, as was the norm in this series, batted superbly in scoring 82 in three hours and forty-five minutes. England then slipped badly until that man again, Trevor Bailey, put down his anchor and steadied the ship being 35 not out at close of play.

We then saw the most superb day of Test cricket. Tony Lock was out quickly in Lindwall's 2nd over without adding to the score leaving England at 237–8. We then saw Bailey at his very best with that classic forward defensive stroke time and time again thwarting the hostility and brilliance of

Lindwall, Miller and Johnston, not to mention Davidson, Archer and Hole. He was well supported, initially by Fred Trueman with whom 25 precious runs were added and then by Alec Bedser with whom 44 runs were added for the last wicket, thereby giving England the precious lead of 31 runs. Every run was cheered with equal recognition for the superlative fielding by Australia. Trevor Bailey was finally bowled by Ron Archer for a priceless 64, worth a century at any other time.

The next hour or so was the deciding period for the whole series and perhaps since the end of the War in 1945. Hutton allowed Bedser just 3 overs and Trueman only 2, before bringing on Laker and Lock, those superb spinners who were so familiar with the wicket at The Oval. How well these two wonderful bowlers responded. In a period of 14 minutes Australia lost 4 wickets, the cream of their batting, for a mere 2 runs. To witness Australian batting collapsing in such a manner was unbelievable for both my father and grandfather and even at the age of 11, I could share their excitement. With Australia at 61–5 Hassett decided to instruct his young batsmen to go on the offensive and how well they responded! At tea the score had shot up to 131–6. The tea-break brought England the respite it needed and soon after wards Australia was bowled out for 162, Archer scored 49 and Davidson 21. This left England needing 132 runs to regain the Ashes for the first time in nineteen years. Lock had taken 5 wickets for 45 and Laker had taken 4 wickets for 75.

England went into bat on the evening with fifty minutes remaining, Hutton and Edrich added 24 runs with comparative ease until Hutton was run out. What disaster for the full crowd of mostly England supporters? Edrich and May safely saw

England through to the close at 38–1. May continued to stay with Edrich until the score reached 88 on the final morning.

Denis Compton then joined Bill Edrich, with a further 44 runs needed. These two fine cricketers who had played so many wonderful innings together for both Middlesex and England, withstood the might of the wonderful Australian bowling to knock off the runs. Australia, never for one instance until Hassett and Morris bowled the final two overs, gave an inch and England's scoring rate was just about 2 runs per over.

1953 Final Test The Oval August 15th-19th ENGLAND v AUSTRALIA. England win the Ashes after 17 years.

Australia

A.L.Hassett c Evans b Bedser	53	lbw b Laker	10
A.R.Morris lbw b Bedser	16	lbw b Lock	26
K.R.Miller lbw b Bailey	1	c Trueman b Laker	0
R.N.Harvey c Hutton b Trueman	36	b Lock	1
G.B.Hole c Evans b Trueman	37	lbw b Laker	17
J.H.de Courcey c Evans b Trueman	5	run out	4
R.G.Archer c and b Bedser	10	c Edrich b Lock	49
A.K.Davidson c Edrich b Laker	22	b Lock	21
R.R.Lindwall c Evans b Trueman	62	c Compton b Laker	12
G.R.Langley c Edrich b Lock	18	c Trueman b Lock	2
W.A.Johnston not out	9	not out	6
B 4, n-b 2	6	B 11, l-b 3	14
	275		**162**

England Bowling

	O	M	R	W	O	M	R	W
Bedser	29	3	88	3	11	2	24	0
Trueman	24.3	3	86	4	2	1	4	0
Bailey	14	3	42	1				
Lock	9	2	19	1	21	9	45	5
Laker	5	0	34	1	16.5	2	75	4

England

L.Hutton b Johnston	82	run out	17
W.J.Edrich lbw b Lindwall	21	not out	53
P.B.H.May c Archer b Johnston	39	c Davidson b Miller	37
D.C.S.Compton c Langley b Lindwall	16	not out	22
T.W.Graveney c Miller b Lindwall	4		
T.E.Bailey b Archer	64		
T.G.Evans run out	28		
J.C.Laker c Langley b Miller	1		
G.A.R.Lock c Davidson b Lindwall	4		
F.S.Trueman b Johnston	10		
A.V.Bedser not out	22		
B 9, l-b 5, w 1	15	L-b 1	1
	306	**2 wickets**	**132**

Australia Bowling

	O	M	R	W	O	M	R	W
Lindwall	32	7	70	4	21	5	46	0
Miller	34	12	65	1	11	3	24	1
Johnston	45	16	94	3	29	14	52	0
Davidson	10	1	26	0				
Archer	10.3	2	25	1	1	1	0	0
Hole	11	6	11	0				
2nd Innings Hassett	1	0	4	0				
Morris	0.5	0	5	0				

Looking back over the series after many years and having obtained a far better understanding of the game and the true spirit of cricket, I will always remember the superb bowling of Ray Lindwall and Alec Bedser, the brilliant batting of Len Hutton and the tenacity and skill of Trevor Bailey. What was also remembered was the sportsmanship of the two teams with both captains, Hassett and Hutton being genuine friends and speaking with such grace as they addressed the crowd on the final day. There was no need for the ridiculous sledging that is so common these days. The thoughts of sledging those great players such as Ray Lindwall, Keith Miller or Freddie Trueman are quite amusing, and the responses would have been interesting to say the least! A long stare in those days would have been just as effective as the inane remarks one hears these days.

After nineteen long years, and in Coronation Year, England had finally regained the Ashes. Whilst we still lived in an age of austerity there was much to celebrate in 1953 with Sir Edmund Hillary and Sherpa Tenzing Norgay finally conquering Mt. Everest and Sir Gordon Richards winning the Derby on Pinza. Great Britain and the Commonwealth was beginning to build its way out of the horrific effects of the 2nd World War and with the Coronation of our young Queen there was the beginnings of a new era ahead.

1954 England v Pakistan at The Oval, 16th August 4th Day

I do not remember very much of the cricket played in this match. From later reports it appears that England had rather underestimated the strength of the Pakistan team and in particular the skill of Fazal Mahmood who took six wickets in each innings and Mahmood Hussain who shared the wickets in England's 1st innings. A low scoring game saw England losing by 24 runs. England in their wisdom left out Trevor Bailey and Alec Bedser for Frank Tyson and Peter Loader, who in no way let England down. The lower "tail" starting after Tom Graveney at number five could only score a total of 62 runs in the whole match. A sign of things to come where England has generally been vulnerable to batting collapses. Nevertheless, Fazal had bowled superbly as he did throughout the series, in taking 20 wickets at 20.40 apiece.

With my getting involved with cricket at school and village the Test match against Pakistan was the last watched for many years.

CHAPTER 3

HORSFORD CRICKET CLUB — Early days

Cricket was such a part of my early days and having mentioned previously, the conversation around the table varied between the glorious year of 1947, when Denis Compton and Bill Edrich had their wonderful year in scoring over 7,000 runs and 13 centuries and amassing over 2000 runs against the fine South African team and the crushing of the English team at home in 1948 and away in Australia in 1946–47 and again in 1950–51. From those early days the impression gained was that perhaps Australia was indeed a better team than England.

I was made aware of what a fine player my grandfather had been in his early years starting in the 1920s and continuing right through between the wars. My Father, who can never be regarded as a decent player, was keen and appreciated this wonderful game. My grandfather, Ernest, was a lovely man who had spent over two years in the trenches in the First World War, yet never wanted to talk about his experiences, although we were later to discover that out of a group of about thirty men, only two survived this dreadful war. He worked as a gardener for the Hanbury family in Little Munden and played cricket for the village before and after the First World War right up to the time when we moved to Norfolk in 1946.

My grandfather was a very gentle person, apart from the times when he had a cricket ball in his hand. He bowled left arm at a good pace and for well over thirty seasons he took over 100 wickets in about twenty-two games every year at around 4 runs per wicket. Looking through old newspaper cuttings he regularly took 6 or 7 wickets every innings, the majority clean bowled. He played regularly for Hertford Town having to cycle nearly eight miles each way and was invited to play for the full Hertfordshire County team in the Minor Counties Championship. His employer was not sympathetic to allowing him time off to play and so his talent could not be appreciated at the higher level. He regularly performed well against the top teams in the county when playing for Hertford Town. His other loves in life were my grandmother and bell-ringing. He and his bell-ringing team would regularly ring for a period of four hours and the Belfry at the Parish Church at Dane End was testimony to Ernest's achievements.

  He and his friends would travel, by train from Ware or Hertford, up to Lords or The Oval to see Middlesex or Surrey or on occasions England play. He talked with such admiration for the truly great players that graced this wonderful game during the 1920s and 1930s. His favourite batsman was Sir Jack Hobbs, yet spoke glowingly of Herbert Sutcliffe of Yorkshire, Frank Woolley of Kent, Phillip Mead of Hampshire and Patsy Hendren of Middlesex. His favourite bowlers were Hedley Verity of Yorkshire and Harold Larwood of Nottinghamshire. I am not sure if he saw Sir Don Bradman actually bat but he had no doubts that "he could play a bit!" He talked much about the great Australian fast bowlers, Ted McDonald and Jack Gregory, and those superb Australian spinners Arthur Mailey, Clarrie Grimmett and Bill O'Reilly. The way in which Ernest spoke about cricket was the spur for my enthusiasm of this game loved by many over the centuries and throughout the World.

Establishing of Horsford Cricket Club

The Club was founded in 1947 by four very good friends who spent many evenings in the local public house, The Brickmakers, discussing the prospects of forming a Cricket Club in Horsford. The four individuals involved were Don Rayner, a sales representative for a tarpaulin company who was the first captain of the club and for many years the mainstay of the club. In support of him were Gordon Godfrey, my father. and Wilfred Wilkinson who were both small holders involved in animal husbandry. The last and fourth member of the group was Horace Bowman, the local baker.

The initial challenge the four individuals were faced with was "where are we going to play?"

To this challenge my father said "right, I will go and ask the local Squire of the Manor".

Off he went to the Manor House where he was graciously met by Sir Richard Barrett-Leonard who asked my father "and how can I be of help?"

My Father said, "Well Sir, we would like to start a cricket club and need a field."

Sir Richard was delighted and replied along the lines "what excellent news, you can have the field coming into the estate, but it will cost you the grand sum of ONE SHILLING per year!"

This was reported back to the others and work immediately commenced in laying the first wicket. My grandfather with his experience was very involved and I can remember that several tons of Marl from Nottinghamshire were obtained and rolled into the ground to help to bind the surface together. I can also remember my father persuading the driver of a road roller involved with the new road opposite the ground to assist in the early rolling of the pitch. This was a bit of a disaster as the ground was too soft for the weight of the roller, some seven tons. Whilst the roller provided the compaction required, it did initially leave ridges running down the line of the wicket! Considerable time was required to iron out the ridges but at least we had a well compacted wicket on which we could play cricket.

The outfield was cut with a gang-mower borrowed from the local council. My Father and a friend built the initial wooden pavilion, which was subsequently opened by Michael Falcon, the stalwart of Norfolk cricket for many years, a year or so later. Initially the club played friendlies, which in today's world are a thing of the past. The early matches were played against local villages and teams from Norwich and generally a very useful team from the pilots and air-crew at RAF St Faiths just across the road.

Opening of Horsford Cricket Club Pavilion circa 1949 by Michael Falcon

My father, Gordon Godfrey back row 5th from left, grandfather, Ernest Overall back row 8th from left.

Derek Godfrey standing at front, aged 7–8

Scores of sixty were considered capable of winning most matches, and it was rare if any batsmen were to score a half-century. The cricket was always keenly contested with both sides meeting afterwards at the Red Lion in Drayton. Spectators and players were inconvenienced insomuch that there were no toilets on the ground. The men could normally find a tree and the ladies had to go in a group to a wooded area to enable privacy. The fact that the playing field was sometimes used by the local farmer for grazing his cattle did mean that after the cows had been cleared from the ground great care was needed as to where one put one's feet when chasing the ball. Many a bowler was mischievously given the ball for the next delivery only to discover that the ball had been through a cow-pat! This did not help to keep one side well shined!

It transpired after several months there was a 'right of way' through the line of the wicket area and every Saturday afternoon, a certain lady would walk across the field at around two thirty then back again at about six o'clock! Initially words of protest were uttered until it was established that the lady was within her rights.

These early matches were played in the right spirit, even though some of the umpiring decisions were perhaps what could be regarded as "parochial". There were cries of "how's that, Dad" to which the reply was "that's out Son". Several years later when I was bowling and hit the batsman on his pads, my father, who because of painful knees had stopped playing, was umpiring and shouted "Howzat". I had decided that the batsman was not in front of the stumps and had to give him "Not-out". My Father had his certain ways, and on another occasion, he took a superb catch and bowled when I was bowling, and he was the umpire. He did become a very good umpire and was asked to stand for senior clubs in Norfolk including the local Norwich Constabulary. His eyesight was indeed very good! My father did use a shooting-stick to sit on when he was standing at square-leg, and there was an instance when a very good cricketer, Robin Huggins, who scored over 6,000 runs for Norfolk, pulled a ball which knocked the shooting-stick from under my father, landing him in a heap on the ground.

My Father was a man of principle and with being very involved with the preparation of the wicket, took exception during one match when he was playing, at the Horsford captain's insistence in playing on during a drizzle thereby causing damage to the wicket. This exception took the form of my father going into his van and putting on his raincoat and wellington boots and with his umbrella took up his position in the field! The captain saw his folly shortly after and decided that it was time to call the match off.

My Father's involvement with the local Norwich Constabulary as their umpire came in very useful one night when I was returning in the farm vehicle with 'PINELANDS BOAR SERVICE' on the sides. It was about eleven thirty when driving out of Norwich I saw flashing blue lights in the mirror. I stopped the van immediately and on being asked by one of the officers to get out of the vehicle, I was taken round to the back of the van and one of the officers asked me, "Did you know your rear off-side light is not working?"

"No," I replied.

A little later he drew my attention to the rear number plate and politely said, "Do you realise Sir, that it is an offence to have this fixed with a nail and not properly illuminated?"

Again, I had to reply, "No, officer, I did not"

This very kind officer then took me round to the front of the van and on looking at the registration disc, gleefully exclaimed, "Are you aware that this tax disc ran out some two weeks ago?"

At this stage I thought that the van might be confiscated and that I would have to walk the remaining five miles home. One of the officers then asked me my name and I told him "Derek Godfrey".

The officer said, "Are you Gordon's son?"

"Yes." I replied.

To this the officer said words along the lines of, "Well tell the old bugger to get this van sorted out, and by the way are you playing cricket for us tomorrow evening?"

The following evening the Norwich Constabulary was playing against the Sandringham Estate team at Sandringham. My father had volunteered that I would be able to fill in as a replacement. On walking into the pavilion, I was greeted by these two officers who had stopped me the night before! It was a most enjoyable evening although I have no memory as to the details of the match.

Those early matches were great fun, with the team being made up of Don Rayner, the captain and a capable batsman, Horace Bowman the local baker and also a useful batsman, Kenny Smith who worked for Horace Bowman was the wicket keeper who could play a bit, Gilly Laws a farmer who could hit the ball miles, but alas, only occasionally. The real strength of the team came from the Wilkinson family. Wilfred the father was a fine all-rounder, whilst his son, Malcolm, was a real star.

Malcolm was good enough to play for any senior team within Norfolk and would more than hold his own in the full Norfolk XI. He was a fine hard-hitting batsman and a very accurate and penetrating medium paced bowler. His catching rarely failed. He would regularly hit the biggest sixes into the adjacent wood where many balls were only found thanks to the help of my father's Alsatian after the game.

Whilst Wilfred and Malcolm were the stars, there were also another couple of Wilfred's sons who played good cricket, namely Mervyn and Maxine. A further brother, Marcus, played several years later. The team was made up by my father and grandfather and the local policeman Freddie Banes and the odd stand-in. A motley crew but very keen.

In those early days the key match was against Drayton, next door to Horsford. They were a good team who had two of the best village cricketers around in those days. Billy Hunter was an excellent batsman and Basil Tubby was a most effective bowler. Horsford would usually get beaten regularly by these fine players. Billy Hunter and Malcolm Wilkinson would always score runs and seemed to hold a separate competition as to who could hit the ball the farthest. My special memory of these encounters between Horsford and Drayton was when I was about eleven or twelve and one of the Horsford fielders was injured and I was asked if I would field as a substitute. What an occasion this was. Drayton was chasing a modest Horsford score with Billy Hunter batting and Malcolm Wilkinson bowling. I was down at third-man, the captain thinking this was the safest place for me to field. Billy Hunter tried to hit Malcolm out of the ground and the ball sliced off his bat and went soaring into the stratosphere in the direction of third-man. What a situation this was, I had practised catching with my father and grandfather and was quite relaxed as I got under the catch which was taken. The Horsford team were delighted and Billy Hunter in passing near on his way to the pavilion had the good grace to say, "well caught son!" I felt about 6 feet tall. I am not sure if we won the game or not, it did not really matter at the time.

My grandfather used to open the bowling, left arm medium over the wicket and very accurate. He continued playing until he was sixty-five and only stopped playing after he had a leg broken by a fast delivery when his pads were unable to provide the necessary protection. His skill from the 1920s and 1930s had not gone and in one memorable match against Hingham he took nine wickets very cheaply. He was very fond of remembering the instance when Horsford played Hingham in previous years when Hingham scored 55 all out and at one stage Horsford was 55 for the loss of 5 wickets. The final result was a tie with the Hingham bowler, by the name of Joe Webb taking 5 wickets without conceding another run!

In those early days my grandfather used to bowl his left arm deliveries off a run-up of about ten paces, yet when he batted, he needed a Runner! This was never a problem as he played until he was 65. One particular afternoon, the opposition captain said very kindly, "Hello Ernie, how come you open the bowling, yet you need a runner when you come into bat?"

My grandfather smiled and said, "Well, it's quite simple! When I bowl, I only need to run about ten yards but when I bat, I have to run twenty yards."

The captain scratched his head and smiled at the perfect logic. My grandfather only stopped playing after he was struck on the pad and had his tibia broken. At sixty-five he had had a good innings and retired gracefully from a game he had graced for fifty years.

I started to play for Horsford at the end of the 1955 season for the final two matches. The first game was against Aldborough, a village not far from Cromer. I managed to take six wickets for thirteen runs and felt on top of the world. The following week was the match against Attleborough, who were quite a strong team and included in their team an ex-county player by the name of Freddie Self. I could not get this gentleman out but did manage to take five wickets for six runs. I can vividly remember a particular obdurate left-handed batsman who kept playing and missing outside the off stump. I thought what is needed is an in-swinging well-pitched up delivery. Lo and behold, and without knowing quite how, the next delivery was perfect with the middle stump out of the ground! A combined 11 wickets for a total of 19 runs was a reasonable achievement after the first two games.

Horsford Cricket Team 1958 Derek Godfrey Front Row, 1st on right

CHAPTER 4

Cricket at City of Norwich School and Norfolk County Cricket

1956 was a special year, and besides playing for Horsford on Sundays and mid-week games, I played as a 4th former for the first XI at the City of Norwich School. In previous years the school had provided the full Norfolk County XI with Peter Wesley and Roger Schofield whilst still at school. We had a good team and were unbeaten against other schools. I managed a couple of 6 wickets and generally felt that I had bowled well in taking wickets at around 9 runs apiece. The master in charge of cricket, Bill Haddon was encouraging yet persistent in his call to "pitch the ball up". This was his advice throughout my school days. Towards the end of the season, my father arranged for me to go to the county ground to see the Norfolk professional, Ted Witherden. Ted had recently been released from Kent, without being able to establish himself in their 1st XI despite having scored a very good century against the exceptionally strong Surrey attack in a previous season. Ted watched me bowl and bat and was full of encouragement. Ted never seemed to be concerned as to my action as being "too chest-on". This was the comment made by others after my first season playing for the county. I felt comfortable with my action and could bowl accurately and quickly, imagining that

I was running in like Fred Trueman.

1957 was a special year and in addition to bowling well for the School and Horsford, I was selected to play for the Norfolk Club and Ground against the Cambridge University Crusaders at Trinity College in Cambridge. The Crusaders were virtually the University 2nd XI with certain players who would later gain their 'Blues'. This was quite a day and I managed to bowl pretty well in taking three wickets, two of which were bowled for 39 runs in a total of close on 200. Norfolk collapsed during their innings and as last man I had to try and stay with the remaining batsman for a draw. I had never faced such pace before but somehow, remembering Trevor Bailey's perfect forward defensive stroke of previous years I survived and actually managed a leg glance or perhaps an inside-edge down to fine-leg for a boundary. A friend of my father had promised a half crown for each wicket. What a delight to collect this reward.

The local newspaper, the Eastern Daily Press, was generous in its comments 'the outstanding feature of the Norfolk attack was the most promising performance of the 15-year-old City of Norwich School boy, Derek Godfrey, who captured three wickets for 39 in 15 overs, at a pace similar to that of Coomb.' Arthur Coomb opened the Norfolk bowling for several seasons and was chosen to represent the Minor Counties XI against international touring teams. The newspaper then went onto state "it was left to new boys, Greatrex and Godfrey to play out the last fifteen minutes with much more confidence and certainty than the earlier batsmen.

I bowled well during the season, both for the City of Norwich School and also Horsford and towards the end of the season played a few games for Carrow, a senior team in

Norwich, which played their home matches at Lakenham, the county ground, owned by Colman's the Mustard company. There was one particular game for Horsford that remains in my memory. We played against a strong village team, Hoveton and Wroxham, which played on a lovely little ground within a farm which I believe was owned by Henry Blofeld's family. We used to have tea in a barn sitting on bales of straw. On this day we batted first and were bowled out for just over 60 runs. Our opponents then batted before tea and had scored about 20–1. Their opening batsman, Neville Yellop, was a fine player who scored mountains of runs and could easily have played senior cricket. Neville was not out at tea. After tea, I bowled as quickly and as well as I had ever done. In one over I was twice on a hat-trick, clean bowling every batsman. I managed to finish with nine wickets for nineteen runs, including the wicket of Neville Yellop, caught in the slips. We won the game by about ten runs.

Later in the season, or it might have been 1958, I was selected to play for Norfolk Young Amateurs against Notts Young cricketers at Lakenham. Henry Blofeld was the captain that day, and what a character! Henry had recovered from the most dreadful accident whilst at Eton when he was hit by a bus carrying a party of French ladies and was unconscious for twenty-eight days. Henry's ability may have been badly affected, but on this day he kept wicket sublimely, catching the first three batsmen off my bowling. The game ended in Nott's favour although we did not disgrace ourselves against the stronger Notts team, some of whom were young professionals on the Trent Bridge ground staff.

Norfolk Young Amateurs 1959 Henry Blofeld Captain. Lord Fellowes Back Row 2nd from Left. Derek Godfrey Back Row 2nd from Right

Henry Blofeld was a very fine schoolboy cricketer whilst at Eton and in 1956 scored 104 not out for the Public Schools XI against the Combined Services at Lords. This was a considerable feat as the only other two cricketers at the time who had emulated this achievement were Peter May and Colin Cowdrey, both future England Captains and absolute World class cricketers. The following season whilst Henry was still at Eton, he had that awful life-threatening accident at Eton. Despite this Henry still had sufficient skill to play regularly for Norfolk for a number of seasons and was also good enough to play for Cambridge University during 1958 and 1959 when he was awarded his 'Blue'. Henry batted with great style and showed his enjoyment for the game every time he went out to bat. He continued to play whenever possible for the Norfolk XI until 1965.

'Henry took a job at the merchant bank Robert Benson

Lonsdale for three years, but it was not to his taste and he drifted into sports journalism. He reported on the England tour to India in 1963/4 for The Guardian, and was close to being picked as an emergency batsman to replace the ill Micky Stewart for the 2nd Test in Bombay. When he was told by David Clark, the tour manager, that he might have to play, Henry replied, "I would certainly play if needed, but if I scored 50 or upwards in either innings I was damned if I would stand down for the Calcutta Test." On the day of the Test Stewart discharged himself from hospital and played despite his illness. After tea on the first day, Stewart was rushed back to hospital and played no further part in the tour. Henry continued as a print journalist until 1972 when he joined the Test Match Special team. He had also previously commentated for ITV in the 1960s. The name of Henry Blofeld is now known throughout the cricketing world as one of the most entertaining and knowledgeable commentators ever to have graced this wonderful game.'

Reverting back to my own story, I can remember so clearly the time when the real breakthrough came. This was during the Norfolk Festival Week at Lakenham on August 5th, 1958. I was on duty as a Gate Attendant at the entrance between the public area and the Member's enclosure when I was approached by Mr George Pilch, one of the Norfolk selectors, who mentioned that one of the Norfolk players selected for the following game had been injured and that they would like me to play against Suffolk the following day. I was staggered yet delighted to think that I would be a Norfolk cricketer at sixteen years of age.

I cycled home that evening full of excitement, longing to tell my family that I would be a Norfolk player the following day. My parents and grandparents were so delighted and that evening I made sure that my boots and pads were pristine white, and my mother made sure that my shirt, trousers and sweaters were spotless. We did not have clothing provided by the county in those days and I had a single pair of flannels which had to be washed and ironed each evening. I managed to sleep well that night with no fear of playing the following day.

The following morning was brilliant and full of excitement, together with my father and grandfather we arrived at the ground at around ten o'clock, well in time for the eleven thirty start. Peter Powell, the Norfolk captain was very warm in welcoming me into the Norfolk changing room and introducing me to the rest of the Norfolk team. There was a telegram waiting for me from Don Rayner, the Horsford captain. This was the first I had ever received. During the practising before the game started, I actually signed my first autograph!

Suffolk won the toss and decided to bat first. They scored 270 for nine wickets before declaring after 104 overs. Ian Prior the Suffolk wicket-keeper scored a very fine 137 which included an opening stand of 96 with Keith Girkin who scored 49. I was brought onto bowl first-change and conceded 40 runs in 9 overs. Prior and Girkin were in a different class from batsmen that I had bowled against in the past. I doubt if I was able to get a ball past their bats and it seemed that any delivery slightly short was cut or pushed off the pads for runs and anything slightly over-pitched was driven through the covers for four. I did manage to field very well and so enjoyed chasing and fielding. I had a strong arm and loved to show off by hurling the ball straight and fast right over the stumps.

The Norfolk innings started well and had reached 172–2 with Ted Witherden and Geoff Fiddler batting well. Norfolk then slipped to 172–5 before a very good partnership between Bill Thomas and Ted Witherden added 93 to bring Norfolk to 265. A further flurry of wickets saw Norfolk to 265–9, still 5 runs behind Suffolk's score. In these days' points were awarded for first innings scores. At this stage I walked out to bat and remember facing the Suffolk opening bowler, Bill Whitfield. I was not particularly concerned as the pitch at Lakenham was first class and true and it was safe to play forward without fear of the ball misbehaving. Remembering Trevor Bailey's superb forward defensive stroke I played with confidence and on the fourth or fifth ball I played forward to a ball on leg stump and deviated the ball past the wicket-keeper to the boundary for the runs which gave Norfolk the first innings points. Ted Witherden played so well and scored 133 not out. He managed to score 808 runs in 1958 for an average of 44.88.

The match fizzled out into a draw and Norfolk ended the season near the bottom of the Minor Counties table whilst Suffolk having won a single game finished in the top half.

'A word about Ted Witherden. He played as a professional for Kent from 1951 to 1955, but never established a place in the side. On his first-class debut in 1951 against a Minor Counties XI he took 5 for 32 in the second innings, but after that he seldom bowled in first-class cricket.

He had a purple patch in July 1953 when in three matches in 11 days he scored 310 runs for three dismissals. Against Surrey, who were beginning to dominate county cricket, he scored 26 not out (of a Kent first innings total of 63) and 125 not out in five hours, his first century, almost single-handedly preventing defeat. He then made 8 and 51 against Warwickshire, and 100 (his only other century) in three hours in an innings victory over Worcestershire.

After 1955 he left Kent and joined the Norfolk, where he played as our professional for seven seasons. He was highly successful in his first five seasons, and was the leading run-scorer in the entire Minor Counties Championship in 1958 (808 runs at an average of 44.88), in 1959 (1031 runs at 79.30) and in 1960 (855 runs at 53.43). He was also one of the leading bowlers in 1956, but his bowling became less effective thereafter.'

Ted was a very good county professional for Norfolk and full of encouragement to many young aspiring cricketers.

Going back to my first county game for Norfolk I would like to mention the other members of that team, several of whom I had played with, but several others known by reputation but never having previously met: In batting order.

1 **Alex Cunningham** Master Greshams School Ex RAF pilot

2 **Geoff Fiddler** Norwich Union also excellent rugby player.

3 **Ted Witherden*** County professional, also County Badminton player.

Note: the * denoted that on the scorecard Ted Witherden was referred to as "Witherden E.G" as a result of his being a professional. Perhaps evidence of the "old school tie" so prolific in all forms of cricket in those days.

4 **Henry Blofeld** Cambridge University 'Blue' Kept wicket superbly

5 **Peter Powell** Captain Stanton & Stavely Representative
6 **Andy Corran** Oxford University "Blue" Future Nottinghamshire captain
7 **Bill Thomas** Schoolmaster Greshams School
8 **Joe Campbell Gibson** Export Manager Shoemakers
9 **Roger Schofield** Schoolmaster Thorpe Grammar School
10 **Derek Godfrey** City of Norwich School
11 **Peter Walmsley** Norwich Union Possibly best left arm quick bowler for Norfolk ever. 329 wickets at 21.19 during his superb career with Norfolk.

The next few weeks were a bit of a whirl with the odd games for Horsford at the weekend before going down to stay with my grandparents who had moved back to Hertfordshire, living in a little cottage outside Ware, with no electricity and foul drainage. My grandfather had taken up umpiring for McMullen's Brewery XI in Hertford and became well respected in the local cricketing scene. I used to take my cricket gear with me always hoping there would be a man short. There were some strange looks from both teams when it was discovered that I could in fact play this game!

On 26th August 1958 at about seven o'clock in the evening, I received a telephone call via a lady near to my grandparents. It was my father who explained that as a result of an injury to the county professional, Ted Witherden, I had been asked to take his place in the game starting at Trent Bridge, the following day against Notts 2nd XI! My Father would pick me up in Ware at about seven o'clock the following morning and get me up to Trent Bridge in time for the eleven o'clock start. What excitement at the thought of playing on the same ground where that great fast bowler Harold Larwood had bowled so quickly and effectively, twenty or so years before.

Everything worked out so well the following morning and we arrived in time. The Gateman needed to be reassured that I was in fact playing for Norfolk as the small truck my father was driving had the words 'PINELANDS BOAR SERVICE' in bold letters on both sides! Undeterred we got into the ground and I reported for duty. Notts won the toss and batted and scored 302–9 of which Eric Martin played a beautiful innings of 192. This innings by Martin was a further example of the skill which was expected in a professional game. Whilst being able to bat so beautifully for Notts 2nd XI that day, he had struggled to keep his place in the Notts 1st XI although he did score just under a thousand runs in 1954 with an average of more than 30 during which he was awarded his county cap. The Notts 2nd XI this day included several other players who had received their full caps for Notts 1st team, including Ronnie Giles, Mervyn Winfield, John Springall and Eric Rowe.

I was asked to bowl 1st change from the Radcliffe Road end. What a thrill this was as I felt that I was running in along the same path that Harold Larwood had bowled some twenty years before. I felt good and confident and, in my 2nd or 3rd over I clean bowled John Springall for 25, knocking his leg stump out of the ground. Peter Powell, the captain, ran towards me and said, "well bowled Derek, that's the first of many!" What an encouragement that was. A couple of overs later I bowled Mike Hall, knocking his middle stump out of the ground. The sight of stumps flying out of the ground is priceless for all bowlers especially fast bowlers.

On bowling 24 overs that day and taking 2–61 I felt that I

had bowled well. The Eastern Daily Press commented that I was "rather costly". This comment was unhelpful at the time and was, frankly hurtful for a young aspiring bowler of sixteen years old. Conceding at the rate of two and a half runs an over was not exactly costly. When compared with the very experienced bowlers, Andy Corran who conceded 60 runs in 22 overs and Peter Walmsley who conceded 92 runs in 28 overs my bowling was the most economical of all the bowlers used. I will always remember bowling against Eric Martin and in one over I bowled three, what I thought were decent deliveries which pitched on the middle stump and each time this fine batsman, with a flick of his wrists clipped the ball through mid-wicket for boundaries. This was a painful yet important lesson for any young fast bowler. Norfolk scored 210–5 and I did not bowl in Notts 2nd innings of 69–4. Norfolk ended with 89–2 in their 2nd innings with the game ending in a draw. This concluded a memorable season.

CHAPTER 5

England Schools and Five wickets at Fenners Cricket Ground, Cambridge.

Moving onto 1959 was full of expectation, especially with the announcement that Bill Edrich of Middlesex and England fame was going to become the Norfolk Captain for the new season. I was selected to play for Norfolk Club and Ground against Suffolk Club and Ground and remember walking into the changing room and meeting the great man himself in his MCC touring outfit with the red and gold lines running through his sweater. I bowled well without taking a wicket. With my usual keenness in the field, I felt that I had done reasonably well under Bill's captaincy.

I was selected to play in the early game for Norfolk against Cambridgeshire at Fenners, the famous old ground in Cambridge, the home of the University team. Norfolk batted first and scored 151-3 declared in quick time. Bill Erdrich's whole approach was positive and was always seeking to win games as opposed to mundane draws so prevalent in games lasting two days. Just after lunch on the first day I found myself being given the ball to bowl the 2nd over. Peter Walmsley had bowled the opening over.

In the 1st over I clean bowled the opener with a pitched-up delivery which the opener played over. I felt on top of the world when a couple of overs later I brought a ball back off the seam and struck the Cambridgeshire professional, Eddie Davies, smack in front of the stumps. This was the prize wicket and after another few overs I was rested. Peter Walmsley and Roger Schofield then worked their way through the batting before I was brought back for a second spell. I was still in the groove and bowling as well as I had ever done and Terry Allcock the Norfolk wicket-keeper and Norwich City footballer dropped a catch off my bowling before I clean-bowled the last three batsmen to finish with 5–25 off 14 overs.

Bill Edrich gave me the honour of leading the Norfolk team off the ground and the Cambridgeshire players had the good grace to applaud me into the pavilion. I had never bowled so well in my life and not sure if I ever produced such a performance later in my playing days. The Cambridge press reported as follows 'Hawes who scored 65 out of the Cambridgeshire score of 126, alone succeeded in mastering Norfolk's fine fast bowling attack with 16-year-old schoolboy Godfrey (should have been 17-year-old) particularly outstanding. He took 5–25 and constantly had the Cambs. batsmen groping in despair.'. It was unfortunate that the Eastern Daily Press was on-strike at the time, as a result of which my performance was not reported in the local press.

Norfolk went in again and rattled up 247–7 declared thereby leaving Cambridgeshire to score 276 to win. That Cambridgeshire managed to win was down to fine innings by Dick Hawes and Charles Morris and Maurice Crouch. I only bowled 6.4 overs in the 2nd innings taking 1–22 and dropped a very difficult catch and bowled off Charles Morris in my final over. Bill Edrich kept this game alive by bowling the slower bowlers and had other catches been taken Norfolk could easily have won.

1959 Minor Counties Championship July 1st-2nd NORFOLK v CAMBRIDGESHIRE at Fenners, Cambridge. Cambridgeshire won by 3 wickets.

Norfolk

P.G.Powell	run out	38	b Hoyles	7
W.O.Thomas	lbw b Hoyles	14	st.Reed b Morris	60
Witherden E.G.	not out	39	b Gadsby	62
T.Allcock	not out	54	b Gadsby	50
W.J.Edrich	did not bat		c Crouch b Hoyles	34
G.G.Fidler	did not bat		c Hawes b Hoyles	15
P.C.Jones	did not bat		b Hoyles	2
J.C.Gibson	did not bat		not out	6
R.Schofield	did not bat		did not bat	
D.G.Godfrey	did not bat		did not bat	
P.Walmsley	did not bat		did not bat	
Extras		6	Extras	11
For 2 wickets		**151**	**For 7 wickets**	**247**

Cambridgeshire Bowling

J Hoyles	1 for 30	4 for 59
I.T.Craig	0 for 20	0 for 21
C.B.Gadsby	0 for 41	2 for 72
B.Scott	0 for 54	0 for 19
C.A.Morris		1 for 65

Cambridgeshire

R.Hawes st Allcock b Schofield	65	c and b Witherden	75
C.Reed b Godfrey	0	c Allcock b Godfrey	16
E.Davis lbw b Godfrey	5	c Powell b Witherden	14
R.A.Gautrey lbw b Walmsley	16	lbw b Edrich	29
C.A.Morris st Allcock b Schofield	2	not out	61
M.A.Crouch lbw b Walmsley	0	run out	44
S.Shippey b Godfrey	10	b Walmsley	6
J.Hoyles b Godfrey	12	c and b Edrich	12
I.T.Craig c Godfrey b Schofield	0	not out	12
B.Scott b Godfrey	2		
C.B.Gadsby not out	4		
Extras	10		7
	126	7 wkts	276

Norfolk Bowling

	O	M	R	W	O	M	R	W
P.G.Walmsley	15	4	39	2	7	0	51	1
D.G.Godfrey	14	3	25	5	6.4	2	22	1
R.Scholfield	17	4	52	3	14	1	71	0
J.C-Gibson					12	3	31	0
P.C.Jones					6	2	26	0
E.G.Witherden					18	2	55	2

The enterprising approach adopted by Bill set the pattern for future years ahead including 1960 when Norfolk reached the Challenge Game against Lancashire 2nd XI. My father being a hard-working smallholder could not be present on this day but kept in touch by telephone and was absolutely delighted to hear that I had bowled well.

Returning to school the following day after the Cambridgeshire game, the headmaster announced my performance at morning assembly and so many masters and friends offered their congratulations. There was a particular master with whom I did not particularly get on with, he was the gym master who insisted that after gym sessions everyone went through the cold shower, irrespective of the weather. He was not the most popular teacher in the school. He asked me, rather rudely at the time or so it seemed, "And how did you get your wickets Godfrey?"

With delight I explained, "One LBW and four cleaned bowled Sir!"

Retribution came later in the staff match shortly afterwards when this gentleman opened the batting and my third ball struck him smack in the 'unmentionables' He collapsed in a heap with the whole school quietly sniggering, I politely enquired as to how he was to which he smiled and said in a high-pitched voice, "All right, thank you".

Two balls, or should it be deliveries, later I bowled this gentleman a perfect Yorker which took the middle stump out of the ground. The whole school erupted! I did feel rather sorry for this gentleman, but that's cricket.

My next game was against Buckinghamshire, after schools had broken up for the summer holidays. Buckinghamshire were put into bat and Peter Walmsley whipped out the first three batsmen and I did not get a wicket in my first spell. Coming back with Bucks at around 80-4, shortly after lunch, during which Bill Edrich encouraged his opening bowlers to have a couple of glasses of beer, I managed to take the next five wickets all caught in the slips or behind the wicket. This included getting Fred Harris, their fast bowler, a gentle man, caught behind, yet adamant that he had not hit the ball and said rather a rude word to me as he walked off! My education was continuing! I had bowled well and finished with 5 for 41 in just under 20 overs. Peter Walmsley took the final wicket, and having taken nine wickets between us, we were given the honour of leading the Norfolk team from the field. My father and grandfather were in the crowd and what joy it was to have bowled so well in their company.

Norfolk then rattled up 178-4 at 4 runs an over. A good scoring rate in those days with Ted Witherden scoring 66 and Bill Edrich a very rapid 39 not out. Fred Harris, the Bucks opening bowler bowled aggressively and well to limit the scoring rate. Buckinghamshire, in their second innings batted much better and with centuries from N V Butler and P L B Stoddart both scoring centuries they reached 273-8 in 87 overs leaving Norfolk to score 242 to win in about three hours. Norfolk had a real attempt but against good bowling reached 206-6, the game ending in a draw. I bowled 24 overs in the 2nd innings taking 2-92. The wicket had been good and when batsmen had played themselves in, it was difficult to get a breakthrough.

1959 Minor Counties Championship July 1st-2nd NORFOLK v BUCKINGHAMSHIRE Match drawn

Buckinghamshire

N.V.Butler c Blofeld b Walmsley	7	b Godfrey	121
L Hitchings c Allcock b Walmsley	2	c Allcock b Walmsley	0
P.L.B. Stoddart c Powell b Walmsley	15	c Edrich b Walmsley	104
M.Hardy c and b Edrich	26	b Edrich	3
G.Scott c Edrich b Godfrey	28	c Allcock b Schofield	2
K.W.Butler c Blofeld b Godfrey	18	b Godfrey	11
B.Janes c Allcock b Godfrey	10	c Allcock b Walmsley	6
E.Clifford c Watts b Godfrey	7	not out	5
F.Harris c Allcock b Godfrey	0	c Allcock b Walmsley	12
R.Plested c Blofeld b Walmsley	21	not out	4
R.Avery not out	2		
Extras	10		5
	146	**8 wkts**	**273**

Norfolk Bowling

	O	M	R	W	O	M	R	W
P.G.Walmsley	27	10	50	4	26	9	74	3
D.G.Godfrey	19.3	8	41	5	24	3	92	2
W.J.Edrich	9	1	18	1	19	4	64	2
R.Schofield	4	0	17	0	19	6	36	1

Norfolk

P.G.Powell b Harris	8	c Hardy b Janes	10
H.C.Blofeld c Clifford b Harris	2	c Hitchins b Harris	0
Witherden E.G. c Clifford b N.Butler	66	c Hitchins b Janes	79
A.D.Cunningham c N.Butler b Harris	43	c Scott b K.Butler	5
W.J.Edrich not out	39	b Harris	16
T.Allcock c Hitchins b K.Butler	6	b Harris	38
I.M.Watts not out	8	not out	22
D.M.Rossi did not bat		not out	35
R.Schofield did not bat		did not bat	
D.G.Godfrey did not bat		did not bat	
P.G.Walmsley did not bat		did not bat	
Extras	6		1
5 wickets dec.	**178**	**6 wickets**	**206**

Buckinghamshire Bowling

	O	M	R	W		O	M	R	W
Harris	16	6	48	3		23	5	74	3
Avery	3	2	8	0					
Janes	9	0	45	0		16	2	77	2
K.Butler	12	3	35	1		18	4	54	1
N.Butler	6	0	35	1					

1959 had been such a special year and a few days later I received the most wonderful letter from a Mr. Bunfield from Worcester Royal Grammar School advising that I had been selected to play for England Grammar Schools v Wales Grammar Schools at Colwyn Bay on 24th and 25th August. I was 'over the moon' at the thought of representing my country, albeit at schoolboy level.

The England XI was as follows:
1 H I Moore Carres G S Sleaford Played for Notts. (200 v India)
2 K P Higgins Lancaster R.G S Lancashire Federation
3 G R Bloom Scarborough High School Yorkshire 2nd XI
4 T R Wintle Lydney G S England Rugby International
5 D A Hancock Newcastle High School Staffordshire Cricketer for many years
6 M A Hutson Nottingham High School Notts Youth XI
7 W J Roberts Castleford G S Yorkshire Federation
8 B Poll Cheltenham G S Wicket-keeper. Bucks Minor Counties
9 R J Mulraine K E S Stratford on Avon Warwickshire 2nd XI
10 D G Godfrey City of Norwich G S Norfolk Minor Counties
11 M Quinn Q E G S Mansfield Notts Youth XI

Between the time of being selected and the 24th August, Norfolk Young Amateurs played against Lincolnshire Young Amateurs at Grantham. H. I. (Ian) Moore was playing for Lincolnshire and batted extremely well to score about 70. I tried everything I had but hardly got a single ball past his bat. I did manage to take 4 wickets that day, including one lad who came into bat with a fancy beautiful striped hat who dismissed my first ball with a degree of arrogance through the covers for four. With hackles rising I ran into bowl the next ball as though I was Freddie Trueman himself. The middle stump went flying out of the ground and with a little smile I explained the way to the pavilion! Honour restored. The game petered out into a dull draw.

The big day came and the day before my father drove me in his van, used for transporting pigs up to Colwyn Bay, where I joined the rest of the England team at a very comfortable boarding house run by a Mrs Dobinson. My Father, with funds being short, decided to sleep in his van for the two nights.

The Welsh captain won the toss and decided to bat. We were in for a real surprise as the Welsh team played so very well and reached 283-6 with an excellent piece of batting from Russell Thomas of Rydal School who played beautifully in scoring 77. I did not bowl well and finished with 1-75 off 22 overs. We did not underestimate the quality of the Welsh XI, they just played so well. When the English XI batted, we were shot out by the Welsh bowlers of whom Russell Thomas, again showing his class with his fine medium paced bowling. I managed to stay in with Gary Bloom who scored an excellent 91, adding 49 for the 9th wicket at close of play. I was quickly out the following morning and we finished up having to follow on. Thomas bowled superbly and with a well-controlled away swing which made life difficult for all the batsmen. The England team was bowled out cheaply in the 2nd innings with Wales deservedly winning the match easily.

England Schools v Welsh Schools at Colwyn Bay August 1957
Derek Godfrey back row 3rd from Left

The defeat by Wales was a most chastening experience, we as a team had played badly, apart from Gary Bloom of Yorkshire who had batted beautifully. I had not bowled at all well and found it difficult to bowl a consistent length. In essence I had thought that I had blown a career in cricket "out of the water". It was therefore a considerable surprise to learn a few days later that I had been selected to play for English Schools Cricket Association (ESCA) against Harry Altham's Public Schools XI at the County Ground in Southampton on 31st August 1959. My Father again picked me up from my grandparent's home in Ware and we drove down to Southampton thinking that the game would start at the usual time of eleven thirty.

It had been years since my father had driven to

Southampton and we got hopelessly lost and eventually arrived at the ground just after eleven o'clock, when to our absolute horror discovered that the game had already started! The Manager of the ESCA said, "quickly Godfrey, get changed and get out onto the field". I changed in no time and feeling rather flustered rushed onto the ground. The captain, Ian Powell, of Sussex, welcomed me with a smile and immediately told me to take the next over from the Bannister Park End. My 3rd ball bowled the opening batsman, a certain J Baskervyle-Clegg of Eton and eventually Combined Services. I was then able to settle into bowling long spells and finished with 2-52 off 18 overs. My 2nd wicket was when I bowled Richard Jefferson, who subsequently played for Surrey 1st XI for several seasons and with Norfolk took 100 wickets in two seasons at less than 10 apiece. I subsequently met up with Richard over fifty years later when we met at the Parish Church in Holt, Norfolk. Richard's son, William, played with distinction for Essex for several years and at one time was talked of as being a candidate for the England team.

The Public Schools XI scored 241-8 in 71 overs with Foster of Harrow batting well and scoring 103. The Times reported that 'Godfrey stuck bravely to the task and prevented the enemy from breaking loose'. The ESCA was set to score the target in 170 minutes. This was never easy against very good Public Schools bowling and ESCA finished with 198-1. Moore scored 66, Beacroft 86 not out and Bloom 41 not out. As a team we had played well and knowing that the following day the ESCA was to play at Lords against the MCC Young Professional, we were all trying to get into the team for this chance of a lifetime. We were all relieved to find out that we were all selected to play at Lords the following day.

H S Altham's Public Schools XI v English Schools Cricket Association XI August 31st, 1959 County Ground Southampton
Match drawn
H.S.Altham's XI

J.Baskervyle-Clegg (Eton) b Godfrey	1
J.L.Cuthbertson (Rugby) c Kember b Connett	4
J.W.T.Wilcox (Malvern) c Kember b Connett	38
D.R.J.Foster (Harrow) c Hornsey b Moore	103
C.R.Pilkington (Repton) lbw b Trevett	33
M.L.Dunning (Eton) b Trevett	7
R.J.Jefferson (Winchester) b Godfrey	4
P.R.Boddington (Greshams) not out	19
H.Everard (Repton) st. Kember b Trevett	3
M.Bailey (Malvern) not out	12
C.W.Yeldham (Sherborne) did not bat.	
Extras	16
8 wickets declared	**242**

E.S.C.A Bowling

	O	M	R	W
Connett	12	2	36	2
Moore	12	3	29	1
Godfrey	18	1	52	2
Trevett	22	1	67	3
Dinsdale	9	0	42	0

E.S.C.A

H.I.Moore (Lincolnshire) b Jefferson		66
S.D.Beecroft (Hampshire) not out		86
G.R.Bloom (Yorkshire) not out		41
I.R.Powell (Sussex)	did not bat	
D.R.Shepherd (Devonshire)	did not bat	
J.R.Hornsey (Yorkshire)	did not bat	
O.D.Kember (Shropshire)	did not bat	
J.C.P.Trevett (Sussex)	did not bat	
D.G.Godfrey (Norfolk)	did not bat	
P.Connett (Sussex)	did not bat	
B.V.Dinsdale (Worcestershire)	did not bat	
Extras		5
For 1 wicket		**198**

H.S.Altham's XI Bowling

	O	M	R	W
Jefferson	21	4	59	1
Bailey	10	1	35	0
Yeldham	11	3	24	0
Pilkington	4	0	30	0
Cuthbertson	11	1	35	0
Dunning	2	0	10	0

September 1st, 1959 Lords Cricket Ground. ESCA v MCC Young Professionals

What a wonderful day, the opportunity of playing at the most famous ground in the World, graced by the finest cricketers who had ever played this wonderful game: W G himself, Bradman, Verity, Hutton, Compton, Lindwall, Miller and a host of great players at the time.

Having travelled back from Southampton the previous day and having been told that I had been selected to play against the MCC Young Professionals, I found it difficult to appreciate that within a few weeks I had managed to twice take five wickets in an innings for Norfolk and now had the heaven-sent opportunity of playing at Lords.

We set off from Ware in my father's faithful old pig truck with PINELANDS BOAR SERVICE printed boldly on both sides and drove into Lords. The Gateman was rather taken aback, but after my father explained that I was playing he allowed us, truck and all, into the ground. Going into the lovely old pavilion through the rear door a kindly assistant directed me to the way changing room. This was a wonderful experience. Looking out across the ground we could see that that the wicket had been marked out towards the Grandstand side of the ground. The MCC Young Professionals won the toss and decided to bat and as a team we bowled and caught well and dismissed them for 138. The other opening bowler, P Connett from Sussex took 4-38 and I took 3-42. My 1st wicket was a young man from Norfolk, Evan Hall, whom, at the time, I had not met. Bowling from the pavilion end a ball pitched on the middle stump went down the slope and hit his leg stump.

English Schools Cricket Association v MCC Young Professionals at Lords 1959 My first wicket: Evan Hall bowled by Derek Godfrey

M.C.C Young Professionals

Note: Professionals shown with initials after surnames.

Dindar. A c Trevett b Moore	29
McEntire. J c Lyon b Connett	2
Shepherd. W.H. st Kember b Connett	3
Sheppard.T.W. b Trevett	48
Roberts. D.J. c Powell b Connett	28
Jones.R.E. b Moore	2
Hall.E.R. b Godfrey	0
Mitchell M.F. c Moore b Godfrey	1
Wrack. A. c Prevett b Connett	0
Koefman. D.C. not out	5
Hutton.T. c Moore b Godfrey	0
B 8,l-b 3, w 9	20
	138

E.S.C.A. Bowling

	O	M	R	W
Godfrey	11.3	3	42	3
Connett	11	4	48	4
Moore	12	3	20	2
Trevett	12	5	18	1

E.S.C.A

H.I.Moore (Lincolnshire) c Koefman b Mitchell	0
S.B.Beecroft (Hampshire) c Koefman b Mitchell	1
G.R.Bloom (Yorkshire) c Hutton b Mitchell	0
J.R.Hornsey (Yorkshire) not out	51
I.Powell (Sussex) b Mitchell	1
B.Lyon (Hampshire) c Dindar b Mitchell	6
D.R.Shepherd (Devonshire) c Hutton b Hall	2
D.G.Godfrey (Norfolk) c Dindar b Sheppard	1
O.B.Kember (Shropshire) c Koefman bMitchell	1
J.C.P.Trevett (Sussex) lbw b Mitchell	0
P.Connett (Sussex) c Koefman b Mitchell	0
l-b 3, w 5	8
	71

M.C.C. Young Professionals Bowling

	O	M	R	W
Mitchell	16	6	26	8
Hutton	13	5	26*	0
Sheppard	4	2	6	1
Hall	3	1	5	1

M.C.C Young Professionals win by 67 runs

ESCA XI v MCC Young Professionals at Lords September 1959
David Shepherd Famous Umpire Back Row extreme right. Derek Godfrey Front Row extreme left

This game was also memorable for the fact that the ESCA XI included David Shepherd, the future Gloucestershire cricketer and famous international umpire. With the target of 139 to win, we felt that we were in with a chance of victory. How quickly we became disillusioned as a result of a superb piece of bowling by a lad called Mitchell who in 16 overs took 8-26. He was quick and accurate, and it seems that every chance was taken behind the wicket. I managed a single before being caught off an inside edge onto my pad from the spinner. We were dismissed for 71 with only a lad from Yorkshire, J R Hornsey scoring 51 not out, batting in a manner worthy of such an occasion as playing at Lords. Whilst being disappointed at the result, playing at Lords had been the most wonderful experience. This just about concluded the 1959 cricket season, although I was chosen as the Norfolk Amateur Sportsman of the Year in a poll carried out by the Eastern Daily Press. This was achieved without a doubt as my father visited the local pubs in Horsford, persuading the locals to vote for me! He could be quite persuasive at times. The other memorable event of 1959 was to be chosen for the R G Pilch Cricket prize at the City of Norwich School. The prize was a cricket bat and I remember going into the Pilch Sports shop in Norwich to collect my prize. In the summary of Norfolk cricket at mid-season the comment in the Eastern Daily Press read 'Godfrey played a game or two for Norfolk last season, but this is his first regular county campaign. His speed has increased beyond all expectations since last August, and his accuracy will improve with experience and a tidying up of a much too full-chested action. However, he still has been good enough to rattle out five Cambridgeshire batsmen in an innings on the billiard table that is Fenners, and he had five more in Bucks first innings at Lakenham last week. His standing among schoolboys is shown by his selection, as just about the only representative from the South of England to play for the English Grammar Schools against the Welsh Schools on 24th and 25th August'.

The need 'to tidy up a much too full-chested action' had unfortunate consequences in 1960. From being a natural fast-bowler up to the end of the 1959 season, I lost all my confidence as a bowler at the beginning of the next season as a result of well-meaning yet mistaken coaches attempting to change my action.

With Fred Trueman having just about the perfect action, I

accepted that I should try and get more sideways with my action. Unfortunately, this did not work out, as explained in the next chapter. A word about the legend that is Fred Trueman, with thanks to Wikipedia.

Frederick Sewards Trueman OBE 1931-2006. What a wonderful character and a truly great bowler. He modestly described himself as 'The greatest bloody fast bowler that ever drew breath'.

Harold Wilson, the Prime Minister during his time in office described him as the 'greatest living Yorkshireman'. With the above opinions, albeit both Yorkshiremen, who can argue!

Fred Trueman was a magnificent fast bowler, a brilliant fielder and a batsman with the ability of being able to score three centuries in first-class cricket. He was also a very astute captain whenever the opportunity arose. He was so proud when he led Yorkshire to victory, by an innings and 69 runs, in 1968, against a Test-strength Australian team at Bramall Lane. Fred understood the game so well.

In 1949 at the age of 18 he was selected to play for Yorkshire against Cambridge University. His final match was in 1968. He did play a single match in 1969 and a few games for Derbyshire in limited over competition in 1972. What a wonderful career this man had, despite falling foul of pompous authoritarians yet being lauded by real cricket lovers around the world. Watching him running into bowl, expecting to get a wicket every ball, was a real inspiration to every aspiring young fast bowler.

I was so fortunate to see Fred bowl at the Oval in 1953 when we won the Ashes after so many years of Australian dominance. I vividly recall the time when watching on television the moment he dismissed Neil Hawke, caught by Colin Cowdrey on 15th August 1964, for his 300th wicket in Test cricket. Neil Hawke and Fred Trueman were good friends and the genuine smile and handshake shared by these superb cricketers remains in my mind to this day.

In 67 Tests, Fred took 307 wickets at an average of 21.57 with seventeen times taking 5 wickets in an innings and three times taking 10 wickets in a match. In other first class matches he took 2,304 wickets at 18.29 with one hundred and twenty-six times taking 5 wickets in an innings and twenty-five times taking 10 wickets in a match. With close on 10,000 runs and 500 catches, this man could play. He was a tough character yet had the humility and wisdom to listen to the likes of Bill Bowes and Arthur Mitchell in the Winter of 1950 who helped him to harness his natural speed with full control of the ball. This help did not relate to any change to the beautiful sideways action but enabled his ability to move the ball with a high degree of control. From taking 30 wickets in each of 1949 and 1950 seasons he took 90 wickets in 1951. A rare talent had been honed and the following year he destroyed India in the Test series taking 29 wickets at 13.31 apiece and then by taking 4-86 at the Oval in 1953 enabled England to retain the Ashes. Fred was quick but this was aligned with his wonderful aggression and superb skill. Jack Fingleton, the fine Australian opening batsman of the 1930s described Fred in 1953 as 'Erratic, yes; wild, most certainly; but full of fire and dynamite'.

His 307 wickets at 21.57 puts him in the highest bracket of other great fast bowlers:

Comparison of fast bowlers over the years. To end of 2021

	Tests	Wickets	Average	Strike Rate
J M Anderson	**166**	**632**	**26.62**	**56.60**

It is interesting to note that over the past five years Jimmy Anderson's average has dropped from 29.72 runs per wicket to 26.79. His last 220 wickets have been taken at 21.72 runs per wicket, which places him amongst the finest of all fast bowlers of all times.

	Tests	Wickets	Average	Strike Rate
G D McGrath	124	563	21.64	51.95
C A Walsh	132	519	24.44	57.84
D W Steyn	91	433	22.81	42.19
S C J Broad	143	514	27.64	56.43
R J Hadlee	86	431	22.29	50.85
S M Pollock	108	421	23.11	57.84
Wasim Akram	104	414	23.62	54.65
C E L Ambrose	98	405	20.99	54.57
D K Lillee	70	355	23.92	52.01
A A Donald	72	330	22.25	47.02
M G Johnson	73	313	28.40	51.12
F S Trueman	67	307	21.57	49.43
M D Marshall	81	376	20.94	46.76

This comparison perhaps confirms Fred Truman's opinion of 'The greatest bloody fast bowler that ever drew breath'. Jimmy Anderson can now justifiably challenge Fred's opinion!

CHAPTER 6

<u>1960 What do I do now?</u>

I was running into bowl for the City of Norwich School against Beccles Grammar School. The batsman at the other end was Dougie Mattocks who was a fine player, a brilliant wicket-keeper and a special person. Dougie would play over 200 matches for Norfolk, scoring close on 3,500 runs and taking over 450 dismissals behind the stumps. He died tragically young at the age of fifty-four.

On getting to the crease, I virtually froze and thought "what do I do now?" I somehow got the ball down to the other end and completed the over. Dougie and his partner could easily have hit every delivery to the boundary but sensed there was a problem and graciously played each ball gently back. I could not believe what had happened and never bowled again anywhere as well as I had done in 1959. I was absolutely shattered and bowled very little for the rest of the season.

How did all this happen? The need 'to tidy up a much too full-chested action' was being drummed into me with the best will in the world by those who thought they knew best. The county professional and the school cricket masters were all involved. How well-meaning, but, oh, how disillusioned these kindly men were.

I bowled naturally quick and was accurate. I did not

attempt to swing the ball yet seemed to have a natural away-swing whilst also relying for movement off the seam, not worrying about which way the ball would move.

During the Easter term, the cricket master at school gave up his lunch times to work with me in the school gymnasium getting me to bowl with a more sideway-on action. He was very encouraging and said that "with your natural pace and the right action you can make it in the first-class game". This was just the encouragement that I needed to persevere. Towards the end of the Easter Term, I felt good and with a re-moulded action I looked forward to the 1960 season.

The first game for the school was against one of the senior teams in Norwich, the C E Y M S (Church of England Young Men's Society). We batted first and scored 108. We then bowled out this strong side for 33, the only resistance coming from Roger Schofield, an ex-C N S player and Norfolk County Leg-spinner who scored 15. I bowled as well as I had ever done and took 5-21 in 9 overs, most of these runs coming off the edge. My wickets included clean bowling the Master who had spent time in helping me 'to tidy up a much too full-chested action.'

From the high of bowling the school to victory against this strong Norwich team, this quickly turned to the lowest point of my cricket experience the following week against Beccles Grammar School. Although the news of what had happened to my bowling had reached the Norfolk hierarchy I was selected for a match against Cambridgeshire. I have no doubts that my selection was well intended and perhaps to help restore my confidence.

With Bill Edrich as captain, I played the game in a state of fear dreading the moment when he would ask me to bowl.

The dreaded moment came, and how I managed I do not know. I took a wicket in my first over, almost from memory. My second over was disastrous and I was hit for a couple of boundaries at which stage I was taken off. What a relief this was and knowing that I would not be asked to bowl again I enjoyed the rest of the game and showed off my fielding skill in stopping, chasing and returning the ball over the top of the stumps.

Norfolk had a wonderful season in 1980, heading the Minor Counties table and reaching the Challenge Match against Lancashire 2nd XI. Norfolk won six matches during the season, a real tribute to the positive leadership of Bill Edrich and the excellent cricket played by the whole of the Norfolk team. I was asked to serve as twelfth man for Norfolk at all the home games and what a pleasure this was. I loved fielding and remember one instance when Notts 2nd XI were chasing the Norfolk score with Norman Hill who played regularly for Notts 1st XI and was batting well and guiding his team to victory square cut the ball towards the boundary. I ran a full twenty yards, picked up the ball and hurled it in just over the stumps at the bowler's end to run out his partner going for the 3rd run. The crowd showed their appreciation as did the Norfolk players when Norfolk duly won. It was during this game that one of the Notts players was injured and I actually fielded for the opposition, including taking a catch.

The Challenge Match v Lancashire was quite an occasion, with Lancashire fielding an extremely strong XI, including ex-internationals, Roy Tattersall, Malcolm Hilton and future international Peter Lever. The rest of the team consisted of fine players of the likes of Jackie Bond, Roy Collins, Geoff Clayton, Colin Hilton, Brian Booth and the irrepressible Harry

Pilling. Norfolk was dismissed for 153 and had Lancashire 2nds at 44 for 6 thanks to superb bowling from Peter Walmsley with 4-36 and Andy Corran 4-59. Enter Harry Pilling, at 17 years old, who played so well to score 79 not out in helping Lancashire 2nds to reach 206. This was the key to victory. Norfolk was bowled out for 131 in their 2nd innings with only Bill Edrich able to withstand the brilliant bowling of Roy Tattersall who took 5-17 in 30 overs. The quality of all the Lancashire bowling was so good that on a good wicket 90 overs were bowled in the Norfolk 2nd innings. Bill Edrich had played with both Roy Tattersall and Malcolm Hilton for England in previous years.

The inability to bowl as naturally and as well again was shattering. I know I had a natural talent and determination to bowl quickly and well. I was able to dismiss players with first class experience through sheer speed and with a ball in my hand I felt confident. This natural ability was dismissed by well-meaning people with little if any experience of dealing with natural talent. Looking at the great fast bowlers, there were those such as Ray Lindwall, Freddie Trueman and Dennis Lillee who had classic 'sideway-on' actions. So many great fast bowlers, including Brian Statham, Mike Procter, Malcolm Marshall, Bob Willis and even Sir Ian Botham had actions which were rather 'open-chested'.

It is refreshing to note that the 'MCC Coaching Manual' now states that 'Fast bowlers tend to have an action which leaves them either side-on or chest-on at the end of the run up. While this does not affect the speed at which they bowl, it can limit the style of balls that they can bowl. Effective swing bowling usually requires a side-on action'. How I wish these words had been understood in 1960!

Coaching of young cricketers requires extreme skill. It is not solely a question of getting the technique correct, and whilst there is the obvious need to get the fundamentals right, the main emphasis must always be one of encouragement of natural talent. At the age of 16-18, one is so impressionable and prepared to listen to what is seen as good advice. I only wish that at the time I had the strength of character to tell those who continued to tell me that I was 'too open-chested' to 'eff-off'. My own three sons who were all good cricketers were encouraged to use and trust their natural ability. James, our middle son, at the age of 15 was playing cricket for Penn and Tylers Green in the Mid-Bucks League. He scored a beautifully constructed 60 odd, in one of his early games including on-drives which came so naturally. He continued to score many centuries, hitting the biggest sixes ever seen in Penn. He could bowl well and would catch unbelievably well in the slips. He was never coached, just encouraged.

My youngest son, Tom, could play as well, and one particular match, playing for Penn and Tylers Green against a team in the Mid Bucks League, clean bowled the opening-batsman. The incoming batsman strolled to the wicket confidently, wearing a very impressive ringed cricket cap from a top public school. The first ball was dismissed through the covers with a very fine stroke. The batsman made the fatal mistake of smiling at Tom, who walked deliberately back to his mark, turned and ran in with a determination and bowled the most perfect yorker taking the middle stump out of the ground. Tom, with a few choice words, explained to the batsman, the direction of the pavilion! I was very proud of Tom and I believe Fred Trueman would have approved. Our eldest son, Alex, could bowl very quickly, but not always so accurately. He released his competitive spirit by flying the Apache helicopter for the British Army.

I am very impressed with the coaching being given by Nottinghamshire to my nephew's son, Ben Panter, who is with the Nott's Academy. Ben is 15 and bowls very quickly and well. He has been coached by that excellent bowler, Mike Hendrick. He is being encouraged with no attempt to re-model his action. He is shown how to bowl in-swing, away-swing, slower balls and bouncers. He is taught to vary his length dependent upon the batsmen or the pitch. This is proper coaching. Ben, whilst only 16 has now become the "youngest wicket-taker for Norfolk" during the match between the Norfolk XI against Notts 2nd XI in September 2020

Cricket

Ben Panter, right, with his great uncle Derek Godfrey Picture: ROB PANTER

Ben Panter became Norfolk's youngest wicket-taker last month, taking the record of his great uncle, Derek Godfrey.

Panter made his Norfolk debut against Nottinghamshire second XI last month and dismissed Liam Patterson-White to become the county's youngest ever wicket taker at 15 and 349 days.

The wicket eclipsed Godfrey's record which had stood for more than 60 years when he took took a wicket against Nottinghamshire Second XI at Trent Bridge aged 16 and 208 days.

Godfrey could not be more pleased to lose his record to his great nephew.

"Fast bowling is in the blood – the ability to naturally bowl fast is a gift and Ben has all the attributes needed to succeed," said Godfrey. "He has the skill and determination to improve and with continued encouragement will be an asset for every team he plays for."

Panter is part of the Nottinghamshire Academy and attends Greshams School.

Eastern Daily Press 22.10.2020 Norfolk's youngest wicket takers Ben Panter 2020 Derek Godfrey 1958 62 years apart!

Whilst always knowing that I could bat a bit, I scored good runs for the school and for Horsford and the Barleycorns on Sundays. In 1961 I was elected as captain of the City of Norwich School. This was a real honour and I managed to score very well averaging over 40 in scoring some 400 runs. Being captain, I was also to bowl when needed. Instead of bowling fast I bowled at military medium pace and was very effective managing to bowl economically and at times picking up wickets. I was asked to captain Norfolk Schools against Norfolk Club and Ground at Lakenham and scored 46 after

Mike Oxbury, the future Norfolk opening bowler had whipped out the first two batsmen quickly. Batting with a lad called Pearson from Kings Lynn Grammar School who scored an excellent 76 we reached 174 for 8 before declaring. The Club and Ground XI then batted well and won with the loss of 6 wickets. I bowled well, in my slower style and took 1-19 in 9 overs. I was pleased with my performance.

As a result of this performance, I was picked for the full County XI against Staffordshire on 7 – 8 August at Lakenham in Norwich. This was a real surprise as I had not bowled quick this season and had not produced any wicket taking performances. Nevertheless, I was honoured to play again for the county. Staffordshire were captained by John Ikin, ex-Lancashire and England and who had played with Bill Edrich on the 1946/47 tour of Australia. It was John Ikin who took the 'catch' off Don Bradman when he had started his innings at Brisbane but was controversially given not out and went onto score a century and ensured Australia won the series easily against an England team re-building after the war. The English players were adamant that Bradman had edged the ball directly into Ikin's hands, but Bradman was certain that it was a bump-ball. Wally Hammond and Don Bradman did not get on particularly well and Hammond commented to Bradman "this is a good way to start the series!" These two great cricketers whilst respecting each other's cricketing abilities never really got on.

Staffordshire batted first and scored 315-7 declared off 76 overs and John Ikin scored a lovely 133. I managed to take 3-84 off 15 overs, expensive although I did bowl a maiden over to Ikin when he was on 99. At the end of the over he had the good grace to say, "well bowled son". Also playing in the

Staffordshire team were David Hancock, with whom I had played for England Schools two years earlier and a certain David Steele who later played for Northants and finally with England where he played with such courage and distinction in 1975 against Australia with Lillie and Thompson breathing fire. The scorecard records 'D Steele ct Edrich b Godfrey 14'.

A few words on David Steele.

With credit to Wikipedia they comment as follows: 'Making his debut against Australia at Lord's in 1975, he got lost in the pavilion as he went out to bat. Steele went down one too many flights of stairs and found himself in the basement toilets. He managed to make the field of play without becoming the first Test batsman to be timed out. Once he did arrive at the crease, fast bowler Jeff Thomson gave him a typically Australian welcome. Eyeing Steele's prematurely greying hair at 33, Thomson asked: "Bloody hell, who've we got here, Groucho Marx?"

That summer, however, Steele scored 50, 45, 73, 92, 39 and 66 against the Australians in his trademark staunch, courageous and steady manner. When presenting Steele his cap in the dressing room before his debut, captain Tony Greig felt tears fall on his hand and considered that "Here was a man who would fight for me to the death". His ability to stand up to hostile fast bowling, which other batsmen had struggled to cope and attack with the hook shot, raised morale among his teammates and spectators alike.

In the following year, he commenced against the even more fearsome fast bowling attack of the West Indies by scoring a century at Trent Bridge. Oddly, he was overlooked for that winter's tour to India based on the theory that he could not play spin bowlers. He duly returned to county cricket and finished his career back at Northampton in 1984 by scoring over 22,000 runs, of which 673 came at the top level for England."

David Steele was voted BBC Sports Personality of the Year in 1975, and was named as one of the Wisden Cricketers of the Year in 1976. How I remembered that day in August 1961.'

Norfolk declared their 1st innings some 80 odd runs behind Staffordshire with Bill Edrich 110 not out. Staffordshire rattled up 176-6 in their 2nd innings during which I took 1-21, leaving Norfolk to score 263 to win in 56 overs. Thanks to another not out century by Edrich, Norfolk won the game by five wickets.

This ended my career with Norfolk 1st XI. Later in the season I was selected to play for Norfolk Young Amateurs against the Yorkshire Federation whom we beat by eight wickets. I took 2-26 in 18 overs and then we beat Suffolk the following day, again by 8 wickets, with my taking 2-15 in 13 overs. The following week I took 5-25 against Lincolnshire whom we beat rather easily. It was good to bowl well and take wickets again. It was still exasperating that whenever I attempted to bowl quicker, I lost control; for a natural fast bowler this was difficult to accept.

Earlier in 1981, I had been selected by Norfolk to play against the young South African team called the Fezalas, led by Roy McLean. Unfortunately, because of exams I was unable to play. This was probably a blessing in disguise! The Fezalas was an excellent team, full of young South African players who would go onto grace the cricket fields around the World for many seasons. Players of the like of Eddie Barlow, Denis Lindsay, Colin Bland Peter Pollock, Peter Van Der

Merwe and Jackie Botten became world-class cricketers. On the day when Norfolk played the Fezalas I went to the ground after my morning exams and discovered that by three o'clock Eddie Barlow had taken 6 wickets and scored a century! This young South African team thrashed Norfolk by an innings. They played twenty-one matches during their short tour, including matches against Essex and Gloucestershire, remaining undefeated and always playing positive and attractive cricket. A real testimony to the quality of South African cricket at the time. With players like these young men, soon to be strengthened by players of the calibre of Barry Richards, Mike Procter and Graeme Pollock, South Africa was able to thrash Australia by four Tests to none in 1969/70 and before being isolated in the early 1970s could be regarded as being the best team in the world.

1961 was a climatic year in which I took and passed my final A level in maths, thereby gaining a place at Loughborough College of Advanced Technology to study Civil Engineering. The main reason for choosing Loughborough was its reputation for sport. Having been selected to play hockey for Norfolk at the end of the Hockey season I was looking forward to playing cricket and hockey at Loughborough. Choosing to study at Loughborough was the best decision I ever made for so many reasons. I met my wonderful wife in 1964 and we married on July 30th, 1966, a day made famous by Geoff Hurst scoring a hat-trick in England's famous World Cup victory. I studied a subject which I enjoyed, and which enabled me to have the most fulfilling career and was also able to play excellent cricket and hockey, including the winning of the Universities Athletic Union Hockey Competition and also representing the UAU against Midland Counties.

Cricket in Norfolk had provided many happy and memorable experiences. The experience of playing under Bill Edrich, that superb cricketer, who having flown during the Second World War winning the Distinguished Flying Cross for bravery was quite special. Being given the new ball at Fenners in my first game under his captaincy was something that I will always treasure and being invited by Bill to lead the team off the field after taking five wickets for twenty-five runs remains vivid to this day.

A few words about Bill Edrich, again with thanks to Wikipedia:

'William John Edrich DFC (26 March 1916–24 April 1986) was a first-class cricketer who played for Middlesex, Marylebone Cricket Club (MCC), Norfolk and England.

Edrich's three brothers, Brian, Eric and Geoff, and also his cousin, John, all played first-class cricket. Locally in Norfolk the Edrichs were able to raise a full team of eleven. In 1938 a team composed entirely of Edrichs beat Norfolk in a one-day match.

Born in Lingwood, Norfolk, in 1916, Bill Edrich was an attacking right-handed batsman and right-arm fast bowler. Playing first for Norfolk in the Minor Counties at the age of 16, he qualified for Middlesex in 1937 and was an instant success, scoring more than 2,000 runs in his first full season. The following year, 1938, he scored 1,000 runs before the end of May and made the first of 39 Test match appearances, though with little success. In fact, Edrich achieved almost nothing in Tests until the final "Timeless Test" of the 1938–39 tour to South Africa at Durban, where his 219 enabled England to reach 654 for five wickets, at which point the Test was left drawn to enable the tourists to catch their ship home.

Having finally achieved Test match success, Edrich was promptly dropped for the 1939 series against the West Indians. Even so, he was a Wisden Cricketer of the Year in the 1940 edition of Wisden. Edrich played association football as an amateur for Norwich City and Tottenham Hotspur during the 1930s.]

At the outbreak of war Edrich joined the Royal Air Force, in which he attained the rank of Squadron Leader, operating as a pilot for RAF Bomber Command. On 12 August 1941 he participated in a low-level daylight attack by Bristol Blenheim bombers against power stations in the Cologne area, described by the Daily Telegraph as "the RAF's most audacious and dangerous low-level bombing raid". Of the 54 Blenheims sent on the mission, twelve were shot down. For his part in the war, he was awarded the DFC. He had "an immense relief that he survived" the war and as a result loved to party and lived for the day.

When cricket resumed after the Second World War, he quickly became a regular in the England team, batting at No. 3 and sometimes opening the bowling. He scored centuries against Australia in the 1946–47 Ashes series, two against the South Africans in 1947, another against Australia in 1948 and a final one against New Zealand in 1949. A gutsy batsman he was "almost indifferent to his own safety. No bowler is too fast to hook; no score too large to defy challenge" and was badly bruised standing up to the bouncers of Lindwall and Miller in 1946–47 and 1948.

The post-war years were Edrich's heyday and in 1947 he broke Tom Hayward's record, scoring 3,539 runs in the season and not being much overshadowed by Denis Compton, who scored 3,816. Compton's and Edrich's aggregates remain the highest ever in an English cricket season, and with the reduction in the number of first-class matches seem likely never to be overtaken. In addition to his runs, Edrich also took 67 wickets in the same season.

Edrich's Test career continued until The Ashes tour of 1954–55, but he played less regularly after 1950, when he appeared to have little answer to the West Indian spinners Sonny Ramadhin and Alf Valentine. When England retained the Ashes at Adelaide in 1954–55 the team consumed over 56 bottles of champagne and Edrich — the life and soul of any party — climbed the marble pillar in the lounge of Glenelg's Pier Hotel and sang "Ginger".

All told, Edrich played in 571 first-class matches between 1934 and 1958, scoring 36,985 runs, with a highest score of 267 not out. His run total puts him 29th on the all-time lists. He scored 2,440 runs for England in his 39 Test matches, with the 219 not out at Durban his best. A professional before the Second World War, he turned amateur afterwards and captained Middlesex jointly with Compton in 1951 and 1952, continuing in sole charge from 1953 to 1957. After retiring from Middlesex, he returned to Norfolk and played Minor County cricket until he was 56, captaining the county until 1971.

A famously convivial man, Edrich was married five times and had two sons, Jasper and Justin. He died following a fall at his Chesham, Buckinghamshire home on 24 April 1986, aged 70. The MCC named the twin stands at the Nursery End at Lord's Cricket Ground, in his and Denis Compton's honour.

It was Bill Edrich who was batting with Denis Compton on the famous occasion at the Oval in 1953 when England after

19 years regained the Ashes. What a wonderful day that was. The photograph below gives an indication of the approach adopted by Bill when he batted with such skill and freedom.

Another fine cricketer I can remember with respect was John Ikin of Lancashire and England. Bill Edrich and John Ikin toured Australia in 1946/47. With thanks to Wikipedia:

John Thomas Ikin (7 March 1918 – 15 September 1984) was an English cricketer, who played in eighteen Tests from 1946 to 1955. A "calm, popular left-hander who also bowled leg spin", Ikin played most of his cricket for Lancashire. He was a solid left-handed batsman, whose statistically modest Test record underplayed his contribution to the team as a sturdy foil to such players as Bill Edrich, Len Hutton and Denis Compton.

He played minor county cricket for Staffordshire from the age of sixteen, and appeared for Lancashire in four games in 1939, taking George Headley's wicket as the first of 339 in first-class matches. After losing perhaps his best years to World War II, during which he fought at Tobruk, he resumed his career for Lancashire in 1946 and became a mainstay of the team, recording 1,000 runs in a season eleven times. He toured Australia in the 1946-47 Ashes series, compiling an obdurate 60 at Sydney and featuring in a brave stand of 118 with Norman Yardley in Melbourne.

He was involved in a pivotal incident in the first Test at Brisbane when he claimed to have caught Don Bradman at second slip for 28 from the bowling of Bill Voce, only for the umpire to rule the batsman not out. This claim by Ikin that he had fairly caught Bradman was supported by all the English players, and Wally Hammond commented to Bradman along the lines of "This is a fine bloody way to start a series". Ikin's reputation for playing cricket in the right spirit would never have allowed him to claim a catch which he knew was doubtful. Bradman went on to make 187. Ikin went on MCC's disastrous 1947/48 tour of the West Indies under Gubby Allen and was understandably less successful. One of the highlights of his career was when he scored 625 runs at an average of 89.28 on the Commonwealth XI tour of India and Ceylon in 1950/51.

In Cyril Washbrook's benefit match against the 1948 Australians, Ikin had reached 90 when Bradman instructed Keith Miller to bowl. Miller refused, noting that Ikin had been a "Rat of Tobruk", but his fast bowling partner Ray Lindwall denied Ikin his century, bowling him for 99. Ikin took a hat-trick against Somerset in 1949, and recorded his highest score of 192 against Oxford University in 1951. Gradually, injury and fragile health took its toll, and Ikin retired at the end of the 1957 season, with 17,968 first-class runs to his name. He resumed his minor county career with success for Staffordshire, playing on until 1968 and served as assistant manager on the 1965/66 MCC tour of Australia. Jack Ikin's benefit match was against county champions Surrey in 1953.

As mentioned earlier, I can vouch for John Ikin's integrity when playing for Staffordshire in 1961. He had reached 99 in a beautifully crafted innings and I bowled him a maiden over. At the end of the over he smiled and said, "well bowled son". He duly reached his century. Having lost so much confidence as a result of the attempts to change my action, this simple comment meant far more than I could ever have expected.

Another cricketer who I knew well at school was Clive Radley who went onto play for Norfolk, Middlesex and England with distinction.

Again, with thanks to Wikipedia.

'**Clive Thornton Radley MBE** (born 13 May 1944, Hertford, England) is an English former cricketer, who played eight Tests and four One Day Internationals for England. He was selected as one of the five Wisden Cricketers of the Year in 1979

His batting average in Tests (48.10) was substantially higher than he achieved in all first-class cricket (35.44), despite his not making his Test debut until the comparatively advanced age of thirty-three. Also an acclaimed fieldsman, after years of loyal service to Middlesex, Mike Brearley's accession to the England captaincy did his international cause no harm. His brief Test career, however, was ended prematurely by a bad blow to the head in the first match on the 1978/79 tour of Australia. He is one of the few international cricketers to make a century in his last One Day International, against New Zealand in 1978.

He represented Norfolk in 8 Minor County matches in 1961 and 520 First-class matches for Middlesex 1st XI (1964–87), making 46 hundreds, with a best of 200. He also played for Auckland in New Zealand in 1984/85.

On his retirement as a player, he served as the 2nd XI coach of Middlesex (1988–90) until his appointment as Marylebone Cricket Club (MCC) head coach in 1991 (in succession to Don Wilson) where he remained until his retirement in 2009. He was appointed Member of the Order of the British Empire (MBE) in the 2008 New Year Honours for services to cricket.'

CHAPTER 7

Loughborough College Years 1 and 2

Going to Loughborough in September 1961 was a real change from life on a small-holding in Norfolk. The independence did not take long to get used to and life became very enjoyable. During Freshers Week I registered my interests in hockey and cricket at the respective stalls and was delighted to make an acquaintance with Richard English who was captain of the Loughborough Colleges Cricket team and against whom I had played when he played for Suffolk Young Amateurs. On registering my interests at the hockey stall, I was asked to play in the trial game later in the week for the Loughborough Colleges team.

At the time Loughborough Colleges consisted of the College of Physical Education (the Jocks — Short for Jockstraps!), the College of Advanced Technology, the College of Arts and the College of Further Education. Whilst the College of Advanced Technology had its own sports teams, for competing in the University Athletics Union (UAU) competitions against other universities, the colleges combined as 'Loughborough Colleges'.

The Loughborough Colleges teams were predominately filled by students from the PE College with very occasionally students from the College of Advanced Technology being selected. After the hockey trial I was delighted to find out that I had been selected to play for the Colleges 1st XI against Belper, a very good team from north of Derby. Our team was depleted as a result of several being away on a UAU training weekend. Belper played so well and won 4-0. I had a good game and as reported in the College Newsletter 'Apart from Godfrey who at left back played a superb game, the rest of the college team were slow, lethargic and unconstructive'. As a result of this performance, I was able to maintain my place in the team, although it meant switching to right back. (Photo of Loughborough Colleges Hockey XI, 1962)

The Civil Engineering course was excellent, and I enjoyed the new and different subjects studied, especially strength of materials, surveying, hydraulics and structural design. The 1st year at Loughborough at the time required all students of whatever discipline, Civil, Mechanical, Aeronautical or Electrical, to spend every alternate week in the superbly equipped workshop. The object of the College at the time was to train all engineers to acquire practical 'hands-on' skills. The workshops included pattern making, a foundry and machine-shops with a full range of lathes, drills, presses and other machines. The instructors were excellent, and we were all taught good safety lessons that stayed with us throughout our working careers.

A word of explanation as to why I became a Civil Engineer. Ideally, I would have liked to have become a farmer, but it was clear that our small-holding was not large enough to support the whole Godfrey family. I struggled at school, not because I was unintelligent, but because I lacked confidence to learn new material. When first going to the City of Norwich School I started in the top stream and after the first term I was dropped down to the second stream and by the end of my first year I was dropped to the middle stream, where I stayed through to GCE Ordinary levels. By passing five subjects I managed to scrape into the sixth form, perhaps made easier because of my cricket and the headmaster's keen interest. It was only when I was 18 and having struggled with A levels in maths, physics and chemistry, that my father mentioned that he had spoken to a friend who asked if I had ever considered civil engineering as a career.

I wrote to the Institution of Civil Engineers in Great George Street in London, and they sent me details of how to become a qualified civil engineer. This meant obtaining a degree and the minimum of three years' experience on site and in the design office. The projects involved with civil engineering looked very interesting and quickly dispelled any thoughts of working for Norwich Union pushing paper in an office in Norwich. I will always be indebted to this friend of my father, Albert Hunt, who worked as a Clerk of Works for the Council in Norwich.

I worked hard with my academic studies during my first year and with playing Hockey for the Loughborough Colleges 1st team, life was full and enjoyable. The exams at the end of the year were challenging but I managed to pass, thereby getting through to the next year. We managed to get through to the Final of the UAU Hockey Championship, before losing to a very fine Bristol University team led by their superb centre-half, Hugh Marshall, by three goals to two.

Loughborough Colleges Hockey XI 1961 Losing finalists to Bristol University Derek Godfrey Front row 1st Left

In the summer term of my first year, I played a few games for the Colleges Cricket 1st XI prior to my exams. All in all, I had enjoyed my year at Loughborough and seemed to get the balance right between the course and cricket and hockey.

During the summer holidays I helped my father on the small-holding and played cricket for Horsford and the Barleycorns. I remember a couple of games that summer in which I managed to score some runs. The first was for Horsford against the City of Norwich School Old Boys. They batted first and scored 126, I managed to take 3-27 and when we batted, I scored 92 against a pretty good bowling attack to assist winning by 5 wickets. Don Rayner, the captain, commented to the local press that 'Derek Godfrey had shown great promise as a batsman. A few more innings like that and he will have the County selectors looking at him again'.

The other game which I remember was playing for the

Barleycorns against Castle Rising at their lovely little ground in Norfolk to the East of Kings Lynn. The Barleycorns batted very slowly in this all-day game and after two hours had crawled to about 80 for the loss of 4 or 5 wickets. One of the Castle Rising players, a delightful man by the name of Rufus Leggett, who was a Pilot with the Royal Air Force during the war, made it very clear, as I walked to the wicket, with words along the lines "I hope some bugger is going to start hitting the bloody ball! Our captain, Geoff Fiddler had in fact instructed me to "get a move on", and this was just the cue needed. I scored about 50 very quickly including hitting David Armstrong, a very good friend of mine, three time through the covers in one over.

As we finished our innings Rufus came up to me and said a simple, "well played." We reached a respectable score leaving Castle Rising something like 160 to win in about three hours. To the best of my memory, we narrowly won the game.

Rufus Leggett was quite a character and a fine player. Bill Edrich reckoned that Rufus was one of the finest slip-fielders he had ever seen. Rufus played for the Royal Air Force against the Army in 1955 and scored a century in ninety minutes. Other players in his team were future England players, namely: Trevor Bailey, Ray Illingworth, Martin Horton, Fred Titmus, Freddie Trueman, Alan Moss, John Murray and Jim Parks, quite a pedigree of fine players.

Castle Rising were a useful team and from time to time they invited players from Northamptonshire to play for them. I remember George Tribe, that very fine Australian bowler playing in a previous year, causing absolute bewilderment to all the batsmen with his wonderful Left-arm spin bowling.

With thanks again to Wikipedia, 'Tribe played with great

success for Victoria immediately after the Second World War, taking 86 wickets at 19.25 in just 13 games and playing in three Tests under Donald Bradman in the 1946–47 Ashes series. An all-rounder, he bowled slow left-arm orthodox and chinaman and batted doggedly as a left-hander, mostly at number six or seven, compiling 7 centuries in his first class career. Despite his prolific record in first-class cricket, he was unsuccessful during the series against England and was dropped from the national team. In the Fifth Test in Sydney Ray Lindwall took 9 wickets for 109 but thought that Tribe had bowled better, but with no luck to return 0 wickets for 153.

After failing to achieve further recognition in Australia, Tribe moved to the Lancashire League in 1947. He joined Milnrow in the Central Lancashire League and took 136 scalps in his first season. He followed that performance with a record 148 wickets the following year and 150 in 1950, when he moved to Rawtenstall for two seasons. Although he never toured with Australia, he took 99 wickets on a Commonwealth tour of India in 1949/50. An engineer by trade, he joined a Northamptonshire based firm in 1951 and his prolific record saw Northamptonshire offer him terms for that season. He proved an immediate success and played for the county for nine seasons, achieving "the double" of 1,000 runs and 100 wickets in seven of those seasons. His value to Northamptonshire as the county moved from being one of the weakest teams to being serious challengers for the County Championship was immense. He was awarded his benefit in 1956.

As of 2007, Tribe still holds the Northamptonshire record for best bowling in a first-class match, returning figures of 15–31 (made up of 7–22 and 8-9) against Yorkshire in 1958.] He took a record 175 wickets for the county in 1955. He was a Wisden Cricketer of the Year in 1955.'

Returning to Loughborough in September 1962 at the start of my second year, I found life very difficult and could not get down to work in the same manner as my first year. I still enjoyed playing hockey for the Colleges 1st team, but academic work was a real struggle and I slipped well behind with set work. I struggled through the first term but was unable to complete my second year.

I knew shortly after leaving college in February 1963, that I wanted to pursue my studies to become qualified as a civil engineer. My Father found a job for me with Eastern Counties Farmers (ECF) right through the period from February through to August. I was so fortunate at having missed the end of academic year exams that year as over a third of the students failed and had to leave the course. This was shattering for so many of my friends. It seems that the new Professor of the Civil Engineering Faculty was more interested in producing engineers with a more academic leaning as opposed to the previous leaning towards engineers with practical experience. I paid back my grant from the Norfolk County Education Authority with my earnings from ECF, and started again at Loughborough in September. During my time away from Loughborough that year, I was so surprised and delighted to receive a letter from the retiring captain of the Colleges hockey team inviting me to be captain when I returned. This I readily accepted.

Working for ECF was great fun, with the main work being in assisting a young Technician in installing pumping installations on farms throughout East Anglia for irrigation purposes. I also helped out other Technicians in repairing combined harvesters that seemed to break down regularly during harvesting. This was good work, in the open air and with good people. I met some lovely people during these months. Farming people are "the salt of the earth", working hard, with good humour and straight in their dealings. During this time my father was trying to teach me to drive. We arranged the Driving Test in Norwich and turned up in the pig truck with PINELANDS BOAR SERVICE proudly written on both sides! I went into the testing centre and came out with the driving examiner who asked, "Where is your vehicle sir?"

To which I replied, "Over there, sir," pointing to the truck with PINELANDS BOAR SERVICE on the side.

The examiner looked surprised but nevertheless walked towards the van. On opening the door, he discovered that the front passenger seat had been replaced with a large egg-box on which he was expected to sit! All credit to the examiner for not making a fuss. Health and safety were not an issue in those days!

I then turned the ignition switch and with absolute consternation, the whole van started shaking. The Examiner exclaimed, "What on earth is that?"

To which I explained, "Well sir, there is a boar in the back!"

The Examiner, in a state of shock, said "There is no way you can take your test with a pig in the back!"

By this time my father had seen what was going and innocently enquired if there was a problem?

I replied that, "I could not take my driving test with a pig in the back!"

"No problems," said my father, and dropping the back of the truck, proceeded with getting the old boar, off the truck.

He then spent the next half hour walking the old fellow round the car-park!

Needless to say, I failed my test!

On taking my test again a few weeks later I passed in a proper car this time. This meant that ECF could use my newly established driving ability to collect and deliver equipment whenever needed to farms around East Anglia. This was such an enjoyable way to spend the time until returning to Loughborough in September. I will always remember being asked to pick up an old tractor drawn combine harvester from a farm in St Faiths. On arriving at the farm, I discovered that the harvester was in a barn and that I had to manoeuvre it into the open before being able to tow it back to ECF some five miles away. More by luck than judgement I managed and towed the harvester back along a single-track lane between St Faiths and the main Holt Road. I had to take extreme care and was unable to drive much faster than 5 mph much to the annoyance of car drivers behind!

Being able to drive made such a change to my life, and my parents bought me a very old Ford Anglia car from the early 1950s. It was black, three-gear with a long gear stick, not always easy to engage, yet providing me with the independence needed and a real encouragement for returning to Loughborough to restart my second year.

Returning to Loughborough to continue my studies to become a civil engineer and also to captain the Colleges Hockey team was a real incentive to work hard. I worked very hard and enjoyed every part of the academic year. I passed the end of year exams without difficulties and also captained the colleges hockey team to victory in the UAU Final against the old enemy, Bristol University, who had defeated us two years previously. Enough of this until later. What is even more important is that I met my future wife in the early part of 1964.

I was in 'digs' during my second year at a small house in Loughborough owned by a Mr and Mrs Banks. I shared a room with a lad by the name of John Scott, who was also in his second year doing civil engineering. John was a keen sportsman, a good cricketer and rugby player. John came from Walsall and his father was a Police Inspector with the local constabulary. John went to the same school as David Brown the very fine fast bowler who played twenty-five times for England in the 1960s. We enjoyed our time together at the home of Mr and Mrs Banks and it was comfortable and clean. We both worked hard and passed the end of year exams without too much difficulty. I particularly remember the awful occasion of 22nd November 1963 when President J F Kennedy was assassinated. This was such a shocking event as JFK had led the USA with real courage against the threat of the communist dictatorship of the Soviet Union in the early 60s.

In addition to playing hockey and captain of the side that won the UAU Championship that season, I also played cricket for the College of Technology XI. The standard was not quite as good as that of the full Loughborough Colleges team. We played matches against local mid-week teams and had a game against the full Leicester University 1st XI. We managed to get to the final of the 20-overs knock-out competition for teams around Loughborough before losing to a very good team from one of the nearby towns. I captained the team and scored a fair number of runs and bowled leg-breaks at a quickish pace and took quite a few wickets. Leg-break bowling I found suited my competitive spirit, rather like bowling fast. Bill O'Reilly, the great Australian bowler was possibly one of the most competitive and aggressive cricketers, who bowled leg-spin rather well! Doug Wright of Kent and England also bowled leg-spin at a fair pace, taking seven hat-tricks in first class cricket, a world record. The great Shane Warne bowled his leg-spin at a fair pace with wonderful skill, coupled with a certain degree of competitive intent, perhaps typical of the sporting heritage of this fine nation. Where are the leg-spinners of the modern age?

Towards the end of the summer term, I was asked one Saturday morning if I could play for the Loughborough Colleges 1st team against Burton Town. I willingly said I would, met up with my girlfriend, who became my wife two years later, and joined the team coach to travel to Burton. Burton batted first and scored about 150 and the Colleges team then struggled and lost early wickets to 50 for 4 wickets at which stage I went in. The captain said that we should aim for the win and with this in mind I went for my shots. I was rather fortunate with certain aerial shots falling near to the fielders. It was not a good innings with streaky shots going off the edge to third man or fine-leg. Nevertheless, I reached my half-century and when the last over started we needed 9 runs to win, with my being at the bowler's end. We took a single off the first ball, and my partner took a single off the next. I then played the next couple of good-length balls back to the bowler. I could see the captain getting frustrated on the boundary. I was feeling confident at this stage and straight drove the next two deliveries over the bowler's head for boundaries, thereby winning the game for the Colleges. The Burton team were most gracious in applauding me off the ground. I was chuffed at having scored these runs with my future wife watching!

I mentioned previously that Loughborough Colleges won

the UAU hockey championship this year against Bristol University. This was such a special occasion and one which I will always remember with much pleasure. The game was played on the superb ground owned by Guest, Keen, Nettlefolds (GKN) in Birmingham in April 1964. We had an excellent team, full of county players. Our wingers, one a full international for Wales and the other a flyer from Western Australia, were both sub 10 seconds for the 100 yards. We won by the only goal scored by a delightful young man, Vinny Sethi, from Kenya who was studying Engineering. Our team played so well, and we hardly allowed Bristol a shot at goal.

At the presentation, the Director of GKN, said amongst other things that whilst he congratulated Loughborough on winning "he had never seen a worse game of hockey in his life". As captain I received the cup and whilst not imagining I was at Wembley on Cup Final Day and holding the cup above my head, I did feel that I should say a few words. I thanked Bristol for the way they played the game, and also to the organisers and GKN for putting on this fixture at such a lovely ground. I concluded by saying "as far as the Loughborough team was concerned this was the best game of hockey in our lives". The GKN Director graciously acknowledged my comments. We had a few pints and the journey home was an experience which will never be forgotten.

We were travelling in a hired minibus driven by a delightful driver called Yorkie on the A444 when someone dared me to get onto the roof rack where all of our gear was stowed. Still feeling elated at having won the UAU Championship, and perhaps encouraged by a few celebratory pints at the GKN clubhouse, I opened the rear doors of the minibus and climbed onto the roof lying flat down on the roof-rack to reduce the wind resistance. Car drivers following behind must have thought "damn students, wasting tax-payers money!" Fortunately, no police cars were in the area and after a few miles with honour retained, I clambered back into the minibus with much relief. From that moment on I was known as the 'Roof-Rack Rider'. With great joy I was dropped off at my digs proudly carrying the cup.

The 2nd year at Loughborough was the most enjoyable time of my life. I had captained Loughborough Colleges to the UAU Hockey championship. I had scored my maiden half-century for the cricket team, and had enjoyed the academic side, passing the end of year exams with ease. The most important event however took place around Easter 1964 when I met the young lady who would become my wife!

It was a Saturday evening and I had been playing hockey away from Loughborough in the afternoon. Returning to Loughborough early evening and together with a few of the team dropped off at the Kings Head in town and had a few pints. At around nine o'clock some of us decided that we would go up to the Union Building where there was the usual Saturday dance taking place, where young ladies from all the ladies training colleges for miles around were invited. I was very shy at the time with young ladies. Standing at the edge of the dancing area, I saw this beautiful young lady standing by herself. At this stage I had never ever asked a young lady for a dance. This perhaps showed just how backward my upbringing as a 'good olde Norfolk boy' had been. Struck by the beauty of this young lady and buoyed up with having had a few pints I boldly approach her and said, "would you like to dance?" Very sweetly she accepted, and the rest is history.

We got on so well and stayed together for the rest of the

evening. I asked Jean if I could take her home after the dance to which she replied, "Thank you, but I do have three friends with me!"

"Of course," I said, "and where do you live?"

"Leicester." she said. Leicester was about 15 miles away! Undeterred, I managed to start my old Ford Anglia and with Jean in the front and these other delightful young ladies in the back we set off for Leicester and with no clear understanding of the directions and with not being stopped by the police for being under the influence, this precious cargo was delivered safely. Telephone numbers were exchanged and the return journey to Loughborough was wonderful. On becoming a Christian, and a year later, I realised that God had enabled Jean and I to meet. How thankful I was to have met such a beautiful person as Jean.

Back at my digs I shared my experience with John Scott and when I told him that the name of the young lady was Jean, he quickly said "how congenial", a term which he used every time we subsequently met. I felt on top of the world and knew that I was in love for the first time in my life. I telephoned Jean a day or so later and was so delighted to receive a warm response. We met the following Saturday at the dance in Loughborough and kept in contact during the rest of the academic year. Jean completed her course as Leicester Domestic Science College, and I was delighted when she asked me to be her escort at their Final Ball. Jean did so very well at college and was invited to take up an appointment at Colville School as Head of Home Economics and Needlework. She was chosen specially by her lecturers and this was a tremendous achievement for her first appointment.

During the summer holiday Jean spent a few weeks

staying in Norfolk at the family small-holding in Horsford. This was such a wonderfully happy summer as we got to know each other more and more. With helping on the small-holding and playing cricket and showing Jean the delights of Norfolk, our lives were full. In love and with so much to look forward to. I had told my mother what a superb cook Jean was, and she was asked to make the Yorkshire pudding for the Sunday roast. This was a bit of a disaster as the pudding was flat and soggy! The family still enjoyed the meal. There was another memorable instance when at the breakfast table my mother asked casually if we would like chicken for lunch. We all said that would be very nice. My mother then said, "would you go and get one from the shed on the corner." Of course, I knew what she meant. Jean asked if she could come along. We went up the yard to the shed only for Jean to be shocked to find that the chickens in the shed were running around. I asked her which one she would like, and she just about froze as I grabbed one, wrung its neck and took it back to the kitchen where my mother plucked and prepared it for lunch. Jean put her cares behind her as she enjoyed a chicken lunch, possibly the freshest chicken she had ever had.

CHAPTER 8

Loughborough College Final Year 1964/65

I returned to Loughborough in September 1964 full of optimism on so many fronts. I had met the most beautiful young lady with whom I was very much in love and was enthusiastic about the final academic year. Civil engineering was a career which I was looking forward to starting at the end of the academic year. I was also looking forward to the hockey season, although I had stepped down from being captain.

Shortly into the first term, I was asked if I was interested in standing for Hall Chairman. I agreed to take part in the forthcoming election and was delighted to be elected. The Hall was under the charge of the Hall Warden, an excellent man, Jimmy White, ex-military man who had served in Malaya after the war. The social side of the Hall was run by the Student's Committee. Being Hall Chairman was a wonderful experience in standing up in front of several hundred students and lecturers to give out notices and introduce guest speakers at regular dining-in nights. As per usual, my standing up to give out notices would be greeted by having to dodge bread rolls being thrown! I did on one occasion have the pleasure of introducing Dickie Jeeps, the England Rugby player and what a great evening that was. On another occasion I had to introduce the chairman of a construction company, and we got on so well that on discovering I was studying Civil

Engineering he offered me a job! I could not accept at the time but became aware later that this company closed after a very difficult underground power station contract in Africa went badly wrong.

Work went well during the final year and with Jean being some ten miles away in Coalville this time went quickly and the whole year was the most pleasant ever experienced. We managed to see each other at the weekends and at the end of the term I was invited to go up to Jean's home in Oldham to meet her parents. This was such a special time and Jean's parents were such lovely people and I was warmly welcomed. They were real Northern folk, hard-working and straight as a die, and they loved cricket! Jean's Father had played in club cricket during his early years and her brother-in law, Jack, was playing for Werneth in the Central Lancashire League. Jack was a fast bowler who dismissed the great Sir Garfield Sobers on three occasions. I felt very much at home with Jean's family.

This culminated on Christmas Day 1964 when as tradition demanded, the men in the family went down the local for a celebratory drink. These northerners drank mild beer whereas I always preferred bitter, unaware of the higher alcohol content. The difference became apparent after six pints when we returned to Jean's home for Christmas lunch. It was a beautiful meal with all the trimmings. The Christmas pudding was excellent, and Jean's lovely mother insisted I had a second helping! At this I was not feeling too well and asked to be excused. I went upstairs, went to the WC and then found a bed and fell fast asleep! I sheepishly went downstairs after a couple of hours and was received with such a warmth that I will always remember. With some trepidation I joined the family as we went out to another pub for an evening drink. I drank

Coca-Cola for the evening. It seemed that I had passed the test of a potential son-in law!

Jean and I would drive up to see her parents whenever we could. Jean's father and I got on so well together and he taught me to play crib, a game which was so useful when I started my career later. My old Ford Anglia was proving to be more and more unreliable and on one occasion the gearbox packed up whilst we were up in Oldham. No problem! One of Jean's uncles owned a garage. He arranged for his mechanic to find a second-hand gear box from an adjacent scrapyard and without any great fuss, the gear box was exchanged during a cold winter's day. No charge was made, with sympathy for this poor student. Most journeys were something of a lottery in those days with cylinder head gaskets going regularly. Despite all its shortcomings this old Ford saw us through to the end of my days at Loughborough.

The final year at Loughborough was wonderful, although hockey and cricket played second fiddle to the academic work and my determination to do well with my studies. I also had a certain young lady to see at every opportunity! The work was hard and challenging and I set a timetable to do thirty hours of work every week outside the lectures. This paid off as I finished the course with an Upper 2nd Class DLC Honours. With Loughborough being a College of Advanced Technology at the time, the Institution of Civil Engineers required passes at Honours levels. Twenty or so years later, after Loughborough had achieved University status my DLC was upgraded to BSc. A long time to get a degree!

This year was one of great change. College life coming to an end and the beginning of a career for which I had no real idea as to what would be involved, and most importantly to become engaged to Jean, immediately after my Finals, with our wedding planned for 1966. I bought Jean a beautiful baguette diamond engagement ring for £78, which I had managed to save over the years. We celebrated our engagement initially with friends at the Kings Head in Loughborough, and then up in Oldham at Jean's sister's house after a Central Lancashire league cricket match.

A word about the Central Lancashire league at the time and Werneth in particular. There were two clubs in Oldham at the time, namely Oldham and Werneth, both of whom had good teams and previously won the League and the Wood Cup on many occasions. All the clubs in the League had players of the highest skill. Players of the calibre of Sir Frank Worrell, Sir Garfield Sobers, Fazal Mahmood, Sonny Ramadhin, Basil D'Oliveira, Cec Wright, Roy Gilchrist and more recently Sir Vivian Richards and Ezra Moseley. These great players drew large crowds every time they played. It was a real revelation to see how the young amateurs played against these stars. It was a tough school, and these youngsters treated the stars with respect, but if a ball was pitched up or too short the ball was hit to the boundary. There was one game when Roy Gilchrist the rapid fast bowler for the West Indies of the 50s bowled a 'beamer' at a lower order batsman and the captain took his team off for fear of serious injury.

The Werneth professional in 1986 was a brilliant young West Indian, by the name of Carl Hooper from Guyana. At twenty years of age, he scored a total of 1715 runs at an average of 77.95 and in doing so he beat the aggregate of the great Sir Frank Worrell who in 1951 had scored a total of 1,694. From all accounts the gates at Werneth during this season quadrupled! Carl Hooper went on to play with much success for the West Indies and the Australian legend Shane Warne regarded him as one of the finest of batsmen that he ever bowled against. Carl, when living in Oldham, stayed next door to Jean's sister. The link with cricket continued throughout our lives.

During the final year at Loughborough, many companies of all disciplines would hold interviews at the college for the purpose of recruiting future engineers. I had an interview with the National Coal Board which I found most uninspiring and another with a consulting engineering company when I quickly realised that life at a drawing board would not be to my liking. The interview with my eventual employer, Taylor Woodrow Construction Ltd went like a dream. The interviewer was a gentleman by the name of Ted Boyd, who I believe was an Office Manager within the company. We spoke about everything, especially cricket and we got on so well. He explained the sort of work that Taylor Woodrow was involved with and this really spurred my attention. He asked me towards the end of the interview as to what sort of diploma did I expect to achieve? I replied an 'upper 2nd' to which he said, 'that's good, we don't want too many brains in the industry!' He more or less offered me a job that day and it was confirmed by letter shortly afterwards. I was to start on 1st September 1965 at the grand salary of £850 per year plus £234 per year site allowance.

The exams went well and between the finals and finding out the results we were required to stay in college. This actually involved our staying in Loughborough for several weeks. I was made aware that a company involved with hiring marquees was looking for temporary workers. I applied and having a driving licence I was hired immediately. This turned out to be quite an experience as all of the workforce had experienced life in many forms. They were all very considerate in the way they treated me as a 'green' student with much to learn in life. We were involved in putting up marquees at many places around the country such as university balls, agricultural shows and the British Grand Prix. I generally drove a small truck with the crew in the front and the equipment in the back. For the Grand Prix I was asked to drive a converted dust cart with the gear stick up near my left shoulder and which required double de-clutching to change gear! This was a challenge for a driver with limited experience. Looking back, I am sure that my ordinary driving licence did not cover my driving such a large vehicle, probably weighing over 3 to 4 tonnes.

Dust cart. Similar to that driven round Silverstone 1965

Arriving at Silverstone and having unloaded the marquee, one of the team dared me to drive the dust cart around the circuit! Being a little carefree and with nobody official stopping me I accepted the challenge and drove around the circuit at an average speed of 40 miles per hour. This probably still remains the record for this type of vehicle!

This work lasted about five weeks, during which I earned good money, which was paid in cash every Thursday, in a single week I was able to clock close on 100 hours over a seven-day period, including overtime and Sunday time. Our exam results were duly announced, and the big day came when our diplomas would be presented by the Head of Pilkington Glass. This was the most wonderful occasion, with Jean, my future wife, and both my parents being at the ceremony. My parents were so elated that I had successfully completed my course and that I had met Jean, who they loved and thought just right. They actually stayed on for the evening celebrations, a meal and a dance which went on to midnight and then had to drive back to Norfolk later. I was delighted insomuch that I would now be able to support Jean and our future children when the time came.

The summer of 1965 was such a happy time. Part of the time was spent in Oldham with Jean and her family. We would watch Werneth play in the Central Lancashire League at the weekends and generally chill out after what had been a hard-working year for us both. Jean had enjoyed her first year at Coalville Grammar School and I was so pleased that I had survived my course. We then spent several weeks together down on the small-holding in Norfolk, helping my father with taking boars out in the famous truck with PINELANDS BOAR SERVICE on the sides. We met some wonderful Norfolk characters during these visits.

There was a very special occasion in August 1965 when, together with Jean, we picked up my grandparents in Ware and took them to Lords to watch the first day of the game between Middlesex and the touring South Africans. What an absolute treat this turned out to be. South Africa beat England in this three-match series as a result of the superb batting of Graeme Pollock and the brilliant bowling of his brother Peter at Trent Bridge. Graeme scored 125 in the 1st innings and 59 in the 2nd innings, with Peter taking 5–53 in the 1st innings and 5–34 in the 2nd innings. These performances by the brothers are almost certainly the finest in the history of cricket. Graeme's century was made in two hours against a very good England bowling side. Many seasoned cricketers, as stated in Wisden regarded this innings by the 21-year-old as being one of the finest Test displays of all times. The great Sir Donald Bradman had already written glowingly of Graeme Pollock's brilliance after he saw him bat in the third Test against Australia in the 1963/4 series in Sydney. Pollock made 122 in South Africa's first innings, and the great man commented, "Next time you decide to play like that, send me a telegram". At nineteen years and 317 days he became the youngest South African to score a Test century, a record that still stands.

We arrived at Lords after about an hour of the game starting with Middlesex struggling against the fine South African attack including Peter Pollock, Eddie Barlow, Richard Dumbrill and Mike Macauley. With the score at 72–5 Fred Titmus joined Clive Radley and added 227 at a run a minute. This was batting of the highest class with Radley driving superbly in reaching his maiden first-class century. Fred Titmus played his part admirably in also reaching his hundred. South Africa subsequently won this game thanks to Middlesex being bowled out cheaply in the 2nd innings with South Africa scoring 207–5 to win the game. I was sorry not to see Graeme Pollock bat at the time and finally managed to do so at Kingsmead, Durban in 1980.

At the weekends I played cricket for various teams

including the Norwich Mallards team, a useful side from Norwich. In the final game I ever played in Norfolk we were playing the Ingham Cricket Club, which had as their opening bowlers, Tracey Moore and Roger Goodwin. Tracey finished up taking 474 wickets for the county side and Roger who also played for the county side was considered the quickest around at the time. We managed to bowl Ingham out for 135 and after losing two wickets quickly, a lad called Bill Mather and I shared a partnership of around 120 to win the game by 8 wickets. Bill scored 48 and I ended with 60. I did not bowl in this game but began to feel confident in being able to bowl quick again. I played for the Barleycorns on a Sunday against Thetford Town. We bowled them out for 54 and knocked off the runs for the loss of three wickets. I managed to take 5 wickets for 16 runs, all clean bowled. A few days later, again, playing for the Barleycorns against a Norwich Wanderers XI, which included Clive Radley of Middlesex and England, I opened the bowling and clean bowled the first three batsmen, including Radley. The rain came and the game finished thereby completing my final bowling spell in Norfolk. Having scored 60 not out in my final innings in Norfolk and having taken three wickets, including that of an England Test cricketer, in my final bowling spell, I set off on my career as a civil engineer with a degree of optimism. 'Hope springs eternal'.

CHAPTER 9

September 1965. Anglesey. Start of career as a Civil Engineer

My career as a Civil Engineer started on 1st September 1965. My employer was Taylor Woodrow Construction Ltd, the main Civil Engineering Contractor on the Nuclear Power Station at Wylfa Head, rated at 1000 Megawatts on the North coast of Anglesey. The project had started in 1963 and was completed in 1971 and performed so well until it was finally closed in 2015. I drove across the country from Norfolk and with a certain degree of apprehension parked in the visitor's car park and reported to the Project Manager's office. Dick England was the Project Manager and had many years in the construction industry. He greeted me warmly and welcomed me into the Taylor Woodrow team. He introduced me to the Agent of the Turbine Hall section, Klaas Van der Lee, who seemed very formidable at the time. I was then shown where the Engineer's office was and met the Section Engineer. It was then explained that I would be looking after part of the construction of the Turbine Hall from the engineering perspective.

Everything seemed very strange, and I felt hopelessly out of my depth. Klaas Van der Lee, the Agent, after a couple of weeks asked me how I was getting on and then explained that

I was responsible for the engineering but also the organisation of the labour force within the section. This was most helpful and meant that, with the help of the experienced foremen I would have to plan the work of the twelve labour gangs to ensure they were always fully employed. This was a tremendous opportunity in appreciating just how much work could be done by each gang of workers. At the time every gang received a production bonus in addition to the basic rate, and it was essential that the opportunity for bonus was always available.

The experience gained was invaluable and with the help of excellent foremen and gangers I quickly settled into life as a Civil Engineer. I enjoyed working with these excellent men and was accepted very quickly. The foremen played Crib during the lunch break and one day I asked if I could join in. The stakes were a penny a point. The foremen looked at this green young engineer and thought "here is a chance for some easy pickings". However, I had been taught how to play by Jean's dad and very quickly was accepted as being part of the team!

The experience obtained during the first year was excellent and stood me in good stead for my whole career. Perhaps the best experience gained was how to deal with people. Young engineers on a big construction site are good targets for those who perhaps resent being told what to do by some university toff who "doesn't know his rectum from his elbow". The importance of listening to the foremen and being able to communicate at the same level with the chargehands and gangers was essential. These were intelligent men and respect was gained if they were listened to.

The Summer of 1966 was very special for two reasons.

England were playing possibly the best football ever played by the national team, and in the process reached the final of the 1966 World Cup against West Germany at Wembley Stadium on July 30th. The other reason for this being a special year was that on the same day as England were beating West Germany by four goals to two, Jean and I were getting married at the Oldham Parish Church. Kenneth Wolstenholme's famous statement "They think it's all over-it is now!" as Geoff Hurst crashed the ball into the roof of the West Germany net, echoes in our minds to this day.

At the time of planning the wedding a year before, we never considered the likelihood of England's reaching the Final on the same day. The Wedding was memorable, with family and friends travelling from Norfolk to Lancashire. John Scott was best man. The reception was held in Chadderton Town Hall, all very-low key but so special. I was ill the week before, probably at the thought of having to make the bridegroom's speech!

The time for me to say a few words duly came and I rose to the occasion, and after a few words of thanks to Jean's parents for their beautiful daughter, I launched into a few reminiscences of our experiences. I was pleasantly surprised when people started to clap and cheer. Rather naively I thought this was because of my eloquence but quickly discovered that the clapping and cheering was in response to Geoff Hurst's hat-trick and England's victory! At the end of the reception, we headed off to Manchester for our flight to London and then onto Paris for our honeymoon.

We spent a lovely four days in Paris, such a beautiful place. We headed home to start our life together in the beautiful seaside village of Benllech on the East side of

Anglesey. Our flat was part of the home of Jack and Barbara Mundy, a most kind and considerate couple. Having been in our new home for a few days we had a call from a favourite uncle along the lines, "Hello Derek, It's Uncle Jack here. You remember at the reception you said that if we wanted to visit, we would be very welcome to stay."

I responded with a degree of trepidation and said, "Yes."

To which Uncle Jack said, "Well, will it be all right if Auntie Elsie and I come up on Monday and stay the week?"

I immediately said, "Yes of course, you will be most welcome"

It then dawned on me that we had virtually no spare cash and payday was several weeks hence. That very same day I received an Income Tax rebate for £14.50 for being a married man. This sum, together with a collection from my colleagues at work, typical at the time, enabled us to live like kings whilst Jack and Elsie were with us. Perhaps the timing of the visit from my favourite uncle and aunt, just a few days after returning from our honeymoon was not best judged, nevertheless we had the most wonderful time visiting this beautiful part of North Wales.

Money was tight during these early days and even though Jean was fully qualified as a teacher, she could not find work in Wales because she did not speak Welsh. Not to worry, she helped the budget with her dressmaking skills and helped Mrs Mundy in her little café in the summer. Those early days of married life were idyllic, and despite not having any spare cash, as do most young couples, we were content.

After twelve months I was promoted to Chief Engineer for the Turbine Hall section of the project, which included also the construction of the roads and services on the whole works.

Again, this was another excellent learning experience. In September 1967, after two years working, I was asked to take control of a project in Wisbech, Cambridgeshire — the other side of the country, but not too far from Norfolk. This meant leaving my young bride of a year at midnight on Sundays, travelling through the night arriving for work at about seven o'clock on Monday mornings. The return journey started at five o'clock on Fridays and arriving in Anglesey at midnight. The roads in those days were not the best to say the least.

Having completed the project in Wisbech, I returned to the Wylfa Power Station where my responsibilities increased to looking after three small projects around the island together with completing the work on the Turbine Hall. I was transferred to Head Office at the end of 1968.

What about cricket during my time on Anglesey? At the start of the 1966 season, I approached Bangor Cricket Club and was invited to play for the 1st XI. We played friendly games against other teams from North Wales and also touring teams from the North of England. We had a very good team with two excellent opening bowlers and were generally far too strong for the majority of teams in North Wales. Colwyn Bay and Llandudno also had good teams and games against them were always well fought. Some of the visiting teams from the north were strong and on one occasion several players with Yorkshire League experience came as members of these teams, including a certain allrounder, Peter Stringer who subsequently played for Yorkshire and Leicestershire.

In August 1966 Glamorgan played a home game against Derbyshire at Colwyn Bay, the first time ever that a county championship match had been played in North Wales. This was a closely contested match and contained some excellent cricket with perhaps the bowlers having the upper hand. On a seamer's wicket the bowling of Derek Morgan for Derbyshire and Ossie Wheatley and Don Shepherd for Glamorgan was of the highest order. After playing two seasons for Bangor and doing well, I gained the impression that foreigners, from England, were not welcomed! I played my final season at Trearddur Bay, near Holyhead. This was such a happy season and with my wife expecting our first child in November we enjoyed such a lovely time. I vividly remember the kindness shown when on a particular Saturday my wife was not well and I had to call the captain to explain that I could not play. He understood immediately and a few days later dropped me a line wishing Jean a speedy recovery. These simple acts reflect so much the spirit of the game of cricket as intended.

Our time on Anglesey was so very special, my first experience of Civil Engineering, marriage, the birth of our first child, good quality cricket and hockey. I played hockey for Bangor and captained the North Wales team and played in the Welsh trials where I was actually named as reserve against England. I also captained the home Welsh team against Denmark, losing 2-0 to a very good Danish side. Our first home as a married couple was in a flat owned by a lovely Christian couple, Jack and Barbara Mundy. Our flat overlooked Benllech Bay with views out to Snowdonia and across to Llandudno. Idyllic and a perfect way of starting our married life together. The Mundy's were very involved with the parish church in Benllech Bay and soon after our marriage Jean and I started worshipping at the same church. Our first son, Alexander, was born in our flat, a home delivery superbly supported by the local midwife and doctor, Parry-Jones. Alex was baptised in Benllech and just before Christmas 1968 we left with much sadness for Horsford, Norfolk, where Jean and Alex would stay for a few months on the farm whilst I sorted out a house in Hayes, Middlesex, near to where Taylor Woodrow's office was located.

CHAPTER 10

January 1969 Hayes, Middlesex. Design office experience.

For the purpose of becoming a fully qualified Civil Engineer it was necessary to spend at least three years after completing academic studies gaining experience on site and in the design office. Having experienced three years on site at the nuclear power station on Anglesey, I was transferred to the headquarters of Taylor Woodrow Construction Ltd in Southall. At the time Taylor Woodrow Construction (TWC) had an excellent design office and research laboratories specializing in concrete technology and pre-stressing techniques.

Having purchased our new home in Hayes, about two miles from the office and established Jean and Alex in our new home, I could then settle into my new job. The first few months were involved in the preparation of the tender for the nuclear power station at Heysham in Lancashire, following which I was assigned to design the outfall tunnel on a foul drainage sewer contract at Lowestoft in Suffolk. This project would be the one on which I would submit my design, as part of my application to become a fully qualified Member of the Institution of Civil Engineers (MICE). The design challenges were interesting and unique, and the reference document was based on research carried out by a Professor Sutherland of

Strathclyde University. At the completion of my design period in Head Office, I submitted my application to the Institution of Civil Engineers to become a fully qualified Civil Engineer. The procedure involved submitting a personal statement of your experience, details of your design experience and a Bill of Quantities of a section of work with which one was experienced. This culminated in a professional interview held at the head office of the institution in Great George Street in Westminster.

The day of the interview duly came, and several young aspiring Civil Engineers were waiting in a huddle when an elderly member of the institution wandered up and said to us "Don't worry chaps, they only fail about 20%!". This was not the sort of encouragement we needed at the time. The interview went well, possibly because of the fact that the design I had submitted was unique and that the interviewers did not fully understand the issues. Anyway, all went well and a few weeks later I received the letter saying that I was now a Member of the Institution of Civil Engineers (MICE) I was absolutely delighted. Towards the end of 1970 I learned that Taylor Woodrow had been awarded the contract for the civil engineering construction of Heysham nuclear power station on the Lancashire coast.

I was appointed as Chief Engineer on the Ancillary Works section, involving the works other than the main reactor/services building and the pumping station. We moved our home from Hayes in Middlesex to a friendly little village, Nether Kellet, near Carnforth in early 1971.

During our time in Hayes, I played for Hayes town. All the matches were friendly with leagues not considered necessary in those days. The cricket was of a high standard against teams such as Uxbridge, Southgate, Ealing, Watford and other useful teams from the area. I did not bowl these days and played solely as a batsman. In June 1970 playing against Southgate, I managed to score my first ever century. We had lost two early wickets against a good opening attack with one of the bowlers being quick and aggressive. Together with a lad called Cooper, we put on 123 before he was out for 51. I continued to bat steadily and reached my century with a push through the covers for three. I can see the shot to this day and looked at the scoreboard to confirm my century. The Southgate team was most generous in applauding my performance and their wicket keeper took pleasure when I straight drove their aggressive opening bowler for the biggest six I ever struck, it seemed to be rising as it crossed the boundary rope. We duly managed to score close on 200 to which Southgate survived easily to finish on 164–7.

A couple of weeks later, a very good friend called Perry Montgomery, with whom I had played at Bangor, invited me to play for his company ICI against Pinkneys Green at their lovely ground not far from Maidenhead. We batted first and I batted at third or fourth wicket down and after an hour batting, we were about 60–3 against a very steady bowling attack. The opening bowler had bowled right through and conceded only about 20 runs from his 10 overs. Perry and I had batted well and pushed the scoring along well and with about twenty minutes to go before tea Perry had scored 90 odd and I had just reached my half-century. I walked up to Perry and said, "I will try to let you have the bowling so you can reach your century." This did not quite work out for in the next over against the opening bowler who had bowled so economically, I hit him for five sixes. The boundary was not large, but each shot would have been six on most grounds. I finished up getting to my century before Perry. We walked off for tea with the score of 230–3 to the applause of both teams and were greeted by our wives who inquired "what's all the clapping about?" They had been so involved with looking after our young children, they never had time to look at the cricket! Happy times.

We enjoyed our time in Hayes, we had lovely neighbours and our daughter, Elizabeth, was born in March 1970, some seventeen months after Alex was born. Financially, we struggled but we knew that everything would work out. Elizabeth was born at home without complications. We attended the local church in Hayes and after a short time I was confirmed by an Assistant Bishop of London. Jean had been a Christian throughout her life and up until the time we met I had been a lapsed Christian. I had always believed in Jesus Christ as being the Son of God yet had never seen the need to get more involved.

CHAPTER 11

1971–1973 Heysham Nuclear Power Station. Continuing Civil Engineering experience

We moved to Lancashire around February/March 1971 into our new home in Nether Kellet, near Morecambe and Lancaster. This was a lovely little chalet with three bedrooms and we felt like royalty after our little home in Hayes. We settled down very quickly with our young family and started the work on the new Nuclear Power Station at Heysham. The challenges involved in starting the construction of a vast project were immense, with the main task to quickly establish the workforce needed. The total complement required was well in excess of one thousand with a staff of over three hundred.

I was caught speeding on my way to pick up some men from the station in Morecambe. Showing the ticket to the owner of the hotel in Morecambe he said, "Don't worry old chap, the Chief Constable is a good friend of mine. Let's draft out a letter to him explaining the circumstances and we'll see what he can do"

A couple of weeks later, I received the reply saying that in view of the circumstances the matter would be dropped! Quite a relief.

My initial role was to organise the construction of the

temporary offices, the permanent roads and service, including drains. This was followed by the construction of several ancillary buildings around the site. The agent responsible for this section of the works was an elderly gentleman who left me very much to my own devices in running the section. This very much suited me. In the first year we had to endure virtually six months of strikes, firstly one of three months caused by the local trade unions, calling the men out as a result of a couple of scaffolders being dismissed for breaching safety regulations and the second being the result of a national builder's strike in 1972. Together with numerous design changes, relating to increased safety measures the first power was produced in 1983 and all being well will continue producing until 2025. I enjoyed this project and ended up being promoted as Sub-Agent responsible for all common service across the project, including the concrete production, craneage and transport.

As a family we enjoyed our life in this delightful part of North Lancashire and in July 1972 our Son, James, was born. He was born at home in the middle of the night, and everything went so well that Jean and I were able to go back to sleep so that when Alex and Liz came into our room in the morning, they were delighted to discover their new little brother, fast asleep. James was Baptized in Bolton le Sands, the next village.

Early in 1971 I approached the local cricket club at Carnforth who played in the North Lancashire League. I went along to the early net sessions and was selected to play for the 1st XI. The cricket was of a good standard and most teams had a professional with at least minor counties experience. Our professional was a grand lad called Jeff Bates, a competent allrounder, who I believe had had experience at Old Trafford.

I played quite well despite managing to break a finger on my left hand twice in the season, each time playing forward to a quick bowler with the ball rising rapidly and pinning my finger to the bat handle. The first time I had scored about 25 when struck and could not continue. I immediately went to the Lancaster Hospital, where I was treated by a most delightful doctor of Indian descent. He smiled sympathetically and being a cricketer himself, said in his beautiful accent "goodness gracious me — you are meant to use your bat and not your finger!" We smiled as he put my finger in a splint and told me not to play again for six weeks.

Six weeks later, I played again, I believe against Penrith. Having been at the crease for a time and playing forward again, I was struck by a fast-rising ball on the same finger. Initially the pain was bearable and I actually managed to score 93 before being dismissed. I had considerable difficulty in removing my batting glove as my finger was swollen and very sore. In the field after tea, my hand became extremely painful and every time I ran after the ball was shear agony and a short time later, I was on the way to Lancaster Hospital again. I was delighted to see the same charming Indian doctor again, and one can appreciate the humorous greeting, "I see you prefer using your finger again as opposed to your bat!" He applied another splint and with a further six weeks of not playing, that concluded my season. A bitter-sweet ending to my first season with Carnforth.

At the Annual General Meeting of the club towards the end of 1971, I was approached by several playing members to see if I was prepared to captain the team. I was honoured to be asked but perhaps mistaken in accepting the invitation to stand. I had a very good relationship with Jack Edwards, the previous captain, who had been a stalwart of Carnforth, and captain for several seasons and led the club to success in both the league and the cup in 1966. The vote was taken, and I was elected as captain for 1972. I was sorry that Jack decided that he would play for Penrith in 1972.

The 1972 season was from both a personal and club perspective not successful and we finished up in the bottom half of the North Lancashire League. I did manage to score a century against Haverigg, one of the top teams in the League. Batting first we reached 48 before Jeff Bates was out. A partnership with David Wilson took the score to 104–2 after 43 overs. In the next 7 overs we scored a further 53 of which I managed to score 47 thereby reaching 103 not out at the end of 50 overs. The opening bowlers, Weavers and Sharp, both played for Cumberland and considered to be the best in the league. We bowled Haverigg out for 145 winning a well-fought game by 12 runs, our first win of the season.

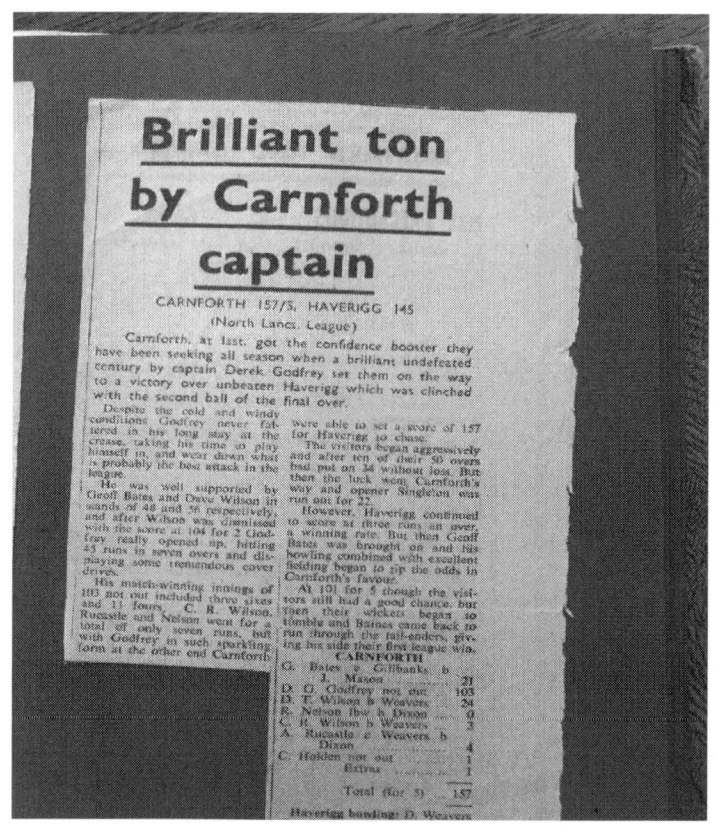

> # Brilliant ton by Carnforth captain
>
> **CARNFORTH 157/5, HAVERIGG 145**
> (North Lancs. League)
>
> Carnforth, at last, got the confidence booster they have been seeking all season when a brilliant undefeated century by captain Derek Godfrey set them on the way to a victory over unbeaten Haverigg which was clinched with the second ball of the final over.
>
> Despite the cold and windy conditions Godfrey never faltered in his long stay at the crease, taking his time to play himself in, and wear down what is probably the best attack in the league.
>
> He was well supported by Geoff Bates and Dave Wilson in stands of 48 and 56 respectively, and after Wilson was dismissed with the score at 104 for 2 Godfrey really opened up, hitting 45 runs in seven overs and displaying some tremendous cover drives.
>
> His match-winning innings of 103 not out included three sixes and 11 fours. C. R. Wilson, Rucastle and Nelson went for a total of only seven runs, but with Godfrey in such sparkling form at the other end Carnforth
>
> were able to set a score of 157 for Haverigg to chase.
>
> The visitors began aggressively and after ten of their 50 overs had put on 34 without loss. But then the next seven, Carnforth's way and opener Singleton was run out for 22.
>
> However, Haverigg continued to score at three runs an over, a winning rate. But then Geoff Bates was brought on and his bowling combined with excellent fielding began to tip the odds in Carnforth's favour.
>
> At 101 for 4 though the visitors still had a good chance, but then their wickets began to tumble and Baines came back to run through the tail-enders, giving his side their first league win.
>
> **CARNFORTH**
> G. Bates c Gillbanks b
> J. Mason 21
> D. O. Godfrey not out 103
> D. T. Wilson b Weavers 24
> R. Nelson lbw b Dixon 0
> C. R. Wilson b Weavers 2
> A. Rucastle c Weavers b
> Dixon 4
> C. Holden not out 1
> Extras 2
>
> Total (for 5) 157
> Haverigg bowling: D. Weavers

Century for Carnforth v Haverigg 1972 North Lancs League

The North Lancashire League involved a good deal of travelling to such beautiful places such as Penrith, Ulverston, Millom, Haverigg, Cockermouth, Carlisle, Workington and Whitehaven. Driving through the Lake District in the summer was always a joy even during the busy tourist season. The cricket was good and competitive yet always played in the right spirit. The Carnforth team was friendly with nine lads from Lancashire, an opening bowler from Yorkshire and myself from Norfolk. The Yorkshireman was a grand lad and a good quick bowler and if ever a catch was dropped it seemed that the War of the Roses was starting again. They were a good bunch of lads and I was made to feel very much at home.

Towards the end of the season and with my job at the power station coming to an end, Jean suggested that next time we move, why don't we apply for an overseas posting. This sounded absolutely right, and I applied to the director responsible. He mentioned that Taylor Woodrow had submitted a tender for a contract in Barrow, and if successful they wanted me to be the Project Manager. We did not win this contract and a few weeks later I was asked if I would be interested in going to South Africa on a secondment with a subsidiary company of the Anglo-American Corporation. After about fifteen seconds of discussion Jean and I agreed. I first had to go down to London to be interviewed by partners of Sir Alexander Gibb and Partners, the eminent Consulting Engineers for the Vanderkloof Underground Power Station project, part of the massive Orange River scheme, in the Northern Cape, designed for irrigation and power production in South Africa. The interview went well and arrangements were made for me to fly to Johannesburg on New Year's Eve, 1972.

CHAPTER 12

January 1973 South Africa Vanderkloof Power Station Northern Cape

The South African company to which I would be seconded to was Shaft Sinkers (Pty) Ltd. This was basically a company which sank shafts throughout the world, some of which were in excess of eight thousand feet (2,440m). Shaft Sinkers had been part of a Joint Venture tendering for the combined dam and power station at Vanderkloof, near Petrusville, one hundred and twenty miles from Kimberley. The other company withdrew from the consortium during the final stages of the tendering process. Shaft Sinkers still wished to submit a tender for the power station. Sir Alexander Gibbs and Partners agreed that Shaft Sinkers could submit a tender provided that they could obtain civil engineering support. The chairmen of Taylor Woodrow and Shaft Sinkers had met previously and agreed that civil engineering assistance would be provided as necessary.

The decision to go to South Africa was the best one Jean and I have ever taken. The last couple of months was involved with my working in Taylor Woodrow's offices in London, perusing the contract documents and meeting with some excellent people who had previous experience in underground construction. The consulting engineers also introduced a significant change to the design which had to be considered carefully and compared with the design of which the tender was based. On the last day of 1972 I travelled down to Heathrow and was stuck in the airport for two whole days as a result of freezing fog with the whole airport at a standstill. From the freezing fog of Heathrow, I arrived in the hot sun of Johannesburg on the morning of January 3rd 1973, not appreciating what a wonderful adventure lay ahead.

I spent six weeks in Shaft Sinker's office in Johannesburg, planning the work and involved in placing orders for long-delivery items such as the formwork for casting concrete to the two tunnels and also for the very large Machine Hall with a span of over twenty metres.

During these early weeks the Derrick Robins XI was playing a game against Transvaal at the Wanderers ground in Johannesburg. The Derrick Robins XI was welcomed warmly by the South Africans and the game at the Wanderers was watched by 17,000 people on the first day. This game was drawn, with my old friend Clive Radley getting a century in the 2nd innings.

The Derrick Robins XI was captained by David Brown and included international players such as John Murray, Robin Hobbs, John Hampshire and Bob Willis. Future England players included Clive Radley and John Lever. The tour was seen as a way to get South Africa back to playing international cricket. In the representative game with virtually a full South Africa XI with players of the likes of Eddie Barlow, Barry Richards, Ali Bacher, Lee Irvine, Andre Bruyns, Ken McEwen, Peter Swart and Rupert Hanley, it was clear that these were players who would compete with any other team at the time. The SA XI duly won this game by an innings and 117 runs.

I subsequently returned home to the UK for a few weeks, to find that Jean had sold the car, and arranged for our home to be let by a most competent estate agents based in Lancaster. Jean also organised vaccinations for herself and the children. With everything sorted, we were driven down to Heathrow to start our new life in South Africa. The intended duration was two years, extended to four years then six then finally seven and a half!

Arriving at Heathrow with plenty of time to spare we were so excited at the prospect of starting a new adventure in a country which we had heard a lot about and where I knew that they played cricket, rather well. Names such as Dudley Nourse, Hugh Tayfield, Neil Adcock, Jackie McGlew, Roy McLean, Trevor Goddard and the recent great players such as Eddie Barlow, the Pollock brothers, Colin Bland, Mike Procter and Barry Richards just leapt off the pages.

My parents and a dear uncle and aunt, came to the airport in a state of frenzy with a few minutes to spare. My father had taken the wrong turning and did not realise that roads around Heathrow had changed over the past thirty years! Anyway, all was well, and we managed to say proper goodbyes knowing that we would not see our family for the next couple of years. For our parents not seeing their grandchildren for this period of time must have been a real wrench. The Taylor Woodrow director also came to bid us farewell and gave me the most valuable piece of advice when he said "Derek, never let the South Africans ever think that they need your advice and always remember that you are there to assist as necessary." This was such apt advice. I found the men I worked with to be so positive and bright with the most wonderful 'can-do' approach. This was so essential for the extremely difficult projects that lay ahead.

With tears all round, we boarded the Jumbo 747, full of mixed emotions and set off for South Africa, some 6,500 miles away. The flight was straightforward with the children being so well treated by the flight attendants, and we arrived safely in Johannesburg the following morning. We were greeted by a member of Shaft Sinkers and driven to a comfortable hotel, The Quirinale, in Hillbrow, a suburb close to Shaft Sinker's office. This was our home for the next weeks during which time I worked in head office planning the construction on the Vanderkloof Power Station. Jean, in the meantime was organising necessities for our new home in the construction village being built for the project. I had been allocated a Ford Ranchero estate type vehicle, with a bench seat in the front and another bench seat fitted specially in the rear. There was a sliding window between the front and the back seats to allow communication with the children.

The journey down to Vanderkloof from Johannesburg went well, with the odd stop for the children at inconvenient places and for food and drink. The journey took about 8 hours. On arriving at Vanderkloof early afternoon we were shown our initial accommodation, a three-bedroomed bungalow furnished and equipped with brand new items. After a couple of months, we then moved to a larger property intended for senior staff. This became our home for the next four years. We settled down very quickly, with Jean establishing our new home and the older children attending the pre-school classes. Shortly after arriving there was a knock on the door and a lovely young African lady by the name of Angela was enquiring through a friend "if Madam needed any help in the house?" Angela was delightful and stayed with us for the next 5 years. She could speak Afrikaans and Xhosa when she first came to us and picked up English very quickly and when we moved to KwaZulu Natal she learned the Zulu language. Her ability to learn new languages put us to shame. She was a real godsend to us as a family, she loved our children which became mutual and was honest as the day would come.

Before leaving England, I had been asked if I would like to take a foreman to help with the practical side of the construction works. I explained to the Taylor Woodrow director that I would like a chargehand with whom I had worked at the Heysham Nuclear Power Station, to join me in South Africa. I had previous discussions with Jim Richardson, and when he knew that I was off to South Africa, asked if I could get him a job. Jim was absolutely first-class in his job as a chargehand carpenter and I knew he would do an excellent job on the project. On discussing with the Project Manager in South Africa it was agreed that there would be a position, provided Jim and his family arranged for themselves to fly over to South Africa.

I kept in touch with Jim during early 1973 and around the middle of the year received the message that Jim, his wife and two children would be flying into Johannesburg and then down to Kimberley on a certain day. I told Jim that I would meet them at Kimberley airport. I duly met Jim, his charming wife, Barbara and the two children and we drove to Vanderkloof about 110 miles away. A short way out of Kimberley we were on dirt roads when Barbara said to Jim in her Yorkshire accent "eer Jim, this is just like the wild west!" They settled into their new home very quickly and Jim was accepted very quickly as the Concreting Foreman, responsible for all the concreting operations. The quality of the finish on the concrete was absolutely first class and everybody, including the client and the consulting engineers were suitably impressed. At the end of the Vanderkloof contract, Jim moved to the Drakensberg project where he was appointed as General Foreman of the concrete works. Again, Jim did a superb job on this much larger project.

There were initial teething problems on the project. The Manager of the mining operations, Cecil Ellis, was a very experienced man with years of production management. Cecil was a tough character, as befits a man who had played Rugby for the Free State and had worked in the mines all his life. I was initially the manager of the Civil Engineering concrete works. The crunch came as a dispute over certain resources, such as compressed air or pumps or transport. I liked Cecil very much and he had the job at heart. Rather than getting involved in open hostility I approached the Project Manager, Peter Weehuizen, and suggested that Cecil should be responsible for all production, including the concreting operations and leaving me to deal with technical, planning and contractual matters. Cecil agreed instantly and we remained good friends whilst retaining mutual respect. The project involving the driving of tunnels into hard dolerite and soft shales which presented problems which were overcome by the "can-do" approach and we finished on schedule and within budget. Contractual matters were discussed and resolved in an amicable manner.

We started a cricket team from the workforce assembled to construct the works. There was a very keen young man, by the name of Scholtz, who took it upon himself to organise matches against teams within a radius of one hundred miles.

He also organised equipment through his employer, ESCOM (Electrical Supply Commission of South Africa). A sports field was prepared with a concrete strip on which coconut matting was laid for cricket matches. We played teams such as Copperton (160 miles), De Aar (60 miles), Hopetown (50 miles) and Koffiefontein (60 miles). The ground at Copperton was rather different from the lush green of an English village ground. There was no grass and the outfield basically a stripped area on the edge of the Kalahari Desert with no concrete strip, just coconut matting!

On one occasion, when Vanderkloof did not have a game, I was asked to play for Hopetown against Copperton. The game was due to start at nine o'clock and intended to be two-innings game. I said goodbye to my wife at four o'clock on the Saturday morning, drove to Hopetown to pick up several players then drove up to Copperton in time for the start. It was a baking hot day and batting first we scored around 200 before declaring at around half past eleven. I managed to score a hundred. Copperton then batted and at around three o'clock in the afternoon had reached around 150-5. With no result in the offing and a dust storm pending the two captains declared an honourable draw and we adjourned to the clubhouse.

South African hospitality is warm, even to a "Rooinek" from England. The South Africans are wonderful and noble people. The men I worked with on the construction site were mostly Afrikaners and those who made up Hopetown cricket team were mostly farmers of Afrikaans and English-speaking stock. After the game we were treated to typical South African "Braaivleis" with lamb and boerewors superbly cooked by men who knew what they were doing. The Lion and Castle lager flowed as also the rum and coke and we eventually got away at around ten o'clock. Thinking that I might get home around two o'clock on Sunday morning I was in for quite a shock. The farmers in our team had arranged to meet up with friends on the way home to Hopetown! We stopped at a couple of farms and friendships, over further cans of Lion and Castle lager, were rekindled. We eventually arrived back in Hopetown at around three a.m. on Sunday morning. With a further hour to get back to Vanderkloof I crept into bed after four o'clock on Sunday morning. I had been away for a full twenty-four hours yet had experienced true South African hospitality.

The Vanderkloof team was quite a mixture, several of us had played at a reasonable level whilst others loved the game but lacked the experience. We had a lad called Keith Miller, named after the great Australian all-rounder, who was himself a very good bowler and who could bat very well. Another fine player was Ronnie Thompson, who could be compared to Eddie Barlow in determination and ability. Our wicket-keeper was Abe Levine who ran the local stores in the construction village. We could generally hold our own against visiting teams.

Whilst living in the Northern Cape, I went with a friend to watch the Derrick Robins XI play against Griqualand West at Kimberley. The Derrick Robins XI was packed with international players, led by the redoubtable Brian Close supported by Younis Ahmed, John Edrich, Bruce Francis, Bob Woolmer, Graham Roope, Mike Smith, John Murray, John Shepherd, John Lever, Graeme Johnson, Peter Lee, Johnny Gleeson and John Snow. This was a very fine team. They scored 197–6 in the 50 overs and restricted Griqualand West to a mere 112–7. In the three representative games against the

SA Invitation XI, the strength of South African cricket was confirmed in the final game at the Wanderers when Messrs Richards, Barlow, Irvine and Procter put the bowlers to the sword in scoring 528–8 declared and bowling the Derrick Robins XI out for scores of around 200 in each innings to win by an innings and 83 runs.

In 1974 the organisers of the Griqualand West Country Districts organised a trial match at the provincial ground in Kimberley for games scheduled against South West Africa (Namibia) in Windhoek and then a week later against the Orange Free State Country Districts in De Aar. I played reasonably well and was selected. We had to travel to Johannesburg, and then take a flight in a Jumbo 747 to Windhoek, to play in the 2-day game. This went well and the team, well kitted out in blazers with the badge on the front, arrived at the hotel in Windhoek where we were warmly greeted by members of the Southwest Africa Cricket Board.

The big day came, and we won the toss and decided to bat. I was opening the batting. Walking to the wicket in front of a large crowd I felt quite confident. The first ball came down on the leg stump, I played forward, the ball came up a bit higher than I expected with the result that I edged the ball straight into the hands of short-leg! I could not believe what happened and dragged myself off to the confines of the dressing room. Over 1,000 miles for a first-baller! We struggled to just over 100 and SWA rattled up a score close to 300 with one of the Ackerman family, all excellent cricketers, scoring a century. We batted again that evening and I managed to survive quite easily. The next morning, we were skittled quickly losing by an innings and plenty. We were disappointed as a team but not disheartened, we had played badly but did not feel any gulf in class, and so with no loss of confidence we looked forward to the game against the Free State the following week.

The game against the Orange Free State Country Districts, in Afrikaans, "the O.V.S. Platteland" was played at De Aar on 15th and 16th November 1974. At the time the full Orange Free State cricket XI was regarded as a second league team in the Currie Cup competition. Section "A" teams consisted of Natal, Transvaal, Eastern Province, Rhodesia and Western Province, whilst Section "B" teams included North-Eastern Transvaal, Border, Natal "B", Transvaal "B", Orange Free State and Griqualand West. This was before the time when the Free State had the great cricketers such as Alan Donald and Hansie Cronje to swell their ranks.

Over recent years the Free State has produced teams good enough to win the League and Cup competitions. In the early 1990s they won the League two years running. The Free State with its capital, Bloemfontein, has for many years been regarded as one of the seats of Afrikanerdom and is the Judicial Capital of South Africa. The people generally are from good solid families going back to their Dutch heritage from the time Jan van Riebeeck landed in Cape Town in 1652 and established the Cape Colony. These people are tough, god-fearing people and strong-principled. They were not prepared to tolerate the British authorities and in the mid-19th century they started the Great Trek into what is now the Orange Free State and the Transvaal. The 'Voortrekkers' or pathfinders, remain as heroes to South Africans these days.

Getting back to the cricket, we won the toss and decided to bat. As for the game against South West Africa, I opened the batting. Facing the first ball, I played forward down the wrong line and looked behind to see my off stump out of the ground. Two first balls in three innings were not exactly what was expected of this "Rooinek", the only non-South African in the team. We were bowled out very quickly, with a very good quick bowler called Norton, taking several wickets for few runs. The Free State then scored over 200 and we had to go in again towards the close of play. We lost a few wickets but with a degree of good fortune, I managed to survive the day. The following morning, we continued to lose wickets steadily, when I decided to play a more attacking game. Bowlers who had seemed difficult to score off seemed to become normal and I managed to hit several boundaries in reaching 49 not out when the innings closed. I had played well in a losing situation. The Free State had to score a few runs to win the game by ten wickets.

The cricket in the Northern Cape continued to be very enjoyable for the whole time we were in this beautiful part of South Africa. Cricket is such an opportunity to make good friends and despite being a 'Rooinek' we were made to feel very much at home in a country we loved then and have done so ever since. There was one special game against Hopetown at their ground, when playing for Vanderkloof, I scored 148 not out, my highest score, out of a total of about 190. We managed to draw this game.

Reverting back to the construction of the underground power station, there were several challenges that needed to be overcome. The capacity of the power station was 240 Megawatts and was started in 1973 with the first power generated in January 1977. See image below. The pictures below show the general layout of the project.

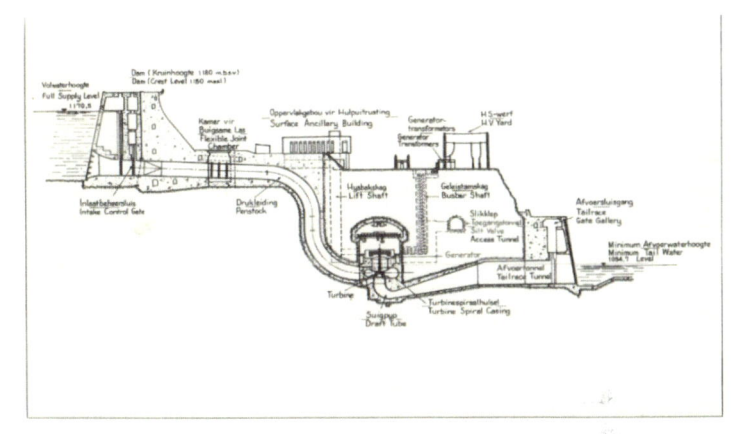

Cross section through Dam and Power Station. Vanderkloof

Overall view of P K Le Roux Dam

Vanderkloof Power Station-as completed 1977

Vanderkloof Power Station during construction

The rock which had to be excavated by means of tunnelling consisted of very hard dolerite and soft highly laminated shales. A similar underground power station was at the time being constructed at the Kariba project on the Zambian side of the River Kariba. Serious rock falls were experienced on the Kariba project, as a result of which the design of the power station at Vanderkloof was changed and the construction method modified. The main contractor at Kariba, Mitchell Construction, was seriously affected by the rockfalls and work was suspended, and subsequently went into liquidation and the project seriously delayed. The contractual position was not adequately resolved, and questions remain unanswered as to the geological conditions known at the time. Mitchell Construction at the time was a well-respected construction company with previous underground experience on the Scottish Hydro-Electric schemes of the 1950s. I could easily have worked for Mitchell Construction, having been offered a job with them whilst at Loughborough in 1965. It is always a crying shame, when a decent company in a high-risk industry is forced into liquidation through no fault of their own.

At Vanderkloof, the change of design and the effects on the construction method was recognised by the client and the consulting engineers, and after negotiation, the additional costs associated with changing the method of construction were agreed satisfactorily. The client was pleased that the works were completed on time, the consulting engineers were relieved that their modified design had been successful, and Shaft Sinkers had succeeded in making a profit.

I enjoyed my role immensely on this project, initially as Chief Engineer, and for the final twelve months, as Project Manager. Life on site was enjoyable and challenging, with being over a hundred miles from major towns such as Kimberley or Bloemfontein. Jean would drive our young daughter over 50 miles each way on dirt roads, to Hopetown for ballet classes twice a week. We would think nothing of driving to Kimberley for a theatre performance.

On one particular trip to Bloemfontein, I had to purchase a couple of bats for the cricket club. I found the sports shop in this lovely city and on entering, found that the shop was owned by a certain great cricketer, Colin Bland. What an absolute gentleman. I explained that I was buying the bats for the Vanderkloof Cricket Club, and after explaining that this was based at the construction village he was so interested and helpful and gave us a discount. Colin Bland was probably the finest fielder ever before another South African, Jonty Rhodes, in the 90s came on the scene. Realising that I was an Englishman, we had a discussion about cricket. It transpired that he was part of that wonderful young South African team, the Fezalas, that toured England so successfully in 1961. When we folded up the Vanderkloof Club in 1976 I was fortunate to hold onto one of the bats from Colin Bland's shop. I treasured this for many years.

With thanks again to Wikipedia.

'Colin Bland was educated at Milton High School in Bulawayo. He made his first-class debut for Rhodesia as a schoolboy against Peter May's English team in 1956–57 and went on to represent them 55 times from 1956 to 1968. He later played for the South African provincial sides Eastern Province and Orange Free State.

A tall and elegant right-handed batsman, Bland broke into the South African Test team in 1961, and was a regular until 1966–67. As South Africa in the apartheid era played Test cricket only against England, Australia and New Zealand, his career was restricted to just 21 Tests, in which he scored 1,669 runs, including three centuries. His highest Test score came in the Second Test against England at Johannesburg in 1964–65; South Africa followed on 214 behind, and was 109 for 4 in the second innings when Bland came in and hit 144 not out in just over four hours to save the match. Colin Bland was a superb batsman, and averaged just below 50 runs per innings, a lasting indication of just what a fine player he was.

Bland's chief fame, though, rested on his fielding. The general consensus is that he was the finest cover fieldsman of his time, and rated by some as the finest ever, he was able to the turn the course of whole matches. His spectacular run out of Ken Barrington in the Lord's Test of 1965, followed by a similar dismissal of Jim Parks, may have prevented England from establishing a match-winning first innings lead, the match eventually being drawn. Brian Johnston recalled of the 1965 tour, "For the first time I heard people saying that they must go to a match, especially to watch a fielder."

Bland was a Wisden Cricketer of the Year in 1966; he is one of only two players so honoured (the other is Stuart Surridge) to be depicted in the accompanying portrait fielding, rather than batting, bowling or keeping. When Wisden asked Peter van der Merwe in 1999 to name the five outstanding cricketers of the twentieth century, he included Colin Bland, saying, "He revolutionised the attitude to fielding, and set a standard not yet equalled."

Bland retired from Test cricket after injury forced him out of the side after the first Test in 1966–67. He continued to play first-class cricket in South Africa until the 1973–74 season.'

Colin Bland greatest fielder ever.

CHAPTER 13

April 1977 South Africa Drakensberg Pumped Storage Scheme Natal

Early in 1977, with the work at Vanderkloof virtually completed, I was asked if I would agree to take on the role as Chief Civil Engineer for the joint-venture of Shaft Sinkers and LBA, both companies within the Anglo-American corporation, on the new underground pumped-storage scheme in the Drakensberg mountains near Bergville in Natal. This was a much larger project than Vanderkloof and Jean and I agreed readily to a further stay in a country which we came to love.

We duly moved to our new home in Natal around April 1977 and settled into this beautiful part of South Africa very quickly. The children soon adapted to their new school, with part of the curriculum being in Afrikaans and part in English. The accommodation was well established and comfortable. I had worked with several of the senior management previously and felt very much at home in my new role.

The Drakensberg Project had two purposes, the first to be able to produce 1,000 megawatts of power and the second to be able to provide water for the Transvaal. The turbines when not producing electricity from the water under a head of four hundred and fifty metres were then reversed and using off-peak electricity pumped water back up the shafts with excess water flowing into the water-ways feeding the Vaal Dam, near Johannesburg in the Transvaal. The scheme is depicted below. When one considers that the whole structure shown in the illustration below is constructed within poor quality rock, it can be appreciated as to the skill involved.

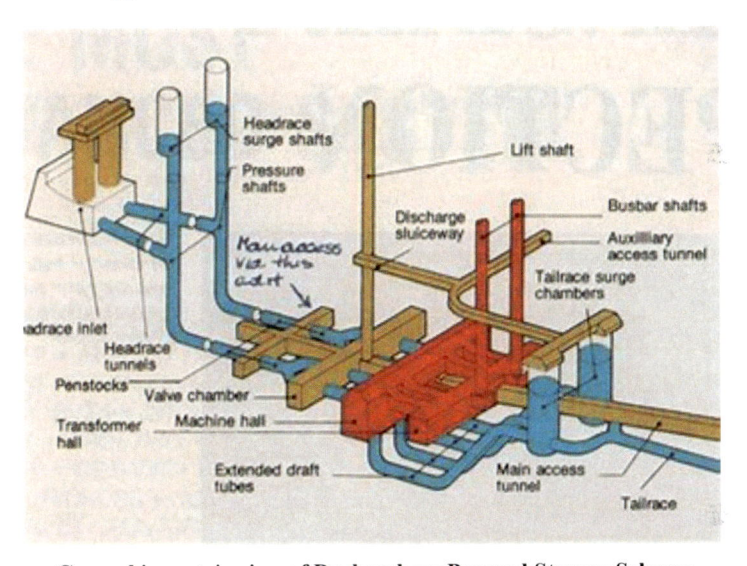

General isometric view of Drakensberg Pumped Storage Scheme

Shaft Sinkers and LTA the partners, named the Consortium as DRAKON, and we set about the massive task ahead with a degree of difficulty. The main access tunnel into the works had not been completed by the French contractors under a separate contract. This meant that we had to use a smaller exploratory tunnel for gaining access into the works. Besides being much smaller, thereby preventing trucks passing in the tunnel, the gradient was much steeper which meant that fully laden trucks had difficulty in exiting the tunnel.

Notwithstanding the lack of use of the Main Access Tunnel, the tunnelling teams worked wonders in completing the excavation works involved with the pressure tunnels and the major separate caverns for the turbines, the valves and the transformers. The rock was a mixture of weak sandstone and siltstone, very friable when exposed to air. It was essential that as soon as rock surfaces were exposed, sprayed concrete was applied immediately. The designers of the project did a brilliant job in understanding that the rock would settle following excavation by drilling and blasting. This movement was limited by immediately sealing the excavated surfaces of the rock with sprayed concrete and then stitching the surrounding rock with 3 to7-metre-long rock-bolts drilled and grouted into the rock. The purpose being to create a "rock-arch" around the excavation. The whole process was monitored by instruments installed into the rock for the purpose of checking movement and any stress build-up. This system on excavations of this magnitude worked so well. When it is considered that the largest cavern, the Machine Hall was 196m long by 16.3m wide and up to 50m deep, the successful completion of the works was a tribute to the skill of the designers and the construction team responsible.

One of the key requirements, insisted upon by the designers, was that the profile of the openings was kept to minimal tolerances and that damage to the surrounding rock, from drilling and blasting was kept to a minimum. This was achieved as a result of the supreme skill and initiative of the Construction Manager, Cecil Ellis, who experimented with drilling spacings and explosives quantities, and in the main excavations devised the optimum scheme of perimeter holes drilled at 225mm spacing and loaded with Cordtex, a detonating cord explosive. This very light explosive charge was set off initially and followed almost instantaneously by the main blast for breaking the rock in the opening. The outcome was perfect with the finished shape of the roof of the main chambers meeting the designer's requirements.

The construction of this very large project was based on the design being modified as a result of the rock encountered and also the finite analysis being carried out at the designer's head office back in London. This did involve significant design changes as to the amount of rock bolts that needed to be installed and also modifications to the sequencing of the works so as to enable geological investigations to be carried out. The lateness caused by the delay in being able to use the Main Access Tunnel and the many design changes resulted in the potential completion date being delayed by as much as twenty-two months. With the client, the Electricity Supply Commission of South Africa (ESCOM) having committed to the contracts for the turbines, generators and other key equipment, together with the need for the power to be available earlier, agreement was reached whereby the works would be accelerated to save fifteen months. Despite further changes to the design this revised programme was kept to. Power from this project became available from October 1980 with the final generator coming on-line in October 1981. The total capacity from the scheme is 1,000 megawatts and can be brought online in a matter of seconds. This scheme has proved to be a great success.

Having described the main reason for our being in this beautiful part of South Africa as my involvement on the Drakensberg Pumped Storage Scheme, may I now revert to my cricketing experiences in this part of the country. We did not have a site cricket team, simply because there was no facility for a cricket field. There was a field where rugby or soccer was played, but it was not suitable for cricket. The nearest town was Bergville, about twenty-five miles away. Contact was made with the cricket club at Bergville and several of us were invited to play for the team.

Most of the Bergville team were farmers and what wonderful characters they were. They played cricket for fun, and several were very fine players. The two opening bowlers were excellent and from memory I believe one had played for Natal Country Districts in previous seasons. We played teams from surrounding areas such as Winterton, Estcourt, Ladysmith and Newcastle. Occasionally teams from further afield would seek a fixture which would be readily accepted.

These local farmers were real characters, and their style of play did perhaps at times not conform to the MCC book of Cricketing Etiquette, especially when the bowler would ask the umpire to hold his cigarette between balls! There was one instance prior to a game starting when one of the players tried to move his pick-up truck. Another player tried to stop him doing so by placing his hand over the exhaust pipe outlet. This worked well and the vehicle remained still. The driver realised what was happening and said something rude in Afrikaans which caused the guilty party to slightly move his hand off the exhaust pipe, at which stage the driver put his foot down, with the result that black soot was shot out over the offender's beautifully laundered cricket whites and face and hands! Talk about the 'Black and White Minstrel show!'

There was another memorable instance when we were playing Newcastle. They had several Indians playing for them by the name of Patel. Playing for Bergville that day was Dodly

Wang who played flank for Natal and was a pretty quick bowler with a competitive nature. A certain Mr Patel, on arriving at the wicket, said very politely to Dodly Wang "please, Mr Wang, don't bowl me a bouncer," shades of the Indian cricketers against Freddie Truman in 1952! Dodly Wang being a gentleman and in no way being aggressive bowled a rather quick bouncer which struck Mr Patel on his head! Mr Patel did not stay at the crease too long.

On another occasion, after an away match at a place by the name of Fort Mistake, several of the players, mostly farmers, decided to stop off at a fishing lake! After catching a few fish, the owner of the fishing lake asked them what they were doing and politely told them to "eff off". It is interesting to note that certain phrases have the same meaning in all languages! He was even more indignant when he was asked if he would cook the fish before they departed! A few pints had been consumed prior to this instance! Fort Mistake was a British signalling post built during the Transvaal War of Independence 1880-1881. It overlooks the Mkupe Pass between Newcastle and Ladysmith. Originally known as Fort One Tree Hill it eventually became known as Fort Mistake and rumour has it that the fort was built on the wrong hill, although no one really knows why. Mkupe Pass is the scene of the last battle of the Transvaal War of Independence when a group of Free State Burghers unsuccessfully attacked the British garrison here shortly after the Battle of Majuba.

There was a very sad occasion when the cricket club at Winterton challenged the workforce on the Drakensberg project to a game on a certain Saturday. We knew several of the Winterton team through their squash court and also through the church where services were held regularly. It was a beautiful sunny day, warm, but just perfect for cricket. We won the toss and decided to bat. We had lost a couple of early wickets when a lovely man called Dudley Roscher joined me at the wicket. We had a good stand putting on about fifty runs before Dudley was dismissed. I watched Dudley walk back to the pavilion. A few minutes later he came out and sat down on a chair and toppled over backwards. Dudley sadly had had a massive heart attack. He was placed in the back of a truck and headed off to the nearest medical centre for treatment. My wife was with Dudley when he died. It subsequently transpired that Dudley's father and grandfather had died at an almost identical age. We immediately called off the game and drove back home. The whole site was shocked at Dudley's death as he was so liked by everybody and absolutely first-rate at his job. His funeral took place in Bergville a short while later. A very sad time for us all, especially for Lyn and the two children. He was sadly missed.

We met some wonderful people during our time in South Africa, and we made good friends with Keith and Merle Miller. Keith had been named after the great Australian all-rounder. We have stayed in touch over many years and have attended the weddings in South Africa of their children. In February 1980 Keith and I spent the day at Kingsmead in Durban to watch the first day of the game between Natal against Transvaal. What an absolute treat lay in store for us that day! We witnessed Graeme Pollock score the most wonderful 168 runs and Clive Rice a robust 110 runs against the bowling of a certain Michael Procter and a lesser-known spinner called Baboo Ibrahim, who Ian Chappell rated as being the best spinner in South African cricket at the time.

Proctor bowled beautifully and was played with much

respect. Early wickets fell before Clive Rice joined Graeme Pollock. The batting was brilliant, and having watched the likes of Len Hutton, Denis Compton, Frank Worrell and Tom Graveney in earlier years, was at least of the quality of these former great players. There was one period when Baboo Ibrahim was bowling beautifully against Graeme Pollock. For over after over the ball was pitched on the perfect length and played with great respect. Twice, during a spell of six or seven overs, the ball was slightly short and on both occasions the ball was pulled with perfect timing over mid-wicket for sixes. The batting of Pollock was sublime. Clive Rice's inning was also excellent, and he was always content in letting Pollock have the strike. Rice's innings was memorable as any loose ball was hit with tremendous force. The batting that day could be described as the "broadsword" of Clive Rice compared with the "rapier" of Graeme Pollock. Transvaal duly won this game by ten wickets.

Again, with thanks to Wikipedia

'Robert Graeme Pollock (born 27 February 1944) is a former cricketer for South Africa, Transvaal and Eastern Province. A member of a famous cricketing family, Pollock is widely regarded as South Africa's greatest cricketer, and as one of the finest batsmen to have played Test cricket. Despite Pollock's international career being cut short at the age of 26 by the sporting boycott of South Africa, and all but one of his 23 Test matches being against England and Australia, the leading cricket nations of the day, he broke a number of records. His completed career Test match batting average of 60.97 remains fifth best after Sir Donald Bradman's (99.94), Steve Smith's, Marnus Labuschagne's and Adam Voges's averages.

Pollock has been the recipient of numerous awards and accolades, including being voted in 1999 as South Africa's Cricketer of the 20th Century, one of Wisden's Cricketers of the Year in 1966, as well as being retrospectively selected in 2007 as the Wisden Leading Cricketer in the World in 1967 and 1969. In South Africa he was player of the year in 1961 and 1984, with special tributes in the S.A. Cricket annuals of 1977 and 1987. Bradman described Pollock, along with Sir Garfield Sobers, as the best left-handed batsman he had ever seen play cricket.

In 2009, Pollock was inducted into the ICC Cricket Hall of Fame.

Pollock was born into a Scottish family in Durban, Natal Province, Union of South Africa on 27 February 1944. His grandfather was a Presbyterian minister, and his father, Andrew, was a former first-class cricketer with Orange Free State and the editor of the Eastern Province Herald. As a youth, Pollock carned the nickname Little Dog:

The name arose when his brother [Peter], with voice still unbroken, made queer-sounding appeals for lbw. The humourist, Springbok Atholl McKinnon, said they sounded like a dog barking, and called him Pooch. When Graeme joined the provincial eleven, they became Big Dog and Little Dog.

Pollock attended Grey High School — a noted sporting school in Port Elizabeth — where he was coached by Sussex professional George Cox. In his first match for Grey Junior, aged 9, he took all ten wickets before scoring 117 not out. At one stage, he hit a six into a neighbouring cemetery and had to fetch the ball himself. He was selected for his first match for the school First XI as a leg spinner, taking six wickets for five runs. At 15, Pollock was selected to represent South Africa schoolboys

In 1960, aged 16 and still attending Grey High School, Pollock was chosen to appear for Eastern Province. His first-class cricket debut was against Border at the Jan Smuts Ground in East London, where he made 54 runs before being run out. He then went on to take two wickets in Border's second innings. Later that season he scored his maiden first-class century, scoring 102 against Transvaal B, becoming the youngest South African to score a first-class century. Pollock played five matches for EP in his debut season, scoring 384 runs at an average of 48.00. In 1961, while visiting Britain with his parents, he played six matches with the Sussex Second XI.

In the 1962–63 South African season, Pollock finished second in the averages, scoring 839 runs including three centuries at an average of 69.66. The highlight of his season was scoring 209 not out for an Eastern Province Invitational XI against the International Cavaliers, which included bowlers such as Richie Benaud and Graham McKenzie. Benaud was to describe the innings as "magnificent", later saying "I knew I was watching a champion. Aged 19, Pollock was the youngest South African to score a double-century in first-class cricket

Debut in Australia

Pollock was 19 when he was selected for the 1963–64 South African cricket team's tour of Australia. He had a disappointing start to the tour, making 1 and 0 against Western Australia, dismissed twice by McKenzie. He recovered in the next match scoring 127 not out against a Western Australia Combined XI. He made his Test debut at the Gabba in Brisbane making 25 in a rain-interrupted match before again being dismissed by McKenzie. The match was an infamous one with the Australian bowler Ian Meckiff no-balled for throwing, effectively ending his career. Pollock was not successful in the Second Test at the Melbourne Cricket Ground, making 16 and 2 as South Africa were heavily defeated by eight wickets.

Pollock's performances in the first two Tests of the series raised questions over the youngster's place, but, in the third Test in Sydney, Pollock made 122 in South Africa's first innings. Bradman commented: "Next time you decide to play like that, send me a telegram". At 19 years and 317 days he became the youngest South African to score a Test century, a record that still stands. In Adelaide, in the fourth Test, Pollock and Eddie Barlow shared a South African third-wicket record partnership of 341; Pollock hitting 175 and Barlow 201. It was during this game that the excellent Charles Fortune was broadcasting for the South African listeners with the renowned earlier Australian captain Victor Richardson, the grandfather of Ian and Greg Chappell. Fortune was passing the microphone over to Richardson, when he understood that Richardson was unable to speak. He was so emotional at seeing the brilliance of Pollock's batting that he had tears in his eyes and could not speak for several minutes. South Africa won the Test at Adelaide by 10 wickets to level the series 1–1. Pollock finished his maiden series with 399 runs to his name, at an average of 57.00. During Pollock's innings of 17 in the drawn fifth Test, he suffered an injury which resulted in his missing the first two Tests of the New Zealand tour which followed.

Charles Fortune was a superb cricket commentator, perhaps the nearest South African to be compared with John

Arlott. There was a classic piece of commentary I recall when he was commentating on a game at Port Elizabeth when Graeme Pollock was batting. For at least 10 minutes after lunch Fortune described what they had had for lunch before he causally announced that Eastern Province were something like 160-2 and Pollock had reached his century!

England toured South Africa in 1964–65 under the captaincy of Mike Smith. Pollock was selected in all five Tests against the tourists. England won the First Test at Kingsmead convincingly by an innings and 104 runs, with Pollock making 5 and a first ball duck. The remaining Tests were all drawn. In the final Test at St George's Park, Pollock made 137 in the first innings, with Wisden Cricketers' Almanack describing it as "a splendid century, distinguished by many drives past cover and mid-on." In the second, he made an unbeaten 77. In the Tests, Pollock made 459 runs at an average of 57.37.

Pollock was included to tour England with the South African team in 1965. In the Second Test at Trent Bridge, Pollock made 125, an innings he described in his autobiography as his best. He made his runs out of 160 added in 140 minutes, the last 91 of his runs coming in 70 minutes. He had come in at 16/2, and the score had declined to 80/5, before his partnerships with the captain Peter van der Merwe and with Richard Dumbrill enabled the score to reach 269. John Woodcock wrote in The Cricketer, "Not since Bradman's day could anyone recall having seen an English attack treated in such cavalier style." while the same correspondent in The Times said, "I can think of no innings played against England since the [Second World] war which was so critical and commanding: I can think of none more beautifully played."] E.W. Swanton wrote in The Daily Telegraph that it was an innings "which in point of style and power, of ease and beauty of execution is fit to rank with anything in the annals of the game." In the second innings, Pollock scored 59. It was a notable match for the Pollock brothers; older brother Peter took 10 wickets in total as South Africa won the match and, therefore, the three Test series 1–0. His performances during that English season saw him named as one of the Wisden Cricketers of the Year in 1966, acclaimed as "one of the most accomplished batsmen in contemporary cricket".

In 1966–67, Bob Simpson led his Australian team to South Africa for a five Test series. The South Africans won the First Test at Wanderers after trailing by 126 after the first innings and scoring 620 runs in the second innings. Pollock scored 90 from 104 balls. Describing Pollock's innings, Wisden said "[he] looked without peer and his timing, placing and wristwork were an object lesson for the purist." In the Second Test at Newlands, responding to an Australian total of 542, Pollock made 209 runs from a team total of 353 despite batting with an injured groin which restricted his footwork and running. South Africa, however, were unable to avoid the follow-on and eventually lost the match by 6 wickets. The Third Test was played at Kingsmead in Durban and Pollock made 67 not out in the second innings, with Ali Bacher batting South Africa to an eight-wicket victory. The Fourth Test saw rain deny South Africa an almost certain victory. The final Test at Port Elizabeth saw Pollock, on his birthday, score another century as South Africa won the match by seven wickets to clinch the series three Tests to one. For the series, Pollock scored 537 runs at an average of 76.71, trailing only Denis Lindsay on both measures for the South Africans.

Pollock and the South Africans were due to play England

at home in 1968–69, but tensions stemming from the South African government's apartheid policy came to a head when South African-born Basil D'Oliveira — of Cape Coloured ancestry — was chosen in the England touring team to replace the injured Tom Cartwright. The South African Prime Minister B. J. Vorster denounced the English team as the "team of the anti-apartheid" movement and refused to allow the team to enter South Africa with D'Oliveira in place. The tour was therefore cancelled.

South Africa's last Test series before their expulsion from international cricket was against Bill Lawry's Australians. The Australians had just completed a gruelling tour of India in vastly different playing conditions before coming to South Africa. Pollock's form continued into the series and he averaged 73.85. Pollock managed to break McGlew's South African Test record of 255 when he scored 274 in the 2nd Test in Durban. When Pollock was batting in this innings with Barry Richards, the opposing captain, Bill Lawry, said about this innings: "Never have I seen the ball hit with such power by two players at the same time." He held this record for nearly thirty years until Daryll Cullinan scored 275 not out against New Zealand in 1999. Pollock was 26 years of age when his Test career was brought to an end.

When the scheduled South African tour of England in 1970 was cancelled, a tour by a "Rest of the World" side was arranged to fill the gap. The side, of which Pollock was a member, played five games against England which were promoted at the time as "Tests," but which are not now recognised as such. Pollock had a poor series by his standards, but he did make 114 in the final match at The Oval, sharing in a fifth wicket partnership of 165 with Gary Sobers.

International isolation was keenly felt by the South African team at the time, including Pollock, and the players took measures to try to reverse the looming sporting boycott. In 1971, Pollock took part in a protest organised by Barry Richards and Mike Procter against the South African government's apartheid policy as it referred to cricket. During a match to celebrate the tenth anniversary of the formation of the Republic of South Africa, the players from both teams walked off after one ball, issuing a joint statement:

"We cricketers feel that the time has come for an expression of our views. We fully support the South African Cricket Association's application to invite non-whites to tour Australia, if they are good enough, and further subscribe to merit being the only criterion on the cricket field."

During South Africa's international isolation, Pollock played in 16 unofficial Test matches against breakaway teams from England, Sri Lanka, the West Indies and Australia. He ended his international career at the age of 42 with a 144 against the rebel Australian team that toured South Africa in 1987. He scored 1376 runs, including 5 centuries, at an average of 65.52.

Pollock continued playing first-class cricket for Eastern Province and Transvaal until his retirement from the first-class game in the 1986–87 season at the age of 43. He made 20,940 runs in first-class cricket, including 64 centuries and 99 fifties, at an average of 54.67. Despite offers, Pollock never played in English domestic cricket, once stating that "the domestic grind was not 'my type of game'." Limited overs matches were introduced sometime after his career began, and he played 112 innings in the shorter form of the game, tallying 4,656 runs at an average of over 50. In 1974–75 Pollock scored 222 not out for Eastern Province against Border in the Gillette Cup, this was the first double century in List A cricket and remained the highest individual innings until 2002 when surpassed by Ali Brown.

By the time of his retirement in 1988, Pollock was already "established in cricket administration: president of the South African Cricket Players' Association, board member and team selector with the Transvaal Cricket Council." He was appointed a Test selector by the United Cricket Board in 2000, a post he held until 2002, at which point he was appointed as a batting coach to the South African team.

Pollock, together with Gary Sobers, was honoured by being chosen to present the match awards following the 2003 Cricket World Cup Final in Johannesburg

On 26 November 2013, the Centurion pavilion at St George's Oval was renamed the "Graeme Pollock Pavilion" in honour of his contribution to cricket.

Standing at 6 feet 2 inches (1.88 m), Pollock used his height well to get to the pitch of the ball, and utilised a strong sense of timing. He had an upright batting stance and his footwork was balanced and correct. He used a heavy bat and liked to play the cover drive. To rectify an apparent weakness on the leg side, Pollock developed a very good pull and leg drive. With his power, he was able to find the gaps in the field, allowing him to score quickly. His style of batting was aggressive, not waiting for poor deliveries when looking to score:

"Pollock does not need a half-volley or a long hop to score fours: he will drive on the up, or cut, force and pull anything even fractionally short of a good length"

— Christopher Martin-Jenkins,

Aside from his batting abilities, Pollock was also an occasional leg-spinner. His teammate Jackie McGlew claimed Pollock could have made an outstanding bowler — He bowled right over the top and really made the ball 'fizz' — but he bowled mainly for enjoyment and with a light heart. In total, he took 4 Test wickets and 43 in first-class cricket. He was also a naturally gifted fielder.

Pollock's Scottish immigrant father Andrew Pollock played cricket for Orange Free State, while his brother, Peter Pollock, was a leading fast bowler who played 28 Test matches for South Africa. Both Graeme Pollock's sons, Anthony Pollock and Andrew Graeme Pollock, played cricket for Transvaal and Gauteng, while his nephew, Shaun Pollock (son of Peter), retired from the South African Test team in 2008, played in 108 Test matches, captained the country from 2000 to 2003 and was South Africa's leading wicket-taker before being overtaken by Dale Steyn.

In 2003, Pollock expressed his thoughts about the sporting boycott of South Africa:

"I was twenty-four. We did not give too much thought to the people who were not given the opportunities. In hindsight we certainly could have done much more in trying to get change to Southern Africa. We had a good series against Australia in '67 and we probably had our best side ever. Poor old Barry (Richards) played just four Tests, Mike Procter seven. But at the same time the protesters got it absolutely right that the way to bring about change in South Africa was in sport. It was difficult for twenty-two years, but in hindsight it was needed and I'm delighted it did achieve change in South Africa."

—Graeme Pollock

Whilst Graeme Pollock had played so beautifully that day in Durban in 1980, his partner Clive Rice should always be remembered as one of the very best all-rounders in World cricket at the time.

During the 1979–1980 season, Clive Rice, in addition to scoring over 500 runs at an average of 53.00 also took the 43 wickets for Transvaal in the Currie Cup competition at the extraordinary low average of 11.76 runs per wicket. An all-rounder, Rice ended his first-class cricket career with a batting average of 40.95 and a bowling average of 22.49.

His career coincided directly with South Africa's sporting isolation, and his international experience was limited to his post-prime days. He played three One Day Internationals for South Africa following the country's return from sporting isolation. He was controversially left out of the squads for the one-off Test against West Indies and the 1992 Cricket World Cup. Despite this he is widely regarded as one of the best all-rounders of his generation, alongside Imran Khan, Ian Botham, Kapil Dev and his county team-mate Richard Hadlee.

Rice played for Nottinghamshire in the English County Championship in a side that also featured internationals Richard Hadlee and Derek Randall. As captain, he led the side to the County Championship title in both 1981 and 1987, winning the prestigious award of being named a Wisden cricketer of the year for his exploits in 1981.

Looking back to that day at Kingsmead in Durban on 9th February 1980, I realise just what a privilege it had been to see one of the greatest batsmen the World has ever seen play such a beautiful innings.

Getting away from cricket for a moment, I would also like to relate another special occasion which had such fond memories. 1980 was the year that the British and Irish Lions Rugby team were in South Africa. A good friend and I drove to Bloemfontein to see the 3rd Test on 14th June.

Again, with thanks to Wikipedia.

'The tour was not a success for the Lions, as they lost the first three tests before salvaging some pride with a win in the fourth. The team did however win all their 14 non-international matches. The Lions were captained by Bill Beaumont.

The tour went ahead in the face of opposition from the British Government and groups opposed to sporting contact with the apartheid regime in South Africa. Britain was a signatory to the 1977 Gleneagles Agreement in which Commonwealth governments agreed to discourage sporting contacts with South Africa. The Government of the Republic of Ireland were also against the tour. The Four Home Unions committee which organises Lions tours decided to go ahead with the planned tour, despite this opposition, in November 1979 and the rugby unions of England (RFU), Ireland (IRFU), Scotland (SRU) and Wales (WRU) all approved the tour by January 1980.'

The tour party was disrupted by an unusually high number of injuries and replacements throughout the 10-week-long tour. The Springboks were fearsome competitors and were anxious to recover their pride from being defeated by Willie John McBride's magnificent team of 1974 when the Lions won the series 3-0, with the last Test being drawn as a result of horrendous refereeing decisions. The Lions had a legitimate try disallowed whilst the Springboks were allowed a try which should have been penalised. Nine players left the tour early, including Mike Slemen who went home due to family illness. Stuart Lane's injury occurred after 55 seconds of the opening game and gave him the shortest career of any Lions tourist. He never played international rugby again. O'Donnell's neck injury ended his rugby career completely. Colin Patterson suffered a knee injury in the penultimate game against Griqualand West which also proved career-ending.

The game at Bloemfontein was won by South Africa in front of a capacity crowd. The Springboks were worthy winners. The Lions scored a very good try, at which stage Jim and I leapt out of seats to applaud the score. There was absolute stony silence around us. We were in the midst of Afrikaners, who loved their rugby with such a passion! We sat down rather quickly for fear of starting another Boer War. The surrounding crowd remained in good spirits and we exchanged pleasantries as we left the stadium.

As an aside, the Lions tour of South Africa in 1974, took South African rugby by surprise. This magnificent team containing Gareth Davies, Phil Bennett, JPR Williams, JJ Williams and Willie John McBride was possibly the greatest team ever to play rugby. Being at Vanderkloof, in the Northern Cape, at the time, the majority of the workforce were Afrikaners and rugby fanatics. A friend from Scotland was a mechanic/welder on the project and had a bet with his Afrikaner friends on every game. He was quite a wealthy man by the end of the series.

During our time on the Drakensberg Pumped Storage Scheme I was fortunate to be invited to play for the Anglo-American Company team to play against their insurance brokers in Johannesburg. What a wonderful experience this turned out to be. I arrived at the ground at precisely the same time as this distinguished looking man carrying his cricket bag. He was very friendly and smiled and said, "are you playing for Anglo-American?"

"Yes," I replied.

He said "welcome, I am Roy McLean". At this stage I recognised this fine cricketer, who had played with such great skill for South Africa. We had a lovely chat about the time when he brought the 'Fezala' cricket team to England in 1961 and he remembered the game against Norfolk. This was the game for which I was selected, yet because of exams I could not play, rather fortuitously, bearing in mind that Eddie Barlow had taken six wickets and scored a century by three o'clock on the first day!

Jackie McGlew was also playing for the Insurance Brokers XI. They were far too strong for our scratch team. I did have the pleasure of bowling several overs of quickish leg-spin against Jackic McGlcw, and cven at the age of 50, he watched each ball as carefully as he had done in his prime and played each ball on its merits. What a privilege it was to play against these superb players.

With thanks again to Wikipedia:

'Derrick John "Jackie" McGlew (11 March 1929–8 June 1998) was a cricketer who played for Natal and South Africa.

An opening batsman with fabled powers of adhesion, suiting his name, McGlew set records in the 1950s for slow scoring. But though his tenacity brought criticism — even from Wisden — he was the linchpin around which the strong South African cricket team of the 1950s was built.

McGlew was picked for the 1951 tour to England on the strength of a century in a 12-a-side match, and was not a success in his two Test matches. But within 18 months, he was both a fixture in the Test side and vice-captain as South Africa held the strong Australians to a series draw in 1952–53. And in the same season he hit what was then South Africa's highest Test innings, an undefeated 255, against New Zealand at Wellington.

McGlew was the South Africans' most successful batsman on his second tour of England in 1955, scoring centuries at Old Trafford and Headingley. He captained the side in two Tests because of injury to the tour captain, Jack Cheetham. South Africa won both matches, and Cheetham wanted McGlew to remain as captain for the Fifth Test even though Cheetham was fit, but he was over-ruled by the other members of the selection committee. In 1956, for his efforts on the tour, McGlew was named as a Wisden Cricketer of the Year with Wisden contrasting the dourness of his batting with the liveliness of his fielding in the covers.

Dourness reached new levels in 1957–58 in the home Test series against Australia: at Durban, McGlew took 313 minutes to reach 50, and the 545 minutes he took to get to 100 was the world record for the slowest century in first-class cricket until declining over-rates in the 1970s took all such timed records away. In all, he batted 575 minutes for 105, but South Africa failed to win because there was not enough time left to bowl Australia out twice. Wisden praised the innings as a feat of concentration and endurance but added: "It is doubtful whether South Africa benefited by it." McGlew's third tour of England in 1960 saw him captain the side. He had a poor Test series, and the tour was blighted by controversy over the bowling action of the South African fast bowler, Geoff Griffin, who was no-balled for throwing at Lord's. McGlew retired from Test cricket after the 1961–62 series against New Zealand, in which he scored his seventh and final Test century. In all, he captained South Africa in 13 Tests, winning four and losing five. He scored 2,440 Test runs at an average of more than 42.

A useful before Lunch and Afternoon Tea bowler, he took no Test wickets with his leg breaks, but did reap a hat-trick for Natal against Transvaal in 1963–64, with the wickets spread over two innings. His best bowling figures in a single innings were only two wickets for four runs.

Batting at number eight or nine, he played some useful innings while leading Natal to victory in the Currie Cup in 1966–67, then retired from first-class cricket.

An excellent tactical captain, he was warm-hearted and devoted to the game. He wrote the books Cricket Crisis (about the 1964–65 series against England) and Six for Glory (about the 1966–67 series against Australia).

In retirement, he briefly threw in his hat with pro-apartheid politics at one point standing as a candidate for the ruling National Party, before moving into business. In 1991–92, when post-apartheid South Africa was re-admitted to world cricket, he was picked as manager of the first visit by a South African team to the West Indies, the Under-19 tour.

With thanks again to Wikipedia

Roy Alastair McLean (9 July 1930–26 August 2007) was a South African cricketer who played in forty Tests from 1951 to 1964. A stroke-playing middle-order batsman, he scored over 2,000 Test runs, but made 11 ducks in 73 Test innings.

McLean was born in Pietermaritzburg, Natal, and

educated at Hilton College. He shone at cricket, hockey and rugby union, and was a strong enough rugby player to represent Natal at fly-half.

As a cricketer, he made his first-class debut for Natal in 1949, and his Test debut on the 1951 tour of England at Old Trafford. He established himself as an exciting and forceful middle-order batsman in the South African team. He was particularly successful on tour, hitting an unbeaten 76 to win the final Test of the 1952–53 tour to Australia, to square the series, despite Australia scoring 520 in their first Innings. He played against the touring Australian rugby union team later in 1953, scoring a drop-goal as fly-half for Natal to win 15–14.

He made his highest Test score in the 2nd Test at Lord's on the tour to England in 1955. Batting against a bowling attack that included Brian Statham, Fred Trueman, Trevor Bailey and Johnny Wardle, he rode his luck, hitting 21 fours and a six but being dropped several times, and scoring 142 of 196 the runs while he was at the wicket, before he was finally bowled by Statham. Nevertheless, England won by 76 runs. In the 3rd Test, at Old Trafford, he hooked Frank Tyson for four several times in the second innings, hitting 50 in 71 minutes before he was run out: South Africa won with 9 balls to spare. He was the South African Cricket Annual Cricketer of the Year in 1955. He and fast bowler Neil Adcock were the only successes of the 1960 tour of England. He reached his highest first-class score, 207, against Worcestershire, and recorded the fastest century that season, in 75 minutes against A E R Gilligan's XI in a festival match at Hastings, despite only scoring 6 runs in the first half an hour. Each was named as a Wisden Cricketer of the Year in 1961.

In 1961 he led an unofficial tour to England by a team of

young players named the Fezelas.

The team contained the nucleus of the great South African side of the late 1960s, with such players as Peter Pollock, Eddie Barlow, Colin Bland, Denis Lindsay and Peter van der Merwe, and was unbeaten on the tour. In the 1966 Wisden Cricketers' Almanack the editor Norman Preston, reflecting on the success of the touring South Africans in 1965, paid tribute to "that exuberant character R.A. McLean... who moulded the new Springboks when he brought the Fezelas side to England in 1961".

He played all five Tests when New Zealand toured in 1961–62, a final two Tests against England in South Africa in 1964–65, and retired from first-class cricket in 1966. He became an insurance salesman.

McLean died in Johannesburg following a long illness. He was survived by his wife of 51 years, Barbara, and their three daughters.'

Playing against such wonderful cricketers such as Jackie McGlew and Roy McLean was such a privilege and they both remembered and spoke fondly of Bill Edrich. Whilst not playing Test cricket against him they would have heard of Bill's double century at Durban in 1938 and his prolific season in 1947 when together with Denis Compton they scored around 2000 runs against South Africa. Roy McLean played with similar panache and freedom of spirit to that of Bill Edrich. Half volleys and short balls were meant to be hit as hard as possible. Even against the quickest, such as Statham, Lindwall and Miller they never considered the danger in hooking these wonderful bowlers!

Early in 1980 we prepared for our return to the UK. We wanted to get back to England so that our eldest son Alex, could settle into his new school before sitting his 12 plus later that year. We also wanted to live in Buckinghamshire, near to the headquarters of Taylor Woodrow Construction. The final months in South Africa were memorable. During the seven and a half years we had met so many wonderful people and our children had started their schooling which was so good that they had little if any difficulties in settling back into the English system on our return. Besides the excellence of the teaching, the teachers commanded respect and encouraged hard work with a good sense of strong morality.

The contract was going well with progress well in line with the agreed programme. The contractual issues were being resolved in a spirit of trust and openness and relations between Contractor, Client and the Engineers were excellent. The Drakensberg project was chosen as the 'Most Outstanding Civil Engineering Achievement of 1981' by the South African Institution of Civil Engineers. The final few weeks were involved with farewell parties held by friends and preparing for our return trip back to the UK. We also planned to stop off in Kenya and Egypt on the way home. This was not easy because of the relationship these countries had with South Africa under the apartheid regime. Leaving the Drakensberg was a very sad day for us all, as we set off for Johannesburg to spend the final night before flying out the next day on around the 23rd June 1980. The final evening Jean and I had been invited to a farewell dinner at the Johannesburg Country Club, attended by the directors of the companies involved with the project. This was such a splendid evening with warm words being expressed. We had come to love this beautiful country and the people we met. Apartheid was so wrong, yet there was little that we could do. We tried to treat everybody with respect and with the job I was required to do, we did not get involved with politics. We always considered that being in South Africa we would respect their ways of doing things, even if we did not agree. Perhaps this showed just how naïve we were at the time. We will however never regret the wonderful years we spent in South Africa.

We flew out of Johannesburg with much sadness, but also with expectation as to a completely new adventure that lay ahead. My job, on returning to head office in Southall in West London, was to be Commercial Manager of the Mining Division. Although Taylor Woodrow was predominantly a construction company, it had also been involved with opencast mining since just after the war and was mining over one and a half million tonnes per year. Our first stop was Nairobi, where we picked up a car from the Taylor Woodrow subsidiary company and went to book into The Norfolk Hotel, only to be told that we were not scheduled to stay until the following evening. We showed the reception staff our booking details, and they accepted their error and booked us into another hotel for the first evening. This was not such a hardship as we were able to check into The Norfolk Hotel the following day. This was a lovely old colonial hotel.

The hotel, built by Maj. C.G.R. Ringer and R. Aylmer Winearls, opened its doors on December 25, 1904 for use by early settlers seeking refuge from the harsh conditions of Kenya. The hotel advertised itself as being the only stone built and tiled roofed hotel in East Africa, sporting forty rooms, a billiard room, and French chef. The hotel was the basecamp of early African explorers who ventured to Masai Mara, Kenya's Coast, and the Great Rift Valley. The hotel also served as a centre for famous hunters. Maj.-Gen. Robert Baden Powell stayed here in Feb. 1906. In 1909, Theodore Roosevelt stayed at the Norfolk before and after his famous safari, following his retirement as the 26th President of the United States.

On December 23, 1980, a man named Muradi Akaali booked a room at the property. Keeping to his room for the duration of his stay, he set up a bomb in his hotel room that he evacuated prior to the explosion, which went at 8:30pm the night of December 31. The bomb exploded, where many people died and destroyed the whole western wing of the property. The hotel's New Year's Eve celebration was scheduled to occur three hours after the explosion occurred. The hotel was re-built shortly afterwards and featured in the 1985 movie "Out of Africa" starring Meryl Streep and Robert Redford. (With thanks to Wikipedia)

We stayed for a couple of days in this very comfortable place, a perfect way to start our new adventure. We drove from Nairobi down to the Masai Mara Game Reserve, some one hundred and fifty miles away and stayed in the lodge at Keekorok. This was a real joy, although not without its challenges. The first being a faulty carburettor on the Peugeot 504 which I had borrowed. I asked the hotel manager if he knew if there was anybody at the Lodge who could have a look. No problem! A lovely, bright, elderly local Kenyan had a look and within a few minutes the problem was solved. The second challenge was the following morning when we arranged for a local Game Ranger to accompany us in the Peugeot 504 on a game drive. His name was Lecavey, my apologies for the spelling, and such a friendly and knowledgeable young man. He spotted vultures circling above, a clear sign that there had been a "kill" somewhere in the reserve. We set off through the bush, and away from the roads. All went well until we came to a stream with a slow trickle of water flowing. I queried with Lecavey if it would be safe to drive through. "No problem baas, you will be fine," he said with a smile Unperturbed I drove into the waterway and found to my alarm that the bed of the stream was rather softer that we had expected, and we were stuck fast!

Rather concerned, we asked Lecavey, "What do we do now?"

"No worry baas, I will go and get a Land Rover to tow us out," Lecavey replied with complete confidence,

This sounded an excellent idea until we remembered that we were in the African bush near to where it was likely that a lion or a leopard had made a "kill" recently. Lecavey was undeterred and set off through the bush to run back to the Keekorok Lodge to get a Land Rover. There we were alone in the Kenyan bush, Jean, myself and our three children. We dread to think what might have happened if Lecavey had been eaten by a lion or a herd of elephants had taken an interest. We could easily have been tipped over and trampled. Perish the thought! We trusted that all would be well and sang a few songs and hymns to keep our spirits high. After about an hour Lecavey returned with a friend and the important Land Rover. We were quickly pulled out; a generous tip was given, and we were away on our safari. Lecavey was brilliant and guided us to the "kill", where a Leopard had taken a small antelope. By the time we arrived he had had his fill and the hyenas and jackals and vultures were squabbling for the smaller morsels. We also saw lions during this trip, so exciting for the children especially. Staying at Keekorok was a wonderful experience, with the local Maasai people proud and distinguished in the way they conducted themselves with such dignity.

After a couple of days, we drove back to Nairobi and caught a plane on the short flight to Mombasa on the coast. We stayed in a hotel literally on the beach for a couple of days and again enjoyed ourselves at this lovely part of Africa. We then flew back to Nairobi to catch the flight to Cairo to spend the final few days of our African adventure. The Egyptian Airways flight was superb, and I will always remember the skill and presence of mind shown by the beautiful Stewardess looking after us. Our young daughter who was 10 had her feet sticking out into the aisle, and the Stewardess tripped and very nearly dropped the tray of drinks she was carrying. Her instant reaction was one of annoyance but turning round and seeing the innocent look on our daughter's face, recovered her poise, smiled and continued with her duties.

Egypt was fascinating, but arriving at Cairo Airport was a bit of a nightmare, as it was in the throes of a major reconstruction. There were no baggage handling facilities and our four suitcases were placed at different places in the concourse. These were duly located and with our three children we hired a taxi to take us to our hotel. We visited the Pyramids, the Sphinx and the world-famous Cairo Museum and had the usual photos taken with us all on camels. I had the best lesson in negotiation I have ever experienced in the museum when I needed to use the toilet. There I was, feeling relieved, before looking round and realising there was no toilet paper! Panic set in before a little knock on the door and a little voice enquired, "Toilet paper Sir?"

I immediately responded, "Yes please."

The charge was the equivalent to one English Pound, which I willingly passed under the door, for which I received a single sheet! It would have finished up cheaper if I had used the local currency instead of the toilet paper. This literally was a case of being caught with one's trousers down!

We had scheduled taking a 'Luxury Train Journey' down to Luxor to see the Valley of the Kings. We were looking forward so much to this, but what a shock we were in for. We arrived at the Cairo station with tickets and managed to find someone in a uniform who directed us towards our train. With three young children, we had been booked into carriages 5, 12 and 13! This was not perhaps the best arrangement. We agreed that we settle ourselves in carriages 12 and 13. The air-conditioning did not work, but on calling the engineer and the payment of "baksheesh", the problem was fixed. There were no sheets on the couches. On further payment of "baksheesh" sheets appeared. The highlight we were looking forward to was dinner in the dining car. Alas, the lights failed and we finished up eating a water melon! We appreciated the history of the Valley of the Kings and Luxor. The guides who helped us in Cairo and the Valley of the Kings were brilliant. At the time tourism was the largest means of trade and each guide was educated to a bachelor's degree. They knew the history of their country so well and were proud to impart their knowledge to those prepared to listen.

We returned to the confusion of Cairo Airport and with all of our luggage still intact we were so pleased to board the British Airways plane for the four-hour flight back to London. We picked up a car at Heathrow and drove to Norfolk to stay with my parents in Horsford. Our wonderful adventure in South Africa was complete, although our connections have remained in place to this present day

CHAPTER 14

August 1980 London Head-Office New life in Buckinghamshire

Arriving back in the UK after seven and a half years in South Africa was a real challenge. Firstly, we needed to find a house, get the children settled into a new school and for myself to adjust to my new role as Commercial Manager of the Mining Division.

Everything worked out very well. Thanks to Jean, we found a lovely home, built in 1922, in Penn about two miles from High Wycombe and six miles from Beaconsfield. It was 50% more than we had budgeted for but with the proceeds from the sale of the house in Lancashire which had been rented out during our time in South Africa, our savings from our time in South Africa and a mortgage we were able to buy Cobwood, Manor Road, Penn.

From the time of arriving back in England in the middle of July 1980 it took us about six weeks to move into our new home. We had furniture coming from our home in Lancashire and also our belongings from South Africa. This all happened on the same day. Our children were staying with my parents in Norfolk, and after a few days, by which time we had sorted out the house, especially the bedrooms, the children joined us. We had made arrangements at the local school in Tylers Green, the next village, within walking distance, for Alex (11), Liz (10) and James (8) to attend at the beginning of September.

We settled in very quickly. Jean sorted out the house in her usual brilliant style, we painted most of the rooms ourselves and after a few months Jean started supply teaching for the local Education Authority. The children seemed to enjoy their new school and quickly made new friends. My job as Commercial Manager of the Mining Division, whilst initially being interesting, was not particularly challenging, when compared to my role as Contracts Manager on the Drakensberg project in South Africa. It seemed strange to have to write out a requisition to be able to obtain a new writing pad, after having had the authority to negotiate millions of rands in South Africa.

My role in the Mining Division was enhanced by being selected to join the Taylor Woodrow Management Training Board and shortly afterwards, my responsibilities were extended to take over the role as Manager of the Nuclear Waste Group, set up with the National Nuclear Consortium. This was an extremely interesting challenge in getting Nuclear Engineers and Research Scientists together in seriously looking at dealing with the question of containing and treatment of low-level radioactive waste. Political arguments took over and the group was disbanded and there still remains an uncertainty in dealing with both low-level and high-level nuclear waste.

During the early 1980s Taylor Woodrow attempted to move into the opencast coal industry in Australia, initially in providing technical services to the established mining companies but with the longer-term view of owning and operating mines. This never worked out, and with the World coal price falling, investment opportunities dwindled and the Australian office in Sydney closed. One of my responsibilities was to report to the director as to what was going on in the Sydney office. This included a couple of visits to Australia, to look at potential opportunities, none of which justified a positive investment in the Australian mining industry.

Taylor Woodrow also had a Mining company in the USA, based in Kentucky. This was established in the 1970s, at the time of the oil crisis. My responsibilities included reporting to the director as to the way in which this company was performing. After three years being back in the UK. I was made a Divisional Director of Taylor Woodrow Energy which included the responsibility for the operation in the USA.

Taylor Woodrow's opencast mining operations in the UK were based near Merthyr Tydfil and Morpeth in Northumberland. We were producing around 50,000 tonnes per month in South Wales and 100,000 tonnes per month in Northumberland. One of the key features of our mine at Butterwell, in Northumberland was 'Big Geordie', a Dragline excavator with a bucket size of 60 cubic metres. Both of our operations were successful in providing coal at around £20 per tonne as compared with an average cost of double this for coal produced from underground mining. Opencast mining was ultimately considered to be environmentally unacceptable with very few mines licensed over recent years.

Butterwell Mine, near Morpeth. 'Big Geordie' in the centre.

My role on both of these contracts was not particularly challenging, except for two instances. The first being to agree an adjustment to take into account inflation on the price of the twelve million tonnes of coal produced at Butterwell. This was assessed and agreed without any rancour very quickly. The second instance was when I was asked to go and negotiate the next three-year contract in South Wales. The director in Head Office had indicated the price we should accept. The meeting with our client, The Opencast Executive of the Coal Board, went very well as we had built up a trust over many years. Without any fuss they offered a price higher than we had expected and we then adjourned for lunch and an afternoon on the golf course!

In 1981 I joined the local cricket club, Penn and Tylers Green, which played in the Mid Bucks League. The teams were mostly village teams, several of whom had good players who had played for Buckinghamshire in their ranks. I played as a batsman with moderate success in a knockout competition against Pinkneys Green, near Maidenhead, the same team against which I had scored a century several years earlier. We were chasing around 150 in the 40 overs and had started very slowly and lost several wickets for a few runs. I joined a friend from Taylor Woodrow and we managed to turn the game round with positive batting. We both scored half-centuries and I played several shots through the covers to balls which were still rising, I had never previously ever attempted to hit the ball "on the up" and was surprised at the results.

The children had settled into their new schools, with Alex and Liz passing their 12 plus exams for entry into the excellent Grammar Schools in High Wycombe. James did not get through the 12 plus and went to the local comprehensive school in the next village, Hazlemere. Early in 1981 Jean discovered that she was expecting our fourth child. We were so delighted, and Tom was born in October 1981. Jean had to stop teaching towards the final stages of her pregnancy.

1981 was the year when Ian (later Lord) Botham performed heroically against the Australians enabling England to retain the Ashes. In case anyone needs reminding of Botham's amazing feats, the details are set out below:

1st Test Trent Bridge Won by Australia by 4 wickets:
England 1st Innings 185 Botham b Alderman 1
Australia 1st Innings 179 Botham 16.5-6-34 -2
England 2nd Innings 125 Botham c Border b Lillee 33
Australia 2nd Innings 162-6 Botham 10-1-34-1
2nd Test Lords Draw
England 1st Innings 311 Botham lbw Lawson 0
Australia 1st Innings 345 Botham 26 -8-71 - 2

England 2nd Innings 265-8* Botham b Bright 0
Australia 2nd Innings 90-4 Botham 8-3-10-1

After this match Ian Botham resigned the captaincy and Mike Brearley took over with the most amazing consequences as a result of shrewd leadership and brilliance of this truly great all-rounder, who showed such resilience in the face of unwarranted criticism from the media and the establishment in the upper echelons of English cricket at the time. Talk about not keeping a good man down! Ian Botham showed just what a man he was against this very fine Australian team, containing the likes of Alan Border, Dennis Lillee, Terry Alderman, Kim Hughes, Geoff Lawson and Rodney Marsh.

3rd Test Headingly Won by England by 18 runs

This one Test could fill a book by itself, and perhaps in the history of this wonderful game, there has never been such a comeback by any team as England managed on the final two days.

Australia 1st Innings 401-9* Botham 39.2-11-95-6
England 1st Innings 174 Botham c Marsh b Lillee 50
England 2nd Innings 356 Botham 149 not out.
Australia 2nd Innings 111 Botham 7-3-14-1. Bob Willis 15.1-3-43-8

At the fall of the 7th wicket at 135 in England's 2nd innings, the deficit was still 92 to require Australia to bat again. Botham with Dilley added 117 runs in 80 minutes, and then with Chris Old a further 67 priceless runs were added and finally with Bob Willis a further 37 runs were added. Bob Willis then bowling the most inspired spell of his career, ran through the

Australian batting to take 8-43 to bring about the most staggering victory. English cricket became alive again, thanks to the brilliance of Ian Botham and Bob Willis.

4th Test Edgbaston Won by England by 29 runs

England 1st Innings 189 Botham b Alderman 26
Australia 1st Innings 258 Botham 20 -1-64-1
England 2nd Innings 219 Botham c Marsh b Lillee 3
Australia 2nd Innings 90-4 Botham 14-9-11-5

Australia, requiring 151 to win had reached 114 for 5 wickets, needing a mere 37 runs to win. Enter Ian Botham, bowling fast and straight, to take the final five wickets at the cost of a single run to win the game for his country. Another amazing recovery by England against an Australian team that was becoming more and more shell-shocked. English cricket became even more alive!

5th Test Old Trafford Won by England by 101 runs

England 1st Innings 231 Botham c Bright b Lillee 0
Australia 1st Innings 130 Botham 6.2-1-28-1
England 2nd Innings 404 Botham c Marsh b Whitney 118
Australia 2nd Innings 402 Botham 36-16-86-2

Botham's superb 118 in the 2nd innings was scored in 123 minutes and included six 6s and thirteen 4s, no mean feat against bowlers of the class of Lillee and Alderman who took 81 wickets between them during the series. From the disaster at Lords in the 2nd Test, Ian Botham had rejuvenated the English team, and by winning three Tests, England had retained the Ashes.

6th and Final Test The Oval Draw
Australia 1st Innings 352 Botham 47-13-125-6
England 1st Innings 314 Botham c Yallop b Lillee 3
Australia 2nd Innings 344-9* Botham 42-9-128-4
England 2nd Innings 261-7 Botham lbw Alderman 16

This ended a most wonderful Test series, which will be remembered by all cricketers from all over the World as the 'Botham Series'. The BBC Sports Personality of the Year award was duly given to Ian Botham for his superlative performances.

In October 1981, our youngest son, Tom, was born. He was baptised around Christmas time when our very good friends, Jim and Barbara Richards from South Africa could be with us and accept the invitation to be Tom's God-parents. This was such a wonderfully happy time for us all as a family.

The next few years were relatively uneventful, my work was not exactly challenging, and my form as a batsman for Penn and Tylers Green fluctuating, although still managing to stay in the first team. With my older sons we had the odd trip up to Lords to see Middlesex play, nothing too exciting. The visit of Australia in 1985 was memorable from an English point of view for the sheer brilliance of the batting by David Gower, supported by Mike Gatting, Tim Robinson, Graham Gooch and the bowling of Richard Ellison with 17 wickets at under 11 runs per wicket and the usual all-round excellence of Ian Botham with 250 runs and 31 wickets. England won the series by three Tests to one and my lasting memory was to see that superb Australian fast bowler Jeff Thomson applauding David Gower after he had caressed him through the covers for yet another boundary. This was the same Jeff Thomson who with the support of Dennis Lillee in the 1974/75 series had blown England away in a four Tests to one win for Australia.

In the 1985 series Gower scored 732 runs, Gatting 527, Robinson 490 and Gooch 487. For Australia, Alan Border scored 597 runs. This was one of those series in which England was able to compete so well against an Australian team, and apart from the 1986-87 series in Australia, we struggled to do so for many a year. The Australian approach to cricket at the time reflected the way they played the game, namely "hard but fair". They had a positive approach and at the time the word "sledging" was not part of cricket. There were the usual humourist remarks exchanged between players, but the barbed comments that intended to break a player's spirit, became a part of the game several years later. The thoughts of the truly great players of the likes of Trueman, Sobers, Laker, Lindwall, Miller, Worrell and Constantine ever indulging in an exercise to destroy a fellow player's confidence was anathema to the way these played the game. Freddie Trueman would have looked at the offender, and without saying a word, it would be unlikely if he would ever be sledged again.

Chapter 15

April 1986 – December 1987 Lexington, Kentucky No cricket in the USA!

In early 1986 I was asked to go to Lexington in Kentucky to take over the Mining Company owned by Taylor Woodrow. I agreed on the understanding that I would spend six weeks in the USA and then 10 days in the UK, with the whole family coming out for the summer holidays. For a time, this worked out well, although there was a strain on the family. Jean was managing to deal with the family so brilliantly. Our young son Tom aged 5 was starting school, our eldest son, Alex was doing A levels and Liz was doing her GCE O levels and our middle son, James, was struggling at school. The mining operation was going badly, and we were losing money and towards the end of 1987, the main board of Taylor Woodrow took the decision to close the operation.

This was a difficult time and I took it upon myself to go down to our mines in Tennessee and West Virginia to explain to the whole workforce that we were closing. This was not easy as we still relied upon the goodwill of the men for the restoration of both the mines. Both mines were in areas where there was little alternative means of employment. The men, over 300 in number, were brilliant and enabled the reclamation work to be completed properly. The closure of the mine in West Virginia was a real shame as we could have had a long-term contract in the mid-1970s for supplying coal at an acceptable price of around $60/tonne. This was not followed up and the decision was taken to sell the coal on the open-market, where prices were higher. Coal prices subsequently tumbled, and we were left in the situation where our production costs were higher than the price we were getting for our coal. With my father dying in January 1987, the time spent in the USA was one of mixed emotions, the joy of seeing my wife and children every six weeks, and being in charge of a challenging operation, intermingled with the sadness of losing my father and the responsibility of having to lay off the workforce.

There was the saving grace experienced during my time in Kentucky, and that was finding a wonderful dynamic church in Lexington, the Christian Missionary Alliance Church. I went along to the church on one of the first Sundays as recommended by a friend and was so warmly welcomed. At the initial meeting all new-comers were asked to introduce themselves and say a few words. The Americans love the way we English people speak and the usual phrase "Gee, I love your accent" becomes quite frequently used. After a short period of time, I was asked if I would serve as an elder, similar to being a mentor, to the younger unmarried members of the church. This was a great experience, and my faith as a Christian grew so much during this time. With my wife and children being so far away, and with the difficulties of running a failing business we trusted that God would ensure that all would be well.

I was asked by the local Bible Training College for trainee Pastors to give a lecture on being a Christian manager in the secular world. I explained that being a Christian meant that I respected people in all parts of life and that I tried to be honest in all my dealings. This all seemed to be going well until a well-intentioned question was raised along the lines of "how can you allow your mines to close at the expense of three hundred men and women losing their jobs?" This rather threw me, as I fully understood the difficulties that the workforce would be faced with, as the mines were the only source of employment for miles. I could only respond along the lines that by taking such decisions to close operations in certain locations we would be protecting many other jobs. Together with the assistance of some of the other students this satisfied the questioner. If I had had the presence of mind at the time, I would have referred to the many mines in the USA and around the world that closed after they could no longer be mined economically.

There was no cricket played in Kentucky, West Virginia or Tennessee, yet on numerous instances I was asked to explain the intricacies of cricket. This usually took place around the dining table. With salt cellars, pepper pots, glasses and cutlery I would attempt to explain how the game was played. The Americans found it so difficult to understand the game and could only relate cricket to baseball. Questions such as,

"You mean the ball can bounce before it reaches the batsman?"

and

"How can a game be drawn after five days?"

Despite there not being any cricket, I used to receive the overseas version of the Daily Telegraph. What an absolute joy it was to read the news of the England trip to Australia for the 1986/87 Ashes tour. This helped to alleviate the problems being experienced with the mining operation and being away from my wife and children.

The 1986-87 tour of Australia started with considerable trepidation as England had lost three series running and had not won a single Test for eleven games. The early performances against Queensland and Western Australia were discouraging for England and its supporters. The Australian press, in their gentle manner, proclaimed that there were only three things wrong with this England team. 'The Pommies can't bat, they can't bowl and they can't field'. How the press had to eat their words throughout the coming months. Credit has to be given to the Australian press for their consistency during the England tour of 2010–11 when they applied the same comments to the Australian team during that series.

1986-1987 England v Australia
1st Test November 14-19 Brisbane England win by seven wickets

England lost the toss, and after losing Broad cheaply, Athey, Gatting, Lamb, Gower and DeFreitas batted very well. Botham again showed his liking for the Australian bowling in scoring 138 in just over four hours with four sixes and thirteen fours, including 22 in an over by Merv Hughes. England scored 456

Australia batted slowly and with half centuries from Geoff Marsh and Greg Matthews were bowled out for 248 scored in 104 overs, all credit to the excellent English bowling, especially by Dilley who took an excellent 5–68. Australia was asked to follow-on, and thanks to an excellent century by Geoff Marsh with a useful contribution by Matthews struggled to 282, again the English bowling was excellent with John Emburey taking 5–80 in 42 overs. England needed to score 75 to win, which was achieved for the loss of three wickets. This was an excellent performance for a team that 'couldn't bat, bowl or field'.

2nd Test November 28-December 3 Perth Draw

England won the toss and batted first, and Broad and Athey opened with 223, with Athey being bowled by Reid for 96. Broad batted beautifully to reach 162, his first Test century. Gower scored a beautiful 136, with even the great Australian commentator, Richie Benaud, glowingly admiring the supreme grace and skill with which Gower batted. His partnership with Jack Richards added a further 207 runs with Richards scoring his maiden and only Test century of 133. England duly declared their innings at 592 for 8 wickets.

Australia, thanks to a fine century from Alan Border with good support from Steve Waugh and Greg Matthews reached 401 in their 1st innings, some 191 behind England. England, in their 2nd innings, scored 199–8* with Gatting scoring an excellent 70 and Gower 48. Australia was set 391 to win. On a slow pitch with little turn Australia struggled but showed their fighting spirit in reaching 197–4 after 96 overs. Perhaps a moral win for England but against a team with the characteristics shown by Australians over the years nothing is certain until the last ball is bowled. Nevertheless, a good performance for a team that 'couldn't bat, bowl or field'.

3rd Test December 12–16 Adelaide Draw

On a beautiful batting wicket both teams revealed their batting strengths. Border winning the toss, allowed his batsmen to show their skill and reached 514–5 before the declaration was made. Boon with an excellent century was well supported by Geoff Marsh 43, Jones 93, Border 70*, Matthews 73* and S.

Waugh 79. Thanks to centuries from Broad and Gatting with solid support throughout England reached 456 to give Australia a lead of 59. Bruce Reid had bowled with skill and perseverance and little luck in taking 4–64 in 28 overs. Australia was thwarted by excellent English bowling in their 2nd innings and despite Border's century, his 7th against England, could only score at the rate of just over 2 runs per over, thereby setting England 261 to win in about 2 hours. England batted out the time losing a couple of wickets. A disappointing match from both team's viewpoint.

4th Test December 26–28 Melbourne England win by innings and 14 runs.

Mike Gatting won the toss and put Australia into bat. On a pitch which was slightly damp, they were bowled out for 141 in less than four hours by Gladstone Small taking 5–48 and Ian Botham taking 5–41. The only batsman to bat with any real skill and determination was Dean Jones who scored 59. No other Australian batsman scored beyond 17. Small, a last-minute replacement for Dilley bowled superb away-swingers and Botham bowling off a shorter run was perhaps surprised at taking his wickets with a combination of medium pace and quick deliveries.

Thanks to another century by Broad and useful contributions from Gatting and Lamb, England scored 349 for a first innings lead of 208. Again, Reid bowled splendidly being well supported by McDermott. Australia's second innings was little better than the first and apart from a very good innings by Marsh in scoring 60 and a fighting innings by Waugh with 49, they were bowled out for 194 with England winning by an innings and 14 runs. Again, the English bowling was excellent, with Emburey, Edmonds spinning the ball beautifully and well supported by Small and DeFreitas. This win meant that England had retained the Ashes, a fitting reward for a team that 'couldn't bat, bowl or field'. The Australian press and the supporters showing their dissent in not paying their Australian dollars to watch their team being beaten by the Pommies. The numbers of people watching this series were down by 125,000 from those watching the 1982-83 series.

5th Test January 10–15 Sydney Australia win by 55 runs

This was a well-fought game of Test cricket, and thanks to a match-winning performance by Dean Jones in scoring 184 out of 343 in Australia's 1st Innings, they won by 55 runs. Small, again bowled well in taking 5–75. Jones innings was exceptional bearing in mind that the next highest score was "extras" with 26. England's 1st innings of 275 was largely the result of Gower with 72, Emburey 69 and Richards 46. Australia's new off-spinner Peter Taylor took 6-78 in his maiden Test, not a bad way to start his international career.

With a lead of 69, Australia was bowled out in their 2nd innings for 251, with Border scoring 49, Waugh 73 and Taylor 42, to show that he could bat as well as bowl, a tremendous debut which perhaps as importantly as Jones was the reason for Australia's win. Emburey bowled beautifully to take 7–78 in 46 overs. Emburey and Edmonds had bowled well throughout the whole of the Test series. England's 2nd innings, apart from Gatting with 96 England did not bat well with Australia being worthy winners.

From England's point of view this had been a successful Ashes series. This final Test at Sydney was the start of Australian dominance for the next nineteen years, during which they retained the Ashes through nine series, until that famous afternoon at the Oval in 2005 when Michael Vaughan's team won the series, against the superb Australian team led by Ricky Ponting with other true greats of the like of Shane Warne and Glen McGrath, not to mention Justin Langer and Matthew Hayden, Adam Gilchrist and others.

Reverting back to life in Kentucky and the open-cast mining industry, the rest of 1987 was a time of considerable difficulties. We were losing money virtually every month and there was little opportunity of the position improving and it was with much regret that I was instructed to start making arrangements to close the operation. I stayed on until December 1987, by which time we had dismissed the majority of the workforce, retaining a suitable number of staff and machine operators to deal with the restoration of the sites.

I had enjoyed the responsibility of being in charge of the mining operation in Kentucky and had met some excellent people. Being away from Jean and the children for long stretches, and the failing business was a strain. I know that during this time my Faith as a Christian grew through my involvement with the Christian Missionary Alliance Church in Lexington. I came to realize more and more that whatever the situation that one finds oneself in, God is always there. God's Promise that "never will I leave you or never will I forsake you" has remained so close to this present day. Many a time I have had to attend a difficult meeting yet have gone into the meeting knowing that God is next to me. What a blessing this has been.

Chapter 16

January 1988 – March 1993 London Taylor Woodrow Head Office

The initial months back in the UK were difficult and after working on several projects, which were not challenging and rather mundane I asked the director about my future. He offered two alternatives, the first being a project manager on projects with a subsidiary engineering company and the second to join the Estimating Department as a Senior Estimator, which I accepted. Whilst being trained and qualified as a Civil Engineer, I had always been interested in the commercial side of engineering. My experience in South Africa had honed my skill in the commercial and contractual side. I felt absolutely at home in the Estimating Department and knew that this was the right place to be over the next five years. It was during this time that I successfully applied to the Institution of Civil Engineers for admission as a Fellow. I was proud to be able to add F.I.C.E after my name in 1989.

The first project I was involved with was the tender for the Docklands Light Railway from Canning Town to Beckton. Taylor Woodrow was in a joint venture with Mowlem Construction at the time, and the tender was being put together at Mowlem's office in Bracknell. The team worked so well and our tender was accepted. The construction work involved on this project was completed successfully within the tender price as submitted. Another most interesting project on which I was the Senior Estimator responsible was the refurbishment of the three-mile-long Woodhead 2 tunnel, in the Peak District, originally constructed in the mid-1850s for the purpose of running trains between Sheffield and Manchester. The tunnel was closed in 1953 as a result of the size being insufficient to accommodate the overhead lines for electrification. The contract we tendered for was the refurbishment of the tunnel to enable cables to be installed for the National Grid. This tender was successful and the work duly completed.

Taylor Woodrow was also invited to submit a tender for the design and construction of a very large multimillion water treatment plant for Thames Water at Ashford Common in West London. This was a most interesting project involving the submission of an outline design associated with costs. The final contract price would be negotiated on a "target price" basis as the design became finalised. The principle being that with the "target price" agreed with the client, Thames Water, any savings to the overall cost of the works would be shared between the client and the contractor. Again, we were awarded the contract and I was asked to lead the negotiations to agree the "target price". This project worked so well, with the work being completed on time and within the budget.

The final large project with which I was involved at the tender stage was the London Bridge station part of the Jubilee Line extension. Taylor Woodrow was involved with Costain on this project and were successful in being awarded the contract, which started at the end of 1993. During the early stages of the stage, the contract was dramatically affected as a result of a tunnel under construction at Heathrow collapsing.

This entailed the London Bridge construction being suspended whilst a modified design of the tunnels was agreed. The delay caused, together with the design changes, rendered our submitted tender virtually impossible to work with and we were involved in submitting a proposal by way of a revised programme and price for completing the works. I was asked to head up the price renegotiation. With an open and fair-minded approach, a satisfactory settlement was amicably reached.

I had decided to retire from Taylor Woodrow in March 1993 at the age of 51. This was initiated as a result of my being asked to act as an Expert Witness on a tunnelling dispute on the Hex River tunnel in South Africa. This involved two visits to Johannesburg for discussions with the legal team working for the client, South African Railways. My role as an expert witness, was based on my experience gained in South Africa between 1973-1980, and entailed assessing the contractor's claim for additional costs as a result of changes to the rock conditions as encountered when compared with those expected at the time the tender was submitted.

As an expert witness, the requirement is to provide independent assessment as to the validity of the contractor's claim for increased costs. This was a real challenge, but by using the experience gained, I was able to prepare a report, together with an assessment of the realistic additional costs which seemed to be accepted by the Client. With Nelson Mandela becoming President of South Africa in 1984, it was agreed that full arbitration procedures would not be initiated and an amicable agreement was reached between the client and the contractor. I would like to think that my assessment of the additional costs was taken into account in reaching the final settlement.

I had retired from serious cricket prior to going to the USA in 1986 and for the following years was content with watching and encouraging our two older sons in their cricket. I played the occasional game for the local church in Tylers Green and actually started bowling quick again. I was able to forget all about my action being "too open-chested" and whilst not being as quick as I was previously, could still bowl accurately with a fair degree of success. What a joy it was to be able to run in and bowl with no inhibitions. One particular game that will always be remembered was a game against Penn Street when my son James and I put on about a hundred in an evening 20 over match. The final game that I played was for a friend's XI of Engineers against a team of Architects at Fenners. The Architect's XI included a certain Darren Bicknell, ex-Surrey, who scored a double hundred. There was no way we could get close to their massive score and we managed to draw the game with my struggling to 40 without middling a single ball. Fenners held such happy memories going back to 1959 when I took 5–25 playing for Norfolk against Cambridgeshire.

Chapter 17

March 1993–2020 Life as a self-employed Consulting Engineer

Having retired from Taylor Woodrow, I was left to my own devices at the age of 51. I drew a pension from Taylor Woodrow which was not adequate to support the family at the time. The Taylor Woodrow pension was generous and with a lump sum was sufficient to cover the immediate period ahead. My final pension was agreed with the Pensions Manager after several discussions over my entitlement to additional years as a result of having spent time in South Africa. From the original Staff Handbook when I joined the company in 1965 it was understood that for every four years spent overseas, one was entitled to an extra year on pension entitlement. The Manager argued that South Africa was a civilised country and as such the rule did not apply. I argued that we lived in remote parts of South Africa with poisonous snakes and scorpions around! On a particular Friday afternoon, the Manager, a charming man, exasperated with my persistence, took out his book and added the two extra years to my entitlement!

I was also cushioned with regards of a regular income by fees being received for my work as an expert witness on the Hex River dispute in South Africa. During the early 90s I had decided to become an osteopath and after five years became a qualified registered osteopath. The purpose of my becoming an osteopath was to be part of a healing ministry at the local church in Tylers Green, Buckinghamshire.

The combination of working as a consulting engineer and osteopath worked well for a time, but gradually with calls from the construction industry increasing and an ever-increasing threat of litigation within the osteopathic profession I decided to concentrate solely on the construction industry. This has worked so well and enabled my being able to be involved with so many large projects such as the CERN project near Geneva, Crossrail, HS2, the refurbishment of Brunel's Tunnel under the Thames between Wapping and Rotherhithe, Channel Tunnel Rail Link and several London Underground projects. I have also been very fortunate in being involved in arbitrations on large projects in South Africa, Ireland and Botswana. The long running connection with the South African construction industry was so useful in 2003 when the Cricket World Cup was held in South Africa.

A very good friend with whom I had worked in the 1970s was the Managing Director of a large construction company in Cape Town, which happened to have a box at Newlands. He casually mentioned "why don't you and Jean come out and watch some cricket?" We took about five seconds to reply and made plans to spend a month in the country we had come to love and understand more and more. After staying with our good friends in Newlands, a suburb of Cape Town and within walking distance of the cricket ground we moved into a lovely old flat in Strand, on the coast about 25 miles from Cape Town.

The flat was full of books relating to the Apartheid era, and it was quite apparent that the majority of the books were supporting the views of those who opposed the ways in which African people, whether they be Afrikaans, English Speaking, Coloureds, Indians or those from traditional African tribes, were treated as a result of the colour of their skin. Looking back over the time we came to realise just how much talent had been overlooked by South African authorities not recognising the talent of so many millions of people other than Afrikaans and English speakers. One only needs to look at the superb South African born Springboks that defeated the mighty English team in the World Rugby Cup Final of 2019 to see just what was being overlooked. The South African cricket team has been enhanced by the likes of Makhaya Ntini who was the first ethnically black player to play for the South African national cricket team. He took 390 wickets in Tests and 266 in one-day internationals. The other superb non-white cricketer of recent times is Hashim Amla. This fine player has stood out in a wonderful South African team over the last 10-15 years with the likes of Graeme Smith, Jaques Kallis, Dale Steyn, Morne Morkel and more recently Kagiso Rabada and Vernon Philander.

Hashim Amla's performances in both Test matches and one-day Tests place him in the higher echelons of superb cricketers from his country. 9,282 runs in Tests with an average of 46.64, twenty-eight centuries and a highest score of 311 against England in 2012. His success in one-day Tests was equally as impressive with 8,113 runs at an average of 49.46 and twenty-seven centuries.

The Cricket World Cup 2003 South Africa v West Indies Cape Town

The first match we saw was the opening match at Cape Town on February 9th 2003. We were unable to see the opening ceremony, the day before, which according to Wisden 'was an evangelical campaign and Olympic-standard opening ceremony, a world away from the half-hearted fiasco at Lords four years earlier'. Whilst Wisden may be critical of the opening ceremony at Lords in 1999 the political decisions taken by the ICC proved too far-reaching.

It would appear that the ICC was far more interested in making profits as opposed to the cricket being the showcase in which the cricket took centre place. The profit made from this World Cup, as stated by Wisden was $US 194m compared to the $US 51m made in 1999. The line adopted by the ICC was that they were only concerned with cricketing related activities, and not politics. This attitude failed to recognize the atrocities that were taking place daily in Zimbabwe and more recently in Kenya. The ICC failed to convince the English and New Zealand players as to their security and as such took the moral decision of refusing to play in Harare and Nairobi respectively. With a degree of flexibility two games could have been relocated. All credit to New Zealand as they managed to qualify for the Super Sixes.

The whole organisation for the actual games of cricket were so well organised and there were many smiling and helpful young people ready to help spectators to find their way around this beautiful ground. The view of Table Mountain in the background was the perfect backdrop. Even the sight of the Newlands Brewery established in 1820 does not spoil the spectator's enjoyment, especially bearing in mind the quality of the Lion and Castle Lager consumed by many a cricket fan at this ground.

Newlands Cricket Ground Cape Town

Newlands hosted its first Test match on 24 March 1889 when England defeated South Africa by an innings and 202 runs.

There have been 55 Test matches played at the ground of which South Africa has won 23, their opponents 21 and 11 which ended in a draw. The last team to beat South Africa there was England in January 2020. The current seating capacity is 25,000

The opening game of the 2003 World Cup was between South Africa and the West Indies at this beautiful ground. This was a truly tremendous game of cricket. West Indies won the toss and decided to bat in this day/night match. Brilliant bowling by Pollock and Ntini reduced West Indies to 7-2 and after 15 overs only 30 runs had been scored. Lara had come in at first wicket down, having not played a competitive innings for five months since being taken ill in Sri Lanka. Together with Chanderpaul, he continued to bat carefully and after 25 overs the score was still only 67. The next 25 overs saw the West Indies reach 278 for the loss of five wickets.

To witness Brian Lara that evening against the bowling of Pollock, Ntini, Donald, Kallis and Klusener was as good a piece of batting as one could ever see. Shades of the wonderful batting by Graeme Pollock against Natal in 1980 and by Len Hutton against Australia at Lords in 1953. This great player began circumspectly against Pollock and Ntini, before moving into a higher gear and brilliance against Donald, Kallis and Klusener. He reached his 116 off 134 balls and a straight-driven six off Donald will be remembered for ever. The whole crowd gave him a standing ovation, knowing they had witnessed something very special. The other West Indies batsmen, Chanderpaul, Hooper, Powell and Sarwan all batted well, and Hooper played one late cut between the wicket-keeper and first slip with the finesse of the finest swordsman. The last 10 overs went for 110 runs and that superb fast bowler,

Sean Pollock, was hit for 23 runs off his penultimate over.

Set to score 279 to win, with an over deducted for a slow over rate, South Africa struggled to 160 for 6. Gary Kirsten, that wonderfully resilient batsman battled well for 69, but Kallis, Rhodes and Pollock with 19 runs between them failed to contribute. Boucher (49), Boje (25*), and Klusener (57) then in typical determined fashion, took the fight to the West Indies. Klusener blasted five sixes. With four balls remaining and eight needed, Klusener was caught on the deep mid-wicket boundary. It was perhaps a lack of cricketing 'nous' that the batsmen had not crossed and as such, Boje was unable to be at the batting end for the final three deliveries. Nevertheless, we had seen a wonderful game of cricket with the West Indies winning by just three runs.

A word about three of the great players in this game. With thanks to Wikipedia, and in no particular order.

'**Brian Charles Lara**, (born 2 May 1969) is a Trinidadian former international cricketer, widely acknowledged as one of the greatest batsmen of all time. He topped the Test batting rankings on several occasions and holds several cricketing records, including the record for the highest individual score in first-class cricket, with 501 not out for Warwickshire against Durham at Edgbaston in 1994, which is the only quintuple-hundred in first-class cricket history. Lara also holds the record for the highest individual score in a Test innings after scoring 400 not out against England at Antigua in 2004. Lara also shares the test record of scoring the highest number of runs in a single over in a Test match, when he scored 28 runs off an over by Robin Peterson of South Africa in 2003 (matched in 2013 by Australia's George Bailey and in 2020 by South Africa's Keshav Maharaj).

In Tests, he scored 11,953 runs at an average of 52.88 with 34 centuries and in One-day Tests he scored a further 10,405 runs at an average of 40.48 with 19 centuries. He scored his runs in the most attractive manner. Shane Warne rated Brian Lara and Sachin Tendulkar as being the best players that he ever bowled against.

The next great player in this game at Cape Town in February 2003 was Jacques Kallis.

Jacques Kallis (born 16 October 1975) is a South African cricket coach and former cricketer. As a right-handed batsman and right-arm fast-medium swing bowler, Kallis is regarded as one of the greatest all-rounders of all time, and as one of South Africa's greatest batsman. As of 2020 he is the only cricketer in the history of the game to score more than 10,000 runs and take over 250 wickets in both ODI and Test match cricket; he also took 131 ODI catches. He scored 13,289 runs in his Test match career and took 292 wickets and 200 catches.

Kallis played 166 Test matches and had a batting average of over 55 runs per innings. From October to December 2007, he scored five centuries in four Test matches. With his century in the second innings of the third Test against India in January 2011, his 40th in all, he moved past Ricky Ponting to become the second-highest scorer of Test centuries, behind only Sachin Tendulkar's 51.

Kallis was named Leading Cricketer in the World in the 2008 Wisden for his performances in 2007 in addition to being the "ICC Test Player of the Year" and ICC Player of the Year in 2005. He has been described by Kevin Pietersen as the greatest cricketer to play the game, and along with Wally Hammond and Sir Garry Sobers is one of the few Test all-rounders whose Test batting average is over 50 and exceeds his Test bowling average by 20 or more. He was a truly great cricketer and respected around the World.

The third great player who played in this game was Alan Donald:

Allan Anthony Donald (born 20 October 1966) is a former South African cricketer who is now a cricket coach. Often nicknamed 'White Lightning', he is considered as one of the South Africa national cricket team's most successful pace bowlers.

Donald was one of the top fast bowlers in Test cricket, reaching the top of the ICC Test rankings in 1998, peaking with a ranking of 895 points the next year. In One Day Internationals (ODIs), he reached 794 points in 1998, ranked second behind teammate Shaun Pollock. He shared the new ball with Pollock from the 1996/1997 tour of India until his retirement in 2002. Since retiring Donald has been a coach with a number of teams, including international sides. From 2018 to 2019 he was the Assistant Coach at Kent County Cricket Club in England.

In 2019, Donald was inducted into the ICC Cricket Hall of Fame.

He made his Test cricket debut on 18 April 1992 in South Africa's first Test since their return to world sport after the abolition of apartheid. South Africa lost to the West Indies in Barbados by 52 runs. Donald took 2–67 and 4–77, including the wicket of Brian Lara. When he retired, he was South Africa's record wicket-taker with 330 Test wickets at an average of 22.25, and claimed 272 One Day International wickets at an average of 21.78. Both of these records have now been overtaken by Shaun Pollock. These records are testimony to the skill of these great cricketers.

During the Trent Bridge Test Match of 1998 South Africa batted first, scoring 374 in their first innings. England responded with 336, with Donald taking 5 wickets. In their second innings, South Africa only scored 208 leaving England a target of 247 to win the match. Michael Atherton was at the crease when Donald began a spell of bowling both would later describe in their respective autobiographies as one of the most intense periods of Test Match Cricket they ever played. It was obvious to all except the Umpire that Atherton had edged the ball off his gloves. Donald was rightly infuriated at this poor decision and Atherton's protested innocence. Great fast bowlers of which Donald, certainly was, bowl with both skill and a passion that can only be understood by those who have ever bowled quickly. The next few overs were as dramatic a spell of Test cricket one could ever witness during which Donald bowled multiple bouncers to Atherton, with the intention of causing bodily damage, but he survived several close chances to remain not out at the end of the day. The next day Atherton along with Alec Stewart were able to score the remaining runs, with Atherton finishing on 98. Several years later, Atherton gave Donald the gloves he wore on this occasion for Donald's benefit year auction. Atherton's skill and tenacity had been witnessed by Donald in the tour to South Africa in 1995-1996 when he batted 11 hours in scoring 185 not out to save the Test match. Test cricket at its very best.

In the 1999 Cricket World Cup semi-final between South Africa and Australia Donald was the last batsman on the South African team. Australia batting first making only 213, Donald taking 4–32 and Pollock 5–36. The game swung back and forth with South Africa eventually needing to score 16 runs off the last 8 balls to win with only one wicket remaining. Lance Klusener and Allan Donald were at the crease. Klusener hit a six and then a single to keep the strike, followed by two fours. The scores were level with four balls left in the game. The next ball resulted in no run. Klusener hit the ball after that straight down the ground and set off for a single, but Donald was watching the ball, and missed the call to run. Both batsmen were at the bowler's end before Donald started running, having dropped his bat. The ball was thrown to the bowler, then to Gilchrist, who broke the stumps at the other end, with Donald only halfway down the pitch. Although the match technically ended in a tie, South Africa had previously lost to Australia in the Super-Six phase, and needed to win outright to progress to the final.'

The Cricket World Cup 2003 England v Pakistan Cape Town

On 22nd February 2003, in a day/night game at Newlands, England took on the very strong Pakistan team. This was England's first match against top-rated teams in the competition, they had played and beaten Holland previously, with Jimmy Anderson taking 4-25 in his 10 overs. Against Namibia on the 19th February, they were not convincing although managed to win by a relatively close margin of 55 runs. The stage was set for a very special game of cricket.

England

M.E.Trescothick c Rashid Latif b Wasim Akram	1
N.V.Knight c. Abdul Razzaq b Waqar Younis	15
M.P. Vaughan c. Younis Khan b. Shoaib	52
N. Hussain c. Rashid Latif b. Waqar Younis	8
A.J. Stewart b Shahid Afridi	30
P.D. Collingwood not out	66
A. Flintoff st. Rashid Latif b. Saqlain	26
C. White c. Younis Khan b. Shahid Afridi	15
A.E. Giles c. Shahid Afridi b. Saqlain	17
A.R.Caddick not out	3
J.M.Anderson did not bat	
L-b 1, w 7, n-b 5	13
8 wickets 50 overs	**246**

Pakistan Bowling

	O	M	R	W
Wasim Akram	10	1	37	1
Shoaib Akhtar	9	1	63	1
Waqar Younis	7	0	37	2
Saqlain Mushtaq	10	0	44	2
Shahid Afridi	8	0	36	2
Abdul Razzaq	6	0	28	0

Pakistan

Saeed Anwar lbw b Anderson	29
Shahid Afridi c Stewart b Caddick	6
Inzamam-ul-Haq c Knight b Anderson	0
Yousaf Youhana b Anderson	0
Younis Khan c Stewart b Flintoff	5
Abdul Razzaq b White	11
Rashid Latif c Stewart b Anderson	0
Wasim Akram c Giles b White	7
Saqlain Mushtaq not out	0
Waqar Younis c Knight b White	2
Shoaib Akhtar b Flintoff	43
B 4, l-b 4, w 11	19
31 overs	**134**

England Bowling

	O	M	R	W
Caddick	7	0	27	1
Anderson	10	2	29	4
Flintoff	9	2	37	2
White	5	0	33	3

England won by 112 runs.

A star, in the form of Jimmy Anderson, was born on that beautiful evening in Cape Town on 22nd February 2003. How well has this young man fulfilled his wonderful promise over the next eighteen years!

England knew that they had to win this game as a result of the fact that as a protest against the dreadful political and humanitarian situation that existed in Zimbabwe, the English players refused to play in Zimbabwe. The players objections were focussed on 'moral, political and contractual grounds'. The players were aware of the atrocities committed under Mugabe's reign of terror and had not been satisfied that adequate security would be in place. They asked that the game be relocated to an alternative venue. England therefore had to forfeit the game with the result that Zimbabwe gained a place in the Super Sixes.

England's early batting against Pakistan was not convincing. Vaughan played a sparkling innings before Collingwood with the support of Stewart and Flintoff batted sensibly to get England to the competitive total of 246. Against the world-class fast bowling of Wasim Akram and Waqar Younis, this was no mean feat. Shoaib Akhtar bowled very fast, but not particularly effective and was credited with the first delivery at 100 mph. This was played with ease by Nick Knight.

With the batting strength of Pakistan, we were expecting a real struggle ahead. The Pakistan batting was formidable with Saeed Anwar, Inzamam, Youhana, Younis Khan and Wasim Akram, all regarded as world-class players with records to justify their reputations. As an English supporter, after the disappointment of the recent Ashes series in Australia when Australia had crushed England in retaining the Ashes by the time Christmas 2002 had arrived, we were not altogether confident. Despite Vaughan's magnificent batting in scoring 633 runs and three centuries, Australia won the series 4-1. According to Wisden, 'England were a rabble compared to Australia's sleek efficiency. If the eleven who took the field looked as though they had never played together before, this was usually true'.

The prospects of England's bowlers being able to prevent this strong Pakistan batting from scoring 247 to win seemed remote. The next hour, however, was a revelation as a young man from Burnley and virtually unknown ripped through the top order with a wonderful piece of bowling. Wisden described this piece of bowling as 'a precocious display of controlled swing by Anderson... his bowling was exceptional... to all intents and purposes Anderson's second over settled matters, when he had Inzamam caught in the slips and cleaned bowled Yousuf Youhana first ball by an impeccable swinging yorker'. Jimmy Anderson had made his mark on this game and a few overs later he again took two wickets, of Saeed Anwar and Rashid Latif, in the same over. His final analysis of 10 overs and four wickets for twenty-nine runs was exceptional. A star had been born that night in Cape Town and eighteen years later Anderson is still opening the bowling for England and has now reached 600 Test wickets. England defeated Pakistan in Cape Town by 112 runs.

I have referred to three great players in the opening game between South Africa and West Indies, namely Lara, Kallis and Donald. It is perhaps necessary to include Jimmy Anderson amongst the list of great cricketers who played in the 2003 World Cup in South Africa:

With thanks to Wikipedia. **James Michael Anderson, OBE** (born 30 July 1982), usually known as Jimmy Anderson, is an English international cricketer who plays for Lancashire County Cricket Club and the England cricket team. Anderson is the all-time leading wicket-taker among fast bowlers surpassing Glenn McGrath (563 wickets) and holds the record of most wickets for England in both Test and One-Day

International (ODI) cricket. He is the first English bowler, and the 6th overall, to pass 500 Test wickets. In September 2020 he was the 1st fast bowler to take 600 Test wickets.

Anderson plays first-class cricket for Lancashire County Cricket Club and since arriving on the international scene in 2002/03 (before his first full season of County cricket) has represented England in over 150 Test matches and nearly 200 One Day Internationals. He is England's all-time highest international wicket-taker when combined across all three formats.

A right-arm pace bowler, Anderson made his international debut at the age of just 20, on England's 2002/03 tour of Australia. When he played his first ODI he had only played five List A matches. Anderson went on to feature in the 2003 ICC World Cup and made his Test match debut against Zimbabwe at Lord's the next summer. Later in 2003, he experienced a dip in form and confidence against South Africa. After this, he was in and out of the team and experienced numerous injuries, including a stress fracture of the back which kept him out of action for most of the 2006 season. He returned to action and is now the opening bowler in England's Test team. He was a regular strike bowler in England's one-day team but has not played in that format since the 2015 World Cup. He is the first English bowler to reach 400 and 500 wickets in Test matches, and on 11 September 2018, he became 4th highest Test wicket-taker of all time. He reached this position when he took his 564th Test wicket, passing Glenn McGrath as the leading wicket-taker among fast bowlers. As of March 2020, he is ranked No.8 in the ICC Test Bowling Rankings, having previously reached the top position at various times between 2016 and 2018.

On 25 July 2016, during the second Test of that year's England-Pakistan series at Old Trafford, he became the first fast bowler to take 50 wickets against all other 7 major Test-playing nations, Australia, India, New Zealand, Pakistan, South Africa, Sri Lanka and West Indies. In December 2019, in the first Test against South Africa, Anderson became the ninth cricketer to play in 150 Test matches. In January 2020, in the second Test of the series against South Africa, Anderson took his 28th five-wicket haul in Test cricket. He surpassed Lord Botham's record of 27, to become the bowler with the most five-wicket hauls for England in Test cricket. As at August 2020 Jimmy Anderson is bowling as well as ever. He is able to bowl in-swing and away swing almost at will, with little if any change of action. His partnership with Stewart Broad makes them the best opening pair in world cricket and with nearly eleven hundred wickets between is as good as any of the great opening pairs from previous times. Gregory and McDonald, Lindwall and Miller, Trueman and Statham, Hall and Griffith and Lillee and Thompson were all wonderful opening partnerships, yet did not have the longevity of the excellence of Anderson and Broad.

The victory over Pakistan at Cape Town in the World Cup was very important for England, bearing in mind that their next two opponents were India and Australia. England had not been convincing in beating Holland and Namibia in their previous games and had forfeited the game against Zimbabwe as a result of their refusal to play in Harare. Zimbabwe had, under Mugabe's rule become a dreadful state, with atrocities committed against rival tribes and politicians and with the declared policy of White farmers being forced off their farms. Henry Olonga, the first black cricketer to play for Zimbabwe, and teammate Andy Flower wore black armbands during Zimbabwe's match on the 10th February in this World Cup to "mourn the death of democracy" in Zimbabwe. With the background of what was happening in Zimbabwe, and the pressure being applied by public protests and media campaigns back in the UK, the English players asked for the game against Zimbabwe to be relocated on "moral, political and contractual grounds". With the safety of the players not being guaranteed, and the ICC refusing to relocate the game, the ECB supported the player's stance. Zimbabwe, thus, with the three points, were able to progress into the Super Sixes stage of the competition. It should also be noted that as a result of violence that had taken place in Kenya, the New Zealand players did not consider that their safety could be guaranteed during their game in Nairobi, with the result that they forfeited the points, allowing Kenya to advance through to the Super Sixes.

England's next match was against India on 26th February in Durban. This was a most disappointing game, and India deserved to win by 82 runs. Winning the toss was important and India batting first, thanks to the brilliance of Sehwag and Tendulkar had reached 75 after eleven overs. Flintoff then bowled a spell which perhaps rivalled his feats against Australia in 2005, and in ten overs took 2 wickets for a mere 15 runs. India rallied, thanks to Dravid and Yuvraj Singh to end with 250-9. England failed completely against the searing pace and swing of Nehra who bowled beautifully in taking six wickets for only 23 runs. Flintoff, the one English player to emerge with any credit, scored 64 to complete a very fine all-round performance. Whereas against Pakistan, England had benefitted with the ball swinging in the late evening, the situation against India was the exact opposite. Notwithstanding the toss, India's fine team deserved to win.

Having lost against India, for England to qualify for the Super Sixes, they had the small matter of beating Australia on March 2nd at Port Elizabeth. How close England came to win this game.

The Cricket World Cup 2003 England v Australia Port Elizabeth

Whilst not being able to see this game we listened intently on the radio. Expectations rose and fell throughout the game but having supported England over seventy years this was nothing unexpected. This game, on March 2nd was played on a typical warm South African day, and after nine overs, Trescothick and Knight had scored 66 against the mighty Glen McGrath and Brett Lee. Sixty-six without loss quickly became 74-4 as Andy Bichel took four for ten. Ponting then took Bichel off, not for one instance with the thought of giving England a chance. Stewart with 46 and Flintoff with 45 with help from the tail took the score to 204. Bichel dismissed both Stewart and Flintoff and finished with 7–20, a truly superlative performance.

When Australia batted, Andy Caddick bowling as well as he had ever done, rocked the upper order batting by taking the first four wickets to finish with 4–35 in his nine overs. His quartet of wickets included Gilchrist, Hayden, Martyn and Ponting, all wonderfully gifted players. At 48–4 Australia were shaking. Australia never gives in to England in any sport and Lehmann and Bevan rallied and took the score to 111–5. Giles and White plus a run-out in quick succession pushed Australia to the precarious position of 135–8. Seventy runs still needed with two wickets remaining. Who should come in at the fall of the 8th wicket but a certain Andy Bichel! With shades of Cliff Gladwin and the famous saying 'cometh the hour, cometh the man', on the 20th December 1948 in Durban, South Africa, when, with 2 wickets standing and 12 runs required off the last three remaining overs, he came into bat and England to a famous victory. Andy Bichel and Michael Bevan, on this occasion guided Australia to a famous victory.

Bichel with Bevan, probably the best "finisher" in limited overs cricket pulled Australia round, so that with two overs to go Australia required 14 runs to win, with Caddick and Flintoff each having an over left to bowl. Hussain, the England captain asked Anderson, the hero against Pakistan, a week or so before, to bowl the penultimate over. Bichel hit a six off the first ball and a four soon followed enabling Australia to win by two wickets. Bichel with 34 not out and Bevan with 74 not out were simply superb. The critics immediately turned their criticism on Hussain for asking the young relatively inexperienced Anderson to bowl this penultimate over. This is unfair and it does perhaps need remembering that great experienced bowlers have been hit for many more than Anderson conceded that day. Sean Pollock had been hit for 23 in an over against the West Indies at this World Cup, and Ben Stokes would be hit for four successive sixes by Carlos Brathwaite in the World Cup 20/20 Final in 2016. That greatest of left-arm bowlers, Hedley Verity who has taken 10 wickets for 10 runs for Yorkshire against Nottinghamshire in 1932 was hit for three sixes and three fours by Jock Cameron of South Africa in 1935. The Yorkshire wicket-keeper, Arthur Wood, cheekily encouraged the bowler with "you've got him in two minds Hedley, he doesn't know if he should hit you for four or six!" Whilst Caddick and Flintoff both had one over remaining there was no guarantee that either could have restricted the scoring.

England were out of the competition. They had played so well against Pakistan and acted with dignity in not playing in Harare. They were beaten by a very good Indian team and gave Australia their biggest fright of the 2003 World Cup. The host country South Africa was also unsuccessful as a dreadful error of judgement in their game against Sri Lanka at Durban on March 3rd. With rain falling the Duckworth/Lewis formula came into play. With South Africa requiring 230 to win, Boucher hit the penultimate ball for a six for South Africa to reach 229. This was the total that they thought had won the game and thinking they had won; Boucher pushed the final ball into the leg-side without attempting to run. With heart-breaking realization Sean Pollock understood, too late, that they needed the extra run. What absolute devastation for this fine South African team?

Australia was the outstanding team and easily qualified to get through to the semi-final, where they defeated Sri Lanka by 48 runs, and in the final, they thrashed India by 125 runs with Ricky Ponting scoring 140 not out with eight sixes and Damien Martyn a beautifully compiled and unselfish innings of 88 not out, giving Ponting the strike as far as possible. India was shattered in chasing 360, when Sachin Tendulkar was dismissed by Glen McGrath with only 4 runs on the board. Their batting never really settled down and against well directed bowling they were dismissed for 234.

Australia, under the excellent leadership of Ricky Ponting, was, by far, the best team in the 2003 World Cup.

According to Ponting their approach was "intent and intimidate". The word 'intent' is understood as meaning to play to the very limit of your own ability and in the best interest of the team. The word 'intimidate' is perhaps unfortunate and suggests that one's opponents should be subjected to threats and bullying. It is very unfortunate that this attitude has been allowed to creep into Australian cricket. They have been the outstanding team in world cricket for the majority of the past hundred years, as a result of their superb cricketing skills coupled with an abundance of determination and grit. The need to attempt to intimidate was mistaken and against the spirit of cricket. Adam Gilchrist will be remembered for his 'walking' after edging the ball in a Test match, rather more than the leadership of Australian captains who have advocated intimidation and attempts to mentally weaken their opponents.

The great Australian fast bowling partnerships, Gregory and McDonald, Lindwall and Miller, Lillee and Thompson imposed their intentions by their fast and at times intimidating bowling. It would be fair to say that they did not attempt to mentally weaken their opponents by the mindless sledging that seems to dominate the game these days. Australian cricketers have been good enough to win through the sheer quality of their ability, without the need to mentally weaken their opponents. It would perhaps be fair to point out that the Australian cricketers do not always react well when they are subjected in intimidatory bowling. The Bodyline series of 1932–1933 was an example when Australia fell afoul of the hostile and superb fast bowling of Larwood and Voce. They were shaken to their roots in 2005 when the superb quartet of English fast bowlers, Harmison, Jones, Flintoff and Hoggard bowled aggressively from the opening overs of the 1st Test, against Hayden and Langer, right through the whole series. Under the excellent leadership of Michael Vaughan, England were not intimidated by Australia and deservedly won a close-fought series. As Corporal Jones said eloquently in Dads Army "they don't like it up em!"

Australian cricketing attitudes had been under the spotlight for several years, when the drama of "Sandpapergate" emerged. In colloquial terms "the day that Cameron tried to get De Koch out". With acknowledgement to Wikipedia, this is explained as follows:

'The 2018 Australian ball-tampering scandal, also known as the Sandpapergate scandal, was a cricket scandal surrounding the Australian national cricket team. In March 2018, during the third Test match against South Africa at Newlands in Cape Town, Cameron Bancroft was caught by television cameras trying to rough up one side of the ball with sandpaper to make it swing in flight. Captain Steve Smith and vice-captain David Warner were found to be involved and all three received unprecedented sanctions from Cricket Australia. Although he was found not to have been directly involved, Australia's coach, Darren Lehmann, announced he would step down from his role following the scandal. Smith was replaced by Tim Paine as Test captain, and Aaron Finch as T20I and ODI captain.

Andy Pycroft, the match referee, charged Bancroft with a Level 2 offence of attempting to alter the condition of the ball. David Richardson, CEO of the International Cricket Council (ICC), charged Smith with "conduct of a serious nature that is contrary to the spirit of the game". Smith accepted the charge and the proposed sanction of two suspension points, which equated to a ban for the next Test match, four demerit points being added to his record, and was fined 100% of his match fee. Bancroft accepted the charge against him, was handed three demerit points and fined 75% of his match fee.

Following Smith's admission, Australia's Prime Minister at that time, Malcolm Turnbull, said it was a "shocking disappointment" .He phoned Cricket Australia (CA) Board chairman David Peever directly to express that disappointment and concern, saying that there has to be the strongest action taken. The Australian Sports Commission requested that Smith stand down immediately, and the incident was widely condemned by former international players and officials.

In a press release dated 25 March 2018, CA CEO James Sutherland apologised to fans and confirmed that both Smith and Warner had agreed to stand down from their roles of captain and vice-captain respectively for the remainder of the match. Tim Paine, the team's wicket-keeper, had been endorsed by the Board of CA to step in as acting captain, and Smith and Warner would take to the field under him. South Africa went on to win the Test match by 322 runs.

Cricket Australia launched its own investigation into the incident.

On 27 March 2018, it was announced that as a result of the preliminary investigation Smith, Warner and Bancroft had been charged with bringing the game into disrepute, suspended and would be sent home. He said that further sanctions against the three players would be announced within 24 hours, and that CA was satisfied that no one else was involved.

During a meeting on 28 March 2018 lasting over two hours, the Cricket Australia Board considered the report. The three players were sanctioned by Cricket Australia for breaching article 2.3.5 of Cricket Australia's Code of Conduct by engaging in conduct that was contrary to the spirit of the game, unbecoming of a representative, harmful to the interests of the game, and/or which brings the game into disrepute.

Warner was found to be responsible for the development of the plan to alter the condition of the ball and instructing Bancroft on how to do it, including demonstrating the technique to him. He was also found to have failed to prevent the plan being implemented, misled match officials by concealing his knowledge of the plan and not voluntarily reporting his involvement. He received a twelve-month suspension from "all international and domestic cricket" and he "will not be considered for team leadership positions in the future." Warner drew flak from a lot of people, many of them his own countrymen, who believed him to be the reason behind the whole scandal.

Smith was found to have known of the plan but failed to take steps to prevent it, told Bancroft to conceal the sandpaper in his trousers, misled match officials and others regarding Bancroft's attempts to artificially alter the condition of the ball, and made misleading public comments regarding the nature, extent and participants of the plan. He received a twelve-month suspension "from all international and domestic cricket" and he "will not be considered for team leadership positions until a minimum of 12 months after the conclusion of [his suspension] from international and domestic cricket. Any consideration of future leadership would be conditional on acceptance by fans and the public, form and authority among the playing group."

Bancroft was found to be a party to the plan to tamper with the ball, that he carried out Warner's instructions, tried to conceal the evidence and made statements to mislead match officials and the public. He received a nine-month suspension from "all international and domestic cricket" and he "will not be considered for team leadership positions until a minimum of 12 months after the conclusion of [his suspension] from international and domestic cricket. Any consideration of future leadership would be conditional on acceptance by fans and the public, form and authority among the playing group."

As well, "all three players will be permitted to play club cricket and will be encouraged to do so to maintain links with the cricket community. In addition, all three players will be required to undertake 100 hours of voluntary service in community cricket."

Before the start of play of the fourth Test between Australia and South Africa on 30 March 2018, newly appointed Australian captain Tim Paine, with the support of his players, approached South African captain Faf du Plessis. After the national anthems were played, both teams shook hands on the field as a gesture of goodwill and respect. Paine hopes that this will become a ritual that symbolises the new direction and attitude his team is taking after the fallout from Cape Town.

While no one contended that the charges and findings against Bancroft, Smith and Warner were not justified, many argued that the sanctions were unprecedented, and that there were flaws in the Cricket Australia (CA) description of the incident. Some did not separate the event—an attempt at ball tampering—from the wider charge brought against the trio of bringing the game into disrepute.

The banning of Smith, Warner and Bancroft, may well appear to be harsh and in addition to these players being unable to play the game they loved, they were harshly penalised financially to the tune of hundreds of thousands of dollars. What was wrong with the olden days when lifting the seam was as natural as Bradman scoring a century every third innings! Umpires knew this was going on and when getting hold of the ball merely pressed the seam flat again. The old adage of "I was just cleaning the seam, Ump." was usually accepted. Then of course we came to the time of the use of bottle tops for altering the characteristic of the ball!

The trio made their returns to the Test arena at Edgbaston on 1 August in the first Test of the 2019 Ashes series, with Smith's scores of 144 and 142 earning him the man of the match award as Australia beat England by 251 runs. Smith played superbly during the series and was the reason for Australia retaining the Ashes. Warner was consistently dismissed by Stuart Broad and Bancroft hardly registered.'

The outcome of the sandpaper incident has reflected very badly on Australian cricket and has caused cricket commentators to look back over the attitudes adopted by Australian cricketers over many years. Australia over the past hundred years has generally been regarded as the best team in the World, apart from the 1980s and 1990s when the superior fast bowling of the West Indies was supreme. England has been the best team for shorter periods, the early 1950s and during certain series such as 2005 and 2010-2011. The question needs to be asked as to why this wonderful cricketing nation has to resort to such actions that undermine the spirit of the game. The introduction of "sledging" and the declared intention of Australian captains to cause mental disintegration of an opponent has no real place in this game. Great Australian cricketers of previous eras, such as Jack Fingleton and Bill

O'Reilly have expressed their disdain for the way in which cricket has changed. International cricket is challenging and tests every part of a player's make-up. When one sees the effect of the pressures felt by fine cricketers such as Jonathan Trott, subjected to personal verbal attacks during the 2013–2014 series, it is surely time for the cricketing authorities to act to instil the true spirit of cricket back into the game. It is also time for umpires to be given the authority to call the fielding captain and explain in no uncertain manner that the actions of sledging, dissent and excessive appealing are tantamount to cheating and bringing the game into disrepute.

CHAPTER 18

The Ups and Downs of English cricket 2003–2005

After the disappointments of being thrashed by Australia in the 2002–2003 Winter Ashes series by four Tests to one and being eliminated from the World Cup in 2003 as a direct result of the player's stance in refusing to play in Zimbabwe, the English cricket authorities arranged for the Zimbabwean cricket team to visit England to play a two match Test series. The reasons given in South Africa during the World Cup a few months earlier for not playing in Harare, namely for "moral, political and security" reasons, seemed to be set aside. Whilst the security of playing in the UK was no real issue, the moral and political situation in Zimbabwe had certainly not changed. People were still being killed and farmers were being pushed out of their farms and the country gradually descending into a state of terror. Cricket had to go on, despite the absolute hypocrisy of giving Mugabe any credence for his being a supporter of cricket in that troubled and beautiful country. The actions of Henry Olonga and Andy Flower taken at the World Cup to show that Zimbabwe was no longer a democratic country did not appear to be considered in allowing the Zimbabwean tour to England to go ahead later in 2003.

England v Zimbabwe May–June 2003 England win series by 2–0

With Andy Flower and Henry Olonga being unavailable, the Zimbabwean team were weakened and lost both Test matches, in an unremarkable series. The outstanding performances for England were Jimmy Anderson's 5–75 in the 1st innings at Lords and Richard Johnson's 6–33 at Durham and Mark Butcher's 137 at Lords. Whilst Zimbabwe had fine cricketers of the ilk of Heath Streak, Stuart Carlisle, Grant Flower, Sean Irvine and Tatenda Taibu and Ray Price they were not able to play to their full potential during this short tour.

NatWest Series (Triangular ODI series Zimbabwe-South Africa-England) June-July England win

England lost a game against both Zimbabwe and South Africa in the preliminary round, yet was able to beat South Africa twice to reach the final at Lords. The final at Lords before a good crowd on a lovely day was from a cricket point of view rather an anti-climax. I was with my good friend, Keith Miller, from South Africa who had organised my wife and myself in being able to watch the World Cup a few months before. During the game he received a call from a friend in South Africa who had seen us on the TV screen back in Cape Town.

    South Africa was bowled out for 107 in 32 overs by Anderson, Gough, Flintoff, Johnson and Giles with none of the batsmen scoring more than 19. After losing Trescothick in the first over by Ntini, beautifully caught by Hall in the slips for a duck, Solanki and Vaughan guided England towards victory, with England winning by seven wickets. My good friend mentioned that the South African captain, Graeme Smith was a player with a real future ahead of him. What a prediction this turned out to be with his scoring double centuries in the first two tests due to start later in July. Double centuries in successive Tests had been achieved previously by Don Bradman, Wally Hammond and Vinod Kambli. Ricky Ponting would join this illustrious group in December 2003.

England v South Africa 2003 Test series drawn. 2 Tests each with 1 drawn

After the first Test, the English captain, Nasser Hussain resigned. He had made the rather rash comment that South Africa was "there for the taking", he also had insulted the South African captain Graeme Smith by not remembering his name during an interview when he referred to him as "whatshisname". Hussain had acted with dignity during the World Cup situation with England not prepared to play in Zimbabwe. He did not act with wisdom when he under-assessed the quality and character of Graeme Smith and his team. These players have strong characters and over the years have shown themselves to be able to compete against the very best.

The 1st Test at Edgbaston was drawn. At the end of the first day, South Africa were 398–1, they reached 594–5 declared. Smith having made 277 and Gibbs 179. The 2nd Day was rained off. England made 408 with Vaughan making 156 and by so doing avoided the follow on. Smith scored a rapid 85 not out and declared at 134–4 leaving England to score 321 to win from 65 overs. Rain and bad light brought the game to a premature end. Smith's total of 362 runs was not a bad start on his debut against England.

The 2nd Test at Lords turned out to be an even bigger shock for England. Having bowled England out for 173, South Africa amassed their record score of 682 for 6 wickets with Smith scoring 259. A total of 621 runs in two completed Tests was a wonderful achievement for this young South African captain of 22 years of age. England batted so much better in the 2nd innings with Flintoff scoring 142 off 146 balls with five sixes and 18 fours. South Africa duly won this match by an innings and 92 runs.

The 3rd Test at Trent Bridge was a strange test. From an English view, it was rather like the 'curate's egg', partly good and partly bad. The batting in the 1st innings was good, yet that of the 2nd innings was bad. England's bowling in the 1st innings was not particularly bad, yet in the 2nd innings was very good. Centuries by Butcher and Hussain enabled England to reach 445 in the 1st innings. South Africa's lower order enabled them to reach 362, before their bowlers shot England out for a mere 118 in the 2nd innings leaving South Africa a relatively low score of 202 to win. With the strength of the batting as already revealed by South Africa, this did not seem a too difficult total. From the Wisden report it seems that Smith got a bad decision, when he was given out LBW having hit the ball. James Kirtley on his debut bowled superbly, swinging the ball both ways and taking 6-34. Anderson also bowled well in taking 7 wickets in the game, including bowling Kallis in both innings. South Africa was bowled out for 131 leaving England the winners by 70 runs. This was quite a turnaround from the thrashing at Lords.

The 4th Test at Headingly was won by South Africa by 191 runs. The stand-out performances by South Africa being the excellent century by Gary Kirsten in the 1st innings and the 99 not out by Andrew Hall in the 2nd Innings. Jacques Kallis bowled superbly in the England 2nd innings to take 6-54. For England good innings were played by Trescothick and Butcher and Flintoff in both innings. Andrew Hall's performance in scoring 99 not out was a tribute to his ability as a cricketer and to his strength of character. He had been involved in two frightful incidents in South Africa during the previous years.

The first incident occurred in 1999, when he had driven to the cash machine near his wife's house. In Andrew's words, with thanks to Wikipedia: "'I finished my transaction, turned around, and there was a guy pointing a gun at me. He raised it, then shot six times. I fell to the ground. They emptied my pockets, took my car keys and drove away. As soon as I began to move, however, they returned, and shone the headlights on me for a moment before turning around and driving off. Perhaps they returned to see if I was still alive. I had no idea where I'd been hit. All I knew was my head pounded, half of my face felt like it was on fire and there was blood everywhere. I was thinking: 'Hang on, have I got half of my head left here?' The really scary moment came when I staggered across the road to a house and a woman answered the door. An awful expression flashed across her face and she began trembling.

I said to her: 'Phone an ambulance, I've been shot.' I was in hospital for three days. While I lay there, I worried whether I would ever be able to play cricket again. But I was lucky. The first bullet had stuck in my left hand as I raised it to protect myself, and the next four somehow missed. The last round, though, grazed my right cheek and left gunpowder burns and shrapnel in my eye and middle finger. Although I was concerned about my hand, I knew I could move it; within two weeks I was back playing cricket. Was I scared? No. There was no time. I said to the press: 'It's not my decision to be unhappy or happy about this. It's happened, it's passed. I'm not a victim, I'm a survivor and I'm not going to let this get me down.' I was lucky I'd survived and could still play cricket, but for it to happen again was pretty unbelievable."

The second frightful incident occurred later, again in his own words: "'my car was for sale and I met two guys who said they wanted to buy it. They asked if they could take it for a test drive and, because you hear of people having their car stolen, I said no. So, one of them pulled out a 9mm gun, stuck it into my side and said: 'Get in the car.' He sat in the driver's seat and his friend got in the back. I was nervous rather than scared, but it's difficult to explain exactly how I felt - it is just an unbelievable feeling that passes through your body. The worst thing was being driven around for 45 minutes with a gun to my head. But they kept saying: 'Look, we just want the car; there's no need to be a hero. Just relax and it will be over soon.' So, I concentrated on trying to keep them, and myself, as calm as possible. When they finally let me go, it was such a relief. They said: 'Get out and lie down on the road. There are some guys following us. If you don't wait half an hour, they'll shoot you.' Well, when they hit the top of the road I was up and running - I didn't give a damn who was around. I ran to the closest garage, phoned my family, and asked them to pick me up. Once again, I'd had a very lucky escape.

All this has taught me a great deal. I used to be the type of guy who lived day to day, but now I reflect more. It caused me to re-evaluate my life. I reassessed my goals, and forced myself to try to push harder to reach them, because I thought:

'This has happened twice, so if I don't pull my finger out, the third time I might not be so lucky.' I am a Christian and my faith has helped me a great deal. Playing for South Africa has also added to my life, and not only from a cricketing perspective. Dewald Pretorius [a fast bowler] grew up in an orphanage and he regularly returns to help out the children there. [Batsman] Gary Kirsten has his own project with street kids. Then there is Shaun Pollock [an all-rounder] and the skipper, Graeme Smith, who are Christians like me.

I have my own organisation, HEAR, that I run with [former South Africa fast bowler] Fannie de Villiers. Fannie initially raised money for his daughter to receive implants that allow her to hear, and now we do the same to help as many children as possible. How do I feel about what happened? Very, very lucky. It was very fortunate that Leanie wasn't with me. I realised instantly that there was a reason for my not dying. I believe I was not alone out there, because, trust me, from point-blank range a blind guy could have hit me six times. The way I view it now is that the Big Man still needs me to bowl some overs for him." That is quite a testimony from a brave young South African, who missed out from scoring a century at Headingly by a single run, yet knows that he, along with several other fine South African cricketers also understand their calling in helping others.

The 5th and final Test match was at the Oval and turned out to be a classic. At the end of the 1st day South Africa's score was 362-4 with Kallis 32 not out. Gibbs had played a wonderful innings of 183 and Kirsten had scored 90. The following morning South Africa was dismissed for 484 with Bicknell and Anderson bowling well. Kallis finished with 66 and Sean Pollock scoring 66 not including a last wicket stand with Ntini of 52. Trescothick then played probably his finest innings for England in scoring 219 and with Thorpe added 268 for the 3rd wicket, and the third day ended with the score at 502–7. With a wicket falling early the following morning it was left to Flintoff batting with Harmison in partnership of 99, of which he smashed the bowling all round this famous old ground to score a priceless 95, the last 85 coming in 72 balls to allow Vaughan to be able to declare at 604–9.

South Africa was shattered and against good English bowling, especially by Bicknell and Harmison were dismissed for 229 leaving England to score 110 to win. With Trescothick in fine form, scoring 69 not out, the runs were scored in 22 overs. This was Alec Stewart's final test, a fitting end for a fine cricketer. England were able to draw the series by playing superb cricket after such a dreadful start against a very good South African team which kept improving over the years ahead. The poor cricket played by England in part of the series was offset by cricket of the highest quality at other times. This seems to have been a characteristic of English cricket for many years, the sheer lack of consistency causing exasperation amongst so many supporters.

Winter tour in Bangladesh and Sri Lanka

At the end of an extremely busy and challenging year for many of the English players, they were required to visit these two countries with perhaps a reduced threat of hostile fast bowling as experienced recently against Australia and South Africa. They knew however that the threat of Muralitharan lay ahead on the slower pitches on Sri Lanka.

England beat Bangladesh in both Tests quite easily, with

margins of 7 wickets and 329 runs. There were good batting performances from the old guard of Trescothick, Vaughan, Thorpe and Hussain. Chris Read kept wicket very competently and the quick bowlers, Harmison, Johnson and Hoggard all took wickets at low cost. The spin bowlers found it more difficult with Batty and Giles taking three wickets between them for 220 runs.

Against Sri Lanka, England found themselves up against a much stronger opposition, with Muralitharan, on his own pitches the most difficult bowler in World cricket. The 1st Test was drawn as a result of heroic defence by the English tail, marshalled by Collingwood on his debut. England fought hard against the brilliance of Muralitharan who took 11–93 in 69 overs. Giles bowled very well for England to finish with match figures of 8–132 in 73 overs.

The 2nd Test also ended with another "great escape" for England when being set 368 to win in four sessions. Michael Vaughan, in describing his innings "as the best of his career" batted nearly seven and a half hours in scoring 105 runs. He was well supported by the tail. John Dyson, the Sri Lanka coach, in a typical Australian attempt to compliment England's achievement by saying that he "was staggered that England did not push for victory on the last day". With Muralitharan taking eight wickets in the match for 124 runs in 96 overs, this may well have been "a bridge too far".

The 3rd Test provided this very gifted Sri Lankan team with the victory they richly deserved. Sri Lanka batted first and scored 628-8 declared with centuries from Samaraweera and Jayawardene and good contributions down the order. With the exception of Vaughan, scoring 70 in the first innings, the English batting failed twice being dismissed for scores of 265 and 148. Muralitharan finished with match figures of 8–103 in 67 overs. In the three-match series Muralitharan took 26 wickets at 12.30 apiece, a truly superb performance and the key to Sri Lanka deservedly winning the series.

After the challenges of Muralitharan and the slower paced wickets experienced during the winter tour England could look forward to playing on their own pitches in 2004.

2004 England's continuing improvement.

This was a year, when under the fine captaincy of Michael Vaughan, England played some excellent cricket with a fine series win in the West Indies then clean sweeps of the Tests against firstly New Zealand and then the West Indies. Over the 2004–2005 Winter against South Africa, they won the series for the first time in 40 years. The series in the West Indies took place in March–May and it is fair to say that the English fast bowlers were superior to their opponents. With the exception of Brian Lara's 400 not out, the English batting was superior.

The 1st Test at Kingston was won by England by 10 wickets with solid but unspectacular batting by England in scoring 339 in response to West Indies score of 311. The West Indies batting in the 2nd innings was simply blown away by Harmison with his magnificent bowling in taking seven wickets for twelve runs. He was well supported by Hoggard and Jones. The bowlers were so well supported by brilliant catching.

The 2nd Test at Port-of-Spain was won by 7 wickets as a result of further excellent fast bowling. In the 1st innings, Harmison took 6–61 and in the 2nd innings Jones took 5–57. The West Indies scored 208 and 209 with England scoring 319 and scoring 99 for the loss of 3 wickets to win the game. Butcher, Hussain and Thorpe all showed the skill and resilience against the very good fast bowling of Collins and Best. At this stage in the series Brian Lara had scored 31 runs in 4 innings.

The 3rd Test at Bridgetown was won by England by the handsome margin of 8 wickets. The excellence of the fast-bowling quartet of Harmison, Hoggard, Flintoff and Jones was the major reason for this English victory, coupled with the superlative batting of Thorpe who scored 119 not out in the total of 226. Flintoff taking 5–58 in the 1st innings and with Harmison and Hoggard in the 2nd innings dismissing West Indies for 94. Lara was beginning to find his form with 36 in the 1st innings and 33 in the 2nd. Shades of things to follow. Thorpe's innings was, in Wisden's words showed "outstanding determination and quality". The West Indies attack was strengthened with the return of Edwards bowling at 90mph, supported by Best, Collins and Collymore. The next highest score for England was extras score of 20.

The 4th and Final Test St. Johns, Antigua was drawn but will always be remembered for Brian Lara scoring 400 not out. After what had been a disappointing series, Lara showed his undoubted class against the fine England attack which had swept England to success in the series. The West Indies total of 751–5 declared, the record score against England. Thanks to a Flintoff century, reached 285 in the 1st innings, a mere 466 behind the West Indies. The English batting in the 2nd innings responded well with Vaughan getting 140 and further solid batting by Trescothick, Butcher and Hussain ensured the match to be drawn.

The series was won as a result of the superb fast bowling

of Harmison, Hoggard, Flintoff and Jones. According to Wisden, this quartet was considered to be the best since the days of John Snow, David Brown and Jeff Jones in the 1967–68 tour to the West Indies. The batting was adequate with excellent performances from Vaughan and Thorpe, supported on occasions by Hussain and Butcher. The wicket-keeping of Read was good although losing his place for the final Test to Geraint Jones who had the pleasure of seeing every one of the 751 runs scored by the West Indies. This series also saw the affirmation of Flintoff as being a World-class all-rounder, capable of scoring centuries interspersed with five wicket hauls. The whole series augured well for the 2004 home series.

England v New Zealand May–June 2004
1st Test Lords England win by 7 wickets

This was an excellent Test match, which saw Andrew Strauss making his debut and Nasser Hussain playing his final game for England. Strauss started with a century and Hussain ended his 96th Test with a century. New Zealand batted first and with fine innings from Richardson, Astle, Oram and Cairns reached 386, scored at the good rate of 3.8 runs an over. When England batted an excellent opening partnership of 190 with Trescothick,86, and Strauss 112, put England on the right path and with good scores from Flintoff and Geraint Jones reached 441, a lead of 55. The New Zealand 2nd innings was dominated by Richardson with an excellent century and Brendon McCullum promoted to No.3 scoring 96.

Strauss, on his debut, was superb with his century in the 1st innings and 83 in the 2nd before being run out by Nasser Hussain. Strauss' cover driving was a joy to behold. England had discovered a gem of an opening batsmen to support Trescothick for years to come. New Zealand was dismissed for 336 in their 2nd innings leaving England to score 282 to win. This was 64 more than the highest total ever chased by England over the previous 105 Tests at Lords. At 35 for 2 England's hopes looked forlorn. Hussain then joined Strauss who had looked more and more assured until a wretched run out caused by Hussain ended Strauss' innings at 83. Hussain was distraught by this incident but was put firmly on the right path by the incoming batsman Thorpe, who told him, "Stop whinging and get on with it". Their partnership of 139 then guided England to an excellent victory.

2nd Test Leeds England win by 9 wickets

This was another triumph for the England captain, Michael Vaughan who led his team to another emphatic victory and was also able to be with his wife when their first child was born. New Zealand again showed that they were a very capable team and on the first day at 202–1 appeared to be in a strong position and by steady batting down the order they reached the acceptable score of 409 against an English attack which gave little away. England responded with 526, Trescothick scoring as quoted by Wisden "a magnificently aggressive century" and Geraint Jones scoring his maiden Test century. Flintoff revealed more of his considerable talent in performing at the highest level in scoring a rapid 94. Earlier Strauss had partnered Trescothick in adding 153 for the 1st wicket and showed more of his assurance in Test cricket. The debate as to Jones' wicket keeping ability when compared to that of Chris Read continued and whilst Read's batting ability at Test level has not been proven there is little doubt that at County level, he constantly showed his class. England has been very fortunate over the years to have so many excellent keepers of the likes of Godfrey Evans, Alan Knott, Jim Parks, Alec Stewart, John Murray, Bob Taylor and James Foster.

New Zealand's 2nd innings was a disappointment and against the excellent bowling of Harmison and Hoggard they were bowled out for 161 leaving England to score 45 to win, achieved for the loss of Strauss. Stephen Fleming the New Zealand captain gave Harmison fulsome praise and described him as "more dynamic than Glen McGrath"

3rd Test Trent Bridge England win by 4 wickets

This was another game in which New Zealand started so well yet was unable to prevent an excellent run-chase by England to win the game on the last day. On the first day, with Fleming and Styris both scoring centuries, the score stood at 225 for one. Persistent bowling by the English attack limited the New Zealanders to a total of 384. When England batted, they quickly lost Strauss and Butcher before solid batting by Trescothick, Vaughan, Thorpe, Flintoff and Giles enabled the score to reach 319, leaving a first innings deficit of 65. Chris Cairns in his final Test took 5-79 on the ground where he had played many games for Nottinghamshire. New Zealand in their 2nd innings increased their advantage through more good batting by Richardson, Fleming and Styris and at one stage were 171 runs in front with only one wicket down. Again, the English bowlers kept to their task and bowled New Zealand out for 218 leaving England to score 284 to win. Harmison with 3 wickets, Flintoff with 3 wickets and Giles with 4 wickets all bowled well.

England did not start well in chasing 284 to win and lost their 3rd wicket at 46. With a fine innings by Butcher with a broken finger scoring 59 with 12 boundaries and a wonderful century from Thorpe in which he combined solid defence interspersed with excellent driving through the covers, England reached their target with 4 wickets remaining. Chris Cairns in his final performance for his country took a further four wickets to end with a match analysis of 9-187.

New Zealand had played excellent cricket throughout the series. By losing certain key sessions in each Test, they gave the initiative to this very good England team shrewdly led by Michael Vaughan. With New Zealand scoring 386, 409 and 384 in the 1st innings of each Test and England having to chase around 280 to win the 1st and 3rd Test gives an indication as to just how close the teams were. The England bowlers were more penetrative than the New Zealanders, who were badly affected by the absence of their quickest and best bowler, Shane Bond. This English team was beginning to show the resilience needed to compete at the highest level.

England v West Indies June–August 2004
1st Test Lords England win by 210 runs

England started the series by scoring 568 with a double-century from Key and centuries from Strauss and Vaughan. Key came in as a late replacement for Butcher who was injured in a car accident. From a score of 527–3 they collapsed losing their last 7 wickets for 41. It seems that one of the inherent characteristics of English batting over the years has been the ability to collapse dramatically. West Indies scored 415 in their

1st innings with Chanderpaul showing resilience and skill in scoring 128 not out. With a lead of 153 England batted again and rattled up 325-5 declared at over four and a half runs an over, with Vaughan scoring his second century of the game. Despite another good innings from Gayle in scoring 81 and the usual determined effort from Chanderpaul with 97 not out, they were bowled out for 267, with Giles taking 5-81 and clean bowling Lara to take his 100th wicket in Test cricket.

2nd Test Edgbaston England win by 256 runs

An excellent batting performance by England in which Trescothick scored 105 and Flintoff a magnificent 167 off 191 balls with 17 fours and seven sixes, which Wisden described as "an innings of pace, strength, variety and ebullience". Flintoff was getting better and better with his batting and bowling and over this period was perhaps the best all-rounder in the World. England declared their 1st innings at 566-9. The West Indies lost 2 wickets quickly before an excellent partnership of 209 between Sarwan with 139 and Lara with 95 taking the score to 221-2. Flintoff dismissed both Sarwan and Lara and despite another stubborn innings from Chanderpaul they were bowled out for 336 to give England a lead of 230. Giles had bowled well in taking 4-65 in 30 overs.

England's batting in the 2nd innings, apart from Trescothick's 2nd century of the match and a half-century from Thorpe, was rather nondescript and they were dismissed for 248, leaving West Indies 478 to win. Gayle, more known for his explosive batting took 5-34, his best bowling performance. West Indies 2nd innings was again disappointing with only Gayle and Chanderpaul again showing the determination needed in Test cricket. Giles bowled well and took 5–57 to finish with match figures of 9–121. The West Indies were dismissed for 222 leaving England the victors by the considerable margin of 256 runs.

3rd Test Old Trafford England win by 7 wickets

This was another game when England showed resolve in recovering from a difficult position to win the match by chasing a challenging total on the last day. With West Indies winning the toss and scoring 395 and having England at 3 wickets for 40 they were in the driving seat. The West Indies batting, apart from Lara being bowled by Flintoff for a duck and Gayle being dismissed by Hoggard for five, was solid. England started badly and were rescued by another good innings by Strauss with 90 and Thorpe with 114 adding 177 for the 4th wicket and enabling the 1st innings to close at 330 giving West Indies a lead of 65 runs, with Bravo taking 6–55. Strauss was confirming his ability to score runs at the top level and Thorpe's innings was confirmation of his skill, guts and determination. A delivery from Edwards, clocked at 93.7mph had broken his hand when he had scored 91.

Excellent bowling by Harmison, Flintoff and Giles, dismissed the West Indies in the 2nd innings for 165, with Sarwan scoring 60. Lara was again dismissed for a low score by Flintoff. England were left to score 231, a record to win in the 4th innings at Old Trafford. A belligerent innings of 93 not out by Key and another excellent 57 by Flintoff saw England win by 7 wickets. Vaughan regarded Flintoff as being "the world's best player" whilst the England coach, Duncan Fletcher, warned the team of "complacency". It was becoming more and more clear that England was developing as a good team under Vaughan with a good pair of openers, solid batting down the order, a world-class all-rounder and a strong fast bowling set-up, with the reliable spin of Giles. Optimism perhaps for the Ashes series of 2005.

4th and Final Test, The Oval England win by 10 wickets

This victory was confirmation of England's continuing improvement. Winning the toss and with solid batting, with each player getting into double figures and Ian Bell scoring 70 on his debut, England reached 470, before shooting West Indies out for a mere 152. Lara returning to form with 79. They could not cope with the searing pace of Harmison and the innings lasted only 37 overs. West Indies, followed on, 318 behind. Gayle then scored a brilliant century off 80 balls with 17 boundaries and a six off Anderson over long-on. This included six successive boundaries off Hoggard's 2nd over. Further good bowling by Harmison and Anderson dismissed West Indies for 318, leaving England to score a single to win.

England had played good cricket throughout the summer and had shown the resilience needed to win matches in which they had had to recover from being behind. Players were maturing all the time and the team responding very well to Vaughan's leadership. Seven wins from seven Tests endorsed England's improvement.

The Winter tour of Namibia, Zimbabwe and South Africa November 2004–February 2005

This tour started in Windhoek where England beat Namibia in both the one-day matches, before moving on to Zimbabwe, where England won all four ODIs quite comfortably. The tour to Zimbabwe was the cause of further controversy and further questioned the ECB's agreement to allow their players to play cricket in a country where atrocities continued to be committed under the reign of terror of Mugabe. Some eighteen months earlier the English players at the 2003 World Cup had refused to play in Harare on the grounds of "moral, political and security reasons". The situation in this beautiful country had most certainly not improved over this time. Further controversy was caused when thirteen British journalists were refused accreditation to enter Zimbabwe at which stage Michael Vaughan made it clear to the ECB chairman that the players would not go, unless the journalists were allowed. With the threat of the tour being cancelled the Zimbabwean officials backed down and the tour went ahead. The tour saw the debut of Kevin Pietersen in the ODIs in Zimbabwe.

England was beaten by South Africa A by 7 wickets in the opening game in South Africa and after the political uncertainties of having played in Zimbabwe and this loss to South Africa A, they headed to Port Elizabeth for the 1st Test against the very capable South African team, strengthened by the debutants, Abie de Villiers and Dale Steyn, both fine players who would show their class in the years ahead.

1st Test Port Elizabeth England win by 7 wickets

South Africa batted first and thanks to 93 from Rudolph and 110 from Dippenaar reached 337. Hoggard and Flintoff both taking three wickets. When England batted Trescothick and Strauss added 152 for the first wicket. Strauss continued his excellent start to Test cricket and reached 126. He showed his ability at this level by reaching 1,000 runs in only his 10th Test, a feat only exceeded by Herbert Sutcliffe 80 years earlier. With Butcher scoring 79 and contributions from Flintoff, Giles, Jones and extras England reached 425, a lead of 88.

With South Africa at 152-2 in the 2nd innings and a lead of 64 with eight wickets standing South Africa was well placed. Simon Jones bowling full, fast and with reverse swing then took 4 good wickets and with contributions from Flintoff and Giles South Africa was dismissed for 229, leaving England to score 145 for victory. Thanks again to Strauss with 94 not out this was achieved for the loss of 3 wickets.

2nd Test Durban Drawn

England was put into bat and bowled out quickly by the excellent South African attack of Pollock, Ntini, Kallis and Steyn for 139. Kallis then played the most superb innings scoring 162 out of the South African total of 332. Batting the 2nd time, Strauss and Trescothick both scored centuries in an opening stand of 273 and with a century from Thorpe and half-centuries from Flintoff and Geraint Jones, England was able to declare at 570-7. Being set 378 to win, South Africa had little difficulty through solid batting and the help of the weather, in saving the game. This completed an excellent year for England in winning 11 tests and drawing twice, firstly through Lara's 400 and secondly through the weather.

3rd Test Cape Town South Africa win by 196 runs

The New Year Test at this beautiful ground showed just how formidable a team South Africa were. Winning the toss and batting first they scored 441, with Kallis scoring a superb 149 and seventies from both Smith and Boje. The fact that this score took 140 overs showed the accuracy of the England bowlers. England's batting failed completely against Ntini and Langeveldt and were bowled out for 163, thereby giving South Africa a lead of 278. Rather than enforcing the follow-on South Africa batted again and ground their way to 222–8 declared in 70 overs, thereby keeping England in the field for the best part of a further day and setting then 500 to win. This became virtually impossible with Trescothick being dismissed 2nd ball. Against a very good South African attack England struggled with no batsman reaching fifty. The highest score was by Harmison batting at no.11 in scoring 42. With both Pollock and Boje taking four wickets South Africa deservedly won by 196 runs.

4th Test Johannesburg England win by 77 runs

This was a stunning win by England, thanks to their batting first with another century by Strauss and eighties from Key and Vaughan, enabling a 1st innings score of 411–8 declared. This was matched by South Africa in scoring 419 with Gibbs scoring an excellent 161, being well supported by Boucher and Boje. The English bowlers struggled with the exception of Hoggard who took 5–144.

England's 2nd innings was dominated by a superlative innings from Trescothick in scoring 180 and well supported by Vaughan and Giles further down the order. They were able to declare at 332–9 leaving South Africa 325 to win in 65 overs. In uncertain light South Africa struggled against the magnificent bowling of Hoggard (7-61), well supported by Flintoff. Gibbs scored an excellent 98 to bring his match aggregate to 259. Smith the captain, shrugging off doctor's orders fought a rear-guard action in scoring 67 not out. With a mere 7 minutes remaining Hoggard dismissed Steyn for an England victory by 77 runs. Hoggard was superb, he swung the ball both ways, hit the perfect length and was able to exploit the wearing wickets where cracks were appearing to further disconcert the batsmen.

5th Test Centurion (Mid-way between Pretoria and Johannesburg) Drawn

This was a game in which Abie de Villiers revealed his class in scoring 92 in the 1st innings and 109 in the 2nd innings. Kallis further confirmed his ability with his 3rd century of the series. The remaining South African batsmen struggled against good English bowling from Hoggard, Harmison, Flintoff and Jones. Encouraging signs for the 2005 Ashes series.

In reply to South Africa's 1st innings of 247, England, with solid batting from Strauss, Thorpe, Flintoff and Geraint Jones reached 359. Andre Nel bowled quickly with real fire and took 6–81 in his first appearance of the series. With 2nd innings centuries from de Villiers and Kallis, South Africa scored 296–6 declared at around 4 runs per over. England was left to score 185 off 44 overs to win. Despite losing Strauss without scoring and three wickets for 20, Vaughan and Flintoff were able to play out time thereby enabling a series win for England. The series against South Africa was the sternest test for England leading into the Ashes series of 2005. During the ODIs that followed, the prodigious talent of Kevin Pietersen was realised in his scoring three centuries against the country of his birth. This talent was to be taken into the Ashes series where Pietersen showed his skill and determination against the finest bowling attack in world cricket at the time.

Chapter 19

2005 Ashes series

The Ashes. Photo from Wikipedia

The Ashes

This little urn is the 'prize' for the winners between Australia and England since 1882–1883. By drawing the initial series 2–2 England held the Ashes until the 1991–1992 series when Australia, under J McC. Blackham beat the England team led by the great WG Grace by 2 Tests to 1.

The idea of the 'Ashes' appears to have been initiated following Australia's defeat of England, at The Oval in 1882, largely as a result of 'the demon bowler-Fred Spofforth' who took 14 wickets for 90 runs.

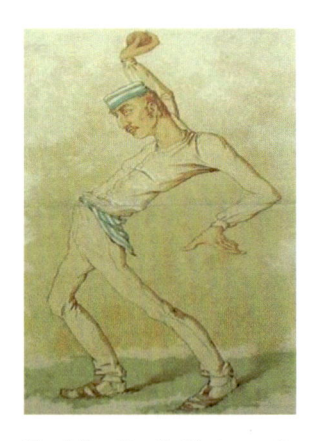

**Fred Spofforth. Not exactly
the classic action.**

At this defeat a mock obituary, written by Reginald Shirley Brooks was published in the Sporting Life which read as follows:

In Affectionate Remembrance

of

ENGLISH CRICKET,

which died at the Oval

on

29 August 1882,

Deeply lamented by a large circle of sorrowing
friends and acquaintances

R.I.P.

N.B.—The body will be cremated and the
ashes taken to Australia.

The origin of the actual Ashes remains a mystery, although it does appear to be 95% certain that the ashes were those from a bail that had been burnt. The container holding the Ashes, was presented to the England captain, the Hon. Ivo Bligh, later Lord Darnley, in an earthenware urn and presented to him by Melbourne residents in 1882. Though the team did not win the series, the urn containing the ashes was sent to him just before leaving Melbourne.

The 2005 series was memorable for so many reasons and from an English view and was the one when the Ashes were regained after 19 years. It is perhaps incidental that when England regained the Ashes in 1953 under Hutton's leadership, Australia had held the Ashes for a similar period of 19 years. It is fair to say that Australia has held the Ashes for significantly longer periods than England. Since the 1st Ashes series of 1882 Australia has held the 'little urn' for approximately 96 years out of the total of 138 years. Under Michael Vaughan's superb leadership, and the ebbing and flowing of the competition, the supporters of both teams were captivated. England went into the series with a very fine bowling attack, an excellent captain, a competent wicket keeper and a batting line-up which seemed to be improving all the time. Most of the batsmen had not recently played against bowlers of the skill of Warne and McGrath and Lee as they entered into the 1st Test at Lords.

1st Test Lords Australia win by 239 runs

The opening morning of this match contained Test cricket at its very best. The English bowling led by Harmison, well supported by Hoggard, Jones and Flintoff, was aggressive and well-directed and reduced Australia to 87–5. Australia rallied by the middle-order took them to 190. England could be well satisfied with dismissing this superb batting team for such a low score. Gilchrist, batting at number seven, was an indication of the strength of Ponting's team.

We then witnessed a piece of bowling by McGrath, which, as superbly as the English pace quartet had bowled, raised the quality to a different level. In 31 balls he took the first 5 wickets for 2 runs. He had both Trescothick and Strauss caught in the slips and then cleaned bowled Vaughan, Bell and Flintoff. At 21–5 Pietersen, on his debut, took the battle to the Australians and playing the most superb and audacious shots in scoring 57 and with the help of both Geraint and Simon Jones took the score to 155, only 35 behind. According to Wisden, the performance of Pietersen reminded many of the previous super-confident South African, Tony Grieg, some thirty years previous.

Australia's 2nd innings of 384 confirmed their strength in scoring with half-centuries from Martyn, Clarke and Katich. This left England 420 to win. Despite an opening stand of 80 between Trescothick and Strauss and another defiant attacking innings from Pietersen, England was dismissed for 180 with Australia winning by 239 runs. The superb McGrath with a further 4 wickets and Warne with 4 wickets were simply too good. A promising start for England had turned into a nightmare. With little more than a week before the next Test at Edgbaston there was a degree of apprehension in the England camp. Credit has to be given to Vaughan and the selectors in picking the same team for the 2nd Test.

2nd Test Edgbaston England win by 2 runs

The question will always be asked "if McGrath had not been injured just prior to the game starting would England have won? The logic says that Australia would have won. The same logic when applied to Headingly in 2019 when Stokes played the innings of his life and Sir Ian Botham's innings at Headingly in 1981 would also point to Australian wins. The facts are that England came out with guns blazing after being put into bat. England with excellent batting from Trescothick, Strauss, Pietersen and Flintoff hammered the Australian attack to the tune of 407 scored in 79 overs. A rate of over 5 runs per over was quite outstanding.

The Australian 1st innings of 308 included good innings by Langer and Ponting. The England attack kept to their task well although the run rate was 4 an over. England's 2nd innings, apart from the brilliance of Flintoff who hit four sixes in scoring 73 and adding 51 for the last wicket with Simon Jones reached 182, thereby leaving Australia 282 to win. Flintoff's total number of sixes in this match was the record in the Ashes series.

Australia struggled in the 2nd innings against the fine and improving English attack. Harmison bowled Clarke with the most outrageous slower ball, beautifully disguised. Going into the final day Australia was 175–8, still requiring another 107 runs to win. Warne, Lee and Kasprowicz took the score to 279, thereby with 1 wicket remaining, requiring just 3 runs to win. The tension around the country and in Australia was unbelievable as Harmison, who had not bowled as well as previously, fired a ball into Kasprowicz's body and hit him on the left glove and caught very well by Geraint Jones. The celebrations were ecstatic, although there was considerable doubt as to the left glove actually being off the bat, in which case the decision should have been not out. Perhaps fortune did favour England in this game, one of the most exciting of all times, and a wonderful advertisement for the three Test matches that followed. This game may well have been affected by the injury to Glen McGrath and the apparent incorrect decision when Kasprowicz was given out, but it is fair to say that over the course of the series there are a host of incidents that can affect the outcome, a dropped catch, an umpiring error, a wrong bowling choice or a bad stroke, all examples of what can alter the course of a game or even the series. England had played good aggressive cricket as evidenced by the 1st innings in scoring over 400 at the rate of over 5 runs an over, something quite exceptional in Ashes cricket.

3rd Test Old Trafford Draw

With just a few days since the dramatic game at Edgbaston, the supporters of both teams were abuzz with excitement when the game at Old Trafford commenced. England kept the same team, whilst Australia brought back McGrath for Kasprowicz. Lee had been on a drip in a Birmingham hospital as a result of an infected knee and McGrath was still struggling with a swollen ankle.

With Vaughan winning the toss and batting first, England scored 444 at the rapid rate of four runs per over. After Lee had bowled Strauss for 6, Trescothick and Vaughan added 137 before Trescothick became Warne's 600th wicket in Tests, a wonderful performance by the best ever leg-spinner in cricket's history. Vaughan was fortunate when after being bowled by McGrath on 45, he was reprieved by the call of "no-ball". He went onto play a beautiful innings of 166. He was well supported by Bell with a well-made 59 and good contributions by Flintoff and Geraint Jones. This England batting performance against an Australian attack which took over 1800 wickets between them, was excellent and showed the intent needed to win the series. After nineteen years of Australian dominance, England showed that they were not going to be pushed around any longer.

Australia responded to England's score of 444 with 302. Shane Warne played magnificently in scoring 90, with the next highest score being 34. English supporters would not have begrudged this wonderful cricketer another ten runs to reach his maiden Test century. Simon Jones, bowling reverse swing at good pace was simply too much for the Australian batsmen and finished with the excellent figures of 6-53. Simon's father Jeff bowled left-arm fast and played with distinction for England during the 1960s and in 15 Tests had taken 44 wickets with his best figures of 6–118 at Adelaide in the 1964–65 Ashes series.

England's 2nd innings rattled along at over four and a half runs an over, with Strauss who was hit on the head by Lee in the first over, scoring his maiden century against Australia. He had struggled against this attack in the earlier matches, but now showed his class and resilience. His partnership with Bell of 127 was of the highest class and enabled England to leave Australia with 423 to win the game. Bell had shown his ability in adding 65 runs to his first innings score of 59, thereby fulfilling the selector's faith in this young player after his low scores in the earlier Tests in this series.

Hayden and Langer, these two established players stayed together to see out the final overs following the declaration. In the 2nd over of the final day Langer was out, thereby bringing Ricky Ponting to the wicket. The crowd, with thousands unable to get into this famous old ground and millions watching and listening in the UK, Australia and around the World, then witnessed one of the most superb rear-guard pieces of batting by Ricky Ponting, who scored 156 out of their total of 371–9. Ponting was magnificent in defying the hostile and skilful England attack, in which Flintoff never let up his endeavours for a second. Ponting was eventually dismissed by Harmison with four overs to go. These overs were defended by Lee and McGrath with skill and determination amidst excruciating tension. The fact that Australia was able to draw this game was a testimony to Ponting's superb innings. It was also quite something to see the Aussies celebrating a draw against the 'old enemy'. The situation amongst those who had supported English cricket over the years was that perhaps the pendulum was swinging towards England re-gaining the Ashes.

4th Test Trent Bridge England win by 3 wickets

Australia had to make two changes with Tait coming in for McGrath, through injury, and Kasprowicz for Gillespie, whilst England was able to name the same team. Vaughan won the toss and scoring again at just under 4 runs an over. Trescothick, Strauss, Vaughan and Pietersen all made good runs, but at 241–5 the game was in the balance. Flintoff and Jones with contrasting styles, the 'broadsword' and the 'rapier' or in more cricketing terms the 'front-foot driver' and the 'back-foot cutter' added 177 in rapid time for England to reach a total of 477. The mighty Australians seemed deflated at yet another onslaught and having to concede over 400 runs for the third time in this series.

Australia was bowled out initially by Hoggard in his

superb spell of 3–32 and then Jones with 5–44. One of the memorable features of the innings was the brilliant catch taken by Strauss off Flintoff to dismiss Gilchrist. Australia was dismissed for 218 leaving a deficit of 259. Vaughan seemed to have few doubts at asking Australia to bat again, the first time they had followed since Karachi in 1988–1989.

The Australian batting in the 2nd innings was solid, with England being sorely affected by the injury to Simon Jones which restricted his bowling to just four overs. They battled their way to scoring 387 with half-centuries from Langer, Clarke and Katich and good contributions from Ponting and Warne. One incident will remain forever in the annals of Ashes history when Ponting was run-out for 48, by the brilliance of the England substitute fielder, Gary Pratt. This young man was on Durham's books at the time and was being used to replace Simon Jones who was injured and effectively out of the England team for the series. Gary Pratt just happened to be a brilliant fielder and Australia objected to his being used and Ponting, after being superbly run out by this young man, made his position clear with a stream of foul language levelled at the English supporters and management. This fine cricketer perhaps over-reacted in the heat of the moment but nevertheless was perhaps un-called for. The newspapers made the comment as to "who's the prat now?" Ricky Ponting was not supported by many other Australians in his objection to England's use of top-class fielders as substitute fielders. Gary Pratt was simply on the field as a legitimate substitute for the injured Simon Jones who was unable to take any further part in the series.

Gary Pratt had been an England Under-19 player and had

scored 1,000 runs for Durham in 2003. He struggled with his form in 2004–2005 and was released. He continued to play with distinction for Cumberland and captained the team for several seasons. It transpires that after this match Ponting spoke to him and congratulated him on his fielding and handed him some mementoes of the occasion. This young man will remain part of cricket folklore for years to come.

With Australia being dismissed for 387, it meant that England had to score 129 to win the game. A relatively simple task perhaps, but against an Australian attack containing Warne and Lee, nothing can be taken for granted. An opening stand between Trescothick and Strauss of 32 in 5 overs quickly became 36–2 with Warne taking the first 2 wickets, including Warne for a duck. The situation worsened to 57–4 when Strauss and Bell were dismissed. A rally by Pietersen and Flintoff took the score to 103 before both were dismissed by Lee to leave England at 111–6, still requiring 18 to win. Geraint Jones was dismissed at 116. At this stage Hoggard joined Giles who casually mentioned that "Lee was reversing the ball at 95mph!", quite an encouragement for a tail-ender. Giles and Hoggard with real guts and application stuck to their task and the runs came in ones and twos before Hoggard got his bat in the way of a Lee full toss and hit it through the covers for four. This lifted the pressure and next over, Giles clipped Warne through mid-wicket to win the game. Warne with 4–31 and Lee with 3–51 had bowled magnificently and had they been supported by more experienced bowlers the result may have been so different. Kasprowicz conceded 19 runs in his 2 overs and Tait 24 runs in 4 overs.

This was a wonderful victory for England and for the first time in nine Ashes series they knew that the series would not be lost. They still had to avoid being defeated in the final Test at The Oval in a few days' time but knew that they had competed so brilliantly in the Tests after Lords.

5th and Final Test The Oval Match Drawn

Vaughan again won the toss and England batted first, and what a competition this turned out to be. Thanks to a superb 129 from Strauss who, in partnership with Flintoff, that man again, added 143, and enabled England to end the first day at 319–7. The English tail continued to wag to reach a score of 373. Shane Warne bowled superbly to take 6–122. The battles between Flintoff and Warne were memorable throughout the series.

Langer and Hayden showed their class and added 185 for the first wicket. They were going well on the 2nd day when they decided to come off for bad light, much to the surprise of the fielders and the crowd. Australia had to win this game to retain the Ashes, yet these two experienced batsmen decided to take the perhaps negative step of going off. Not quite what one would expect of Australia from previous years. With the score at 264–1, we then witnessed a magnificent spell of bowling by Flintoff. He bowled continuously from the Pavilion End until six overs after lunch, dismissing Hayden, Flintoff, Martyn and Katich for 30 runs, in a 14 over spell. Wisden describes his bowling as 'awesome, relentlessly hitting a length, hitting the seam and a hint of swing and with four wickets, a place in Ashes legend'. He finished with 5–78 and with Hoggard chipping in with 4–97, Australia slumped to 367 all out.

On the 4th afternoon, England started their second innings

and lost Strauss, caught off Warne for a single. Trescothick and Vaughan steadied things through to the close of play, ended prematurely and perhaps prompted by McGrath bowling a bouncer in fading light and the threat of rain. Never in Ashes history had the English crowd applauded the fact that play was suspended. The Australian supporters and team wore sunglasses to try and convince the umpires that all was well, whilst the English supporters held umbrellas aloft against the threat of non-existent rain. This pantomime caught on and was conducted in a good spirit.

The following day, the final one of this dramatic series, began with all four results possible. Vaughan and Trescothick took the score to 67 before McGrath dismissed Vaughan and Bell in successive deliveries. 67–3 could easily have become 68–4 had Pietersen been caught off Warne and a few overs later, Pietersen was dropped by Warne off the persevering Lee. As Steve Waugh might have said, as he did to Herschelle Gibbs in an earlier World Cup "You've just dropped the Ashes mate!" England struggled to 109 before Trescothick was out and shortly afterwards Flintoff was dismissed to leave England at 126–5. At lunch with 70 overs remaining England was 133 ahead with the five wickets remaining, any result was still possible. Collingwood then stayed with Pietersen for 72 minutes and eased the score to 186–7. Geraint Jones followed quickly afterwards at 199–7. At tea-time with England 227 ahead and nearly 50 overs remaining, Australia would still have considered the possibility of winning.

Pietersen, playing the innings of his life, up to that time, was finally bowled by the excellent McGrath for 158 which included seven sixes, the highest number by any in an Ashes Test. Warne and other Australians were generous in their applause of this wonderful innings. The partnership of 109 for the eight wicket with Giles, who scored 59 finally ensured that the Ashes were England's. Those magnificent bowlers, McGrath and Warne never gave up for a single moment and Warne finished with 6–124 and the excellent total of 40 wickets for the series.

What a series this had been! The excellence of Warne and Flintoff was perhaps the contest of the season, both exceptional players in any generation. The leadership of Vaughan was a key factor and Ricky Ponting had the good grace in his statement "Apart from when we won at Lords, we were never as good as England and they deserved to win".

Michael Vaughan made the simple statement "We've made people in England really happy — that's the pleasing aspect". Two fine players and captains to whom so much is owed for this memorable series.

These two superb teams provided wonderful entertainment for all cricket supporters around the world. They were so evenly matched with England scoring runs at 29.76 per wicket as compared to Australia at 28.71 per wicket. Australia when bowling took wickets at 31.01 runs per wicket as compared to England taking wickets at 31.29 runs per wicket. The standout performer for Australia was Shane Warne with 40 wickets and 249 runs, and for England, Freddie Flintoff with 402 runs and 24 wickets. Magnificent performances by these superb cricketers.

This magnificent Australian team, containing players who would be considered as greats in any era, such as Ponting, Warne, McGrath and Gilchrist, never ever took a step backwards during this series. They were up against a superbly led English team that performed so well after the first Test at Lords. Australia was unfortunate to lose Glen McGrath for the two games which England won. This series reflected the very best of Test cricket.

The final member of the Australian team was 22-year-old, Shaun Tait, who made his debut at Headingly in this series and took three good wickets in dismissing Trescothick, Bell and Flintoff. This young bowler has been recorded as being able to bowl at 100 mph, thereby joining Shoaib Akhtar and Brett Lee.

The 2005 series will be remembered by many for the quality of the cricket played by both teams and the excellence of so many players who would have held their own in any generation. This series certainly re-kindled the interests of cricket amongst all generations.

CHAPTER 20

The changing faces of English cricket since 2005

England's performances since the heady days of 2005, have been sketchy to say the least. There have been many superb performances by teams and individuals, but these have been inter-laced with disappointing series, when the batting has collapsed, key catches have been dropped and a host of other factors contributing to poor performances. The first Test of several series overseas has been lost as a result of apparent lack of preparation and acclimatization to overseas conditions. The following is a summary of the series played since the Ashes series of 2005.

2005 Nov-Dec. Pakistan away. Pakistan 2 England 0
Captains - Vaughan and Trescothick.Pakistan batting and bowling stronger than England. Simon Jones missed during series.
2006 March. India away. England 1 India 1.
Captain - Flintoff deputising for Vaughan. Cook's debut century. Good batting by Strauss and Collingwood and fine bowling by Flintoff,
2006 May-June. Sri Lanka home. England 1 Sril Lanka 1
Captain - Flintoff deputising for Vaughan. Superb batting by Pietersen countered by Muralitharan 24 wickets in 3 Tests

2006 July-August. Pakistan home. England 3-0
Captain - Strauss. Apart from Mohammad Yousuf and Younis Khan, England's batting stronger, together with fine bowling from Harmison & Panesar.

2006 Nov-Dec 2007. Australia away. Australia 5-0
Captain - Flintoff. Australia showed their superiority in every department and deservedly regained the Ashes lost in 2005.

2007 March-April. World Cup   West Indies
Captain – Vaughan. Disappointing, for England, apart from Pietersen's centuries against Australia and West Indies and good win against West Indies. Losses against top teams. Bowling lacked penetration. Australia brilliant throughout.

2007 May-June. West Indies home. England 3-0
Captains -Strauss and Vaughan. Excellent batting by Pietersen, Prior, Vaughan, Collingwood and Cook, together with fine bowling by Panesar, Sidebottom and Harmison.

2007 July-August. India home. India 1-0.
Captain-Vaughan. Fairly even series. Poor batting by England in 2nd Test and India hanging on for draw in 1st Test, enabled India to deservedly win the series.

2007 World 20/20 South Africa.
Further disappointment for England, with losses against Australia, South Africa, New Zealand and India. Broad hit for six sixes by Yuvraj Singh in one over. India worthy winners.

2007 October - December. Sri Lanka away. Sri Lanka 1-0.
Captain-Vaughan. Superior batting coupled with Muralitharan key to Sri Lankan winning the series.

2008 Feb-March. New Zealand away. England 2-1
Captain-Vaughan. England rallied well after losing 1st Test and with excellent bowling by Sidebottom with 24 wickets in 3 matches were able to win this close fought series.

2008 April-June. New Zealand home. England 2-0
Captain-Vaughan. Superior bowling by Anderson and Sidebottom key to England winning this series.

2008 July-August. South Africa home. South Africa 2-1
Captain-Vaughan/Pietersen. Superb series with Graeme Smith

playing the key innings in scoring 154 not out to win the 3rd Test.

2008 December. India away. India 1-0
Captain-Pietersen. Despite excellent centuries from Strauss (2 in 1st Test) Collingwood and Pietersen, India won series by chasing 387-4 to win 1st Test.

2009 Jan-March. West Indies away. West Indies 1-0.
Captain-Strauss. West Indies won 1st Test as result of bowling England out for 51 and stubborn defence in 3rd and 5th Test. Sarwan outstanding for West Indies. Good batting by England after 1st Test. 2nd Test abandoned after 10 balls because of state of pitch.

2009 May. West Indies home. England 2-0
Captain-Strauss. West Indies were under-prepared for this series. Good batting by Bopara (2 centuries) and 5 wickets for Onions on debut.

2009 July-August. Australia home. England 2-1
Captain-Strauss. Topsy-turvey series. England saved by Anderson/Panesar in 1st Test. Excellent batting by Strauss, Trott, (century on debut) Ponting, Clarke and North (2 centuries in 1st Ashes series) Good bowling by Broad, Swann and Flintoff at times for England and Siddle, Johnson and Hilfenhaus for Australia.

2009 Nov-2010 Jan. South Africa away. England 1 S. Africa 1
Captain-Strauss. England were saved in two Tests by last wicket stands involving Onions. Deserved winners in 2nd Test due to excellent batting and fine bowling by Broad and Swann. South Africa worthy winners of 4th Test through fine batting and superb fast bowling.

2010 March. Bangladesh away. England 2-0
Captain-Cook. Solid English batting and good bowling by Swann was too strong for an improving Bangladesh team.

2010 May-June. Bangladesh home. England 2-0
Captain-Strauss. English batting and bowling generally too strong despite Tamin Iqbal's two centuries.

2010 Jul-August. Pakistan home. England 3-1

Captain-Strauss. Strange series, emmeshed in corruption. England batting too good with centuries from Trott, Broad, Morgan and Prior and fine bowling from Anderson, Broad, Finn and Swann.

2010 Nov -Jan.2011. Australia away. England 3-1
Captain-Strauss. Three wins by an innings by brilliant England, single defeat at Perth when Johnson shot England out with "probably one of the great all-time Ashes spells". Overall England superior in all departments.

2011 Feb-April 2011. World Cup. India.
Captain-Strauss. Another disappointing World Cup. Good wins against South Africa and West Indies and a tie against India. Losses against Ireland and Bangladesh and ten wicket defeat by Sri Lanka in Quarter Final emphasised inconsistency.

2011 May-June. Sri Lanka home. England 1-0
Captain-Strauss. The absence of Muralitharan, Vaas and Malinga seriously affected Sri Lankan bowling. England competent in all departments.

2011 July-Sep. India home. England 4-0
Captain- Strauss-. **ENGLAND NO. 1.** A superb performance and apart from Dravid with three centuries, England better in every department. Fine batting by Pietersen and Bell and excellent bowling by Broad, Bresnan and Anderson

2012 Jan-Feb. Pakistan away-U.A.E. Pakistan 3-0
Captain-Strauss. England out-played by Pakistan. Little answer to fine spin bowling.

2012 Mar-April. Sri Lanka away. England 1-Sri Lanka 1
Captain-Strauss. England out-played in 1st Test. Fine century by Pietersen in 2nd Test and good bowling by Swann enabled England win in 2nd Test.

2012 May-June. West Indies home. England 2-0.
Captain-Strauss. Apart from Samuels and Chanderpaul, England's batting stronger and bowling much more suited to conditions.

2012 Aug-Sep. South Africa home. South Africa 2-0
Captain-Strauss. South Africa superior in all departments, especially catching. Amla and Kallis brilliant.

2012 Nov-Dec. India away. England 2-1
Captain-Cook. Superb leadership and batting by Cook and with Swann and Panesar out-bowling the Indian spinners brought about this excellent series win.

2013 Feb-Mar. New Zealand away. Series drawn 0-0
Captain-Cook. Fluctuating series. New Zealand prevented from winning series by Panesar's defence in final Test.

2013 May. New Zealand home. England 2-0
Captain-Cook. Excellent bowling by Broad and Root's first century enabled England to win this closely contested series.

2013 May-Sep. Australia home. England 3-0
Captain-Cook. Sublime batting by Bell (3 centuries) and fine bowling by Broad, Swann and Anderson key to this series win.

2013 Dec-2014 Jan. Australia away. Australia 5-0
Captain-Cook. England was outplayed by this excellent Australian team. The top six batsmen all scored more than Pietersen for England, and apart from Broad the Australian bowlers were superior. The behaviour of the media and certain of the Australian players was disgraceful and threatening.

2014 June. Sri Lanka home. Sri Lanka 1-0
Captain-Cook. Closely fought series. England defeated off penultimate ball of 1st Test. Sr Lanka survived final over of 2nd Test with last pair at wicket.

2014 Jul-Aug. India home. England 3-1
Captain-Cook. India won 2nd Test and England won next 3 convincingly. Superb batting by Root and Ballance and fine bowling by Broad, Anderson and Ali superior to that of India.

2015 Feb-Mar. The World Cup. Australia and New Zealand.
Captain-Morgan. This was another disappointing performance by England with losses to Australia, New Zealand, Sri Lanka and Bangladesh. Australia deservedly won their 5th World Cup by defeating the excellent New Zealanders in the Final.

2015 April-May. West Indies away. Series drawn 1-1.
Captain-Cook. A resurgent West Indies, with an improving pace attack, played very well to draw this series. Anderson bowled very well and Root, Ballance and Cook scored good runs.

2015 May-June. New Zealand home. Series drawn 1-1.
Captain-Cook. Well contested series. Excellent leadership by McCullum and Cook in restoring the true spirit of cricket and encouraging positive cricket.

2015 Jul-Aug. Australia home. England 3-2
Captain-Cook. After the annihilation of 2013/4 England recovered well to win this fluctuating series. Root and Broad superb for England. Smith, Rogers and Warner excellent for Australia.

2015 Oct-Nov. Pakistan away-U.A.E. Pakistan 2-0.
Captain-Cook. England outplayed by Pakistan despite fine batting by Cook and Root and excellent bowling by Anderson.

2015 Dec-2016 Jan. South Africa away. England 2-1
Captain-Cook. Superb series dominated by brilliance of Stokes, Broad, Amla and emergence of Rabada as a World-class bowler. South Africa affected by absence of Steyn and Philander.

2016 May-Jun. Sri Lanka home. England 2-0
Captain-Cook. England superior in all departments. Excellent performances by Bairstow (2 centuries and average of 129.00) and Anderson (21 wickets at 10.80).

2016 Jul-Aug. Pakistan home. Series drawn 2-2
Captain-Cook. Excellent series, tribute to captains, Cook and Misbah-ul-Haq, played in the right spirit. Root with 512 runs and Woakes with 26 wickets excellent for England and consistent batting by Pakistan.

2016 Oct. Bangladesh away. Series drawn 1-1.
Captain-Cook. Tamil Iqbal superb century in 2nd Test and Hasan's 19 wickets, key to Bangladesh victory. England's all-rounders ensured good competitive cricket.

2016 Nov-Dec. India away. India 4-0
Captain-Cook. India superior in all departments. Kohli brilliant averaging 109.16, matched by Root with 491 runs at 49.10. English bowlers largely ineffective.

2017 Jul-Aug. South Africa home. England 3-1
Captain-Cook. Fluctuating series. Root excellent and well supported by the bowlers. Morkel excellent for South Africa. Woakes injured for whole series.

2017 Aug-Sep. West Indies home. England 2-1
Captain-Root. Continuing signs of West Indies improving with good batting by Brathwaite and S. Hope and quick bowling by Roach and Gabriel. For England Root and Cook and Anderson and Stokes excellent.

2017 Nov-2018 Jan. Australia away. Australia 4-0
Captain-Root. Australia simply too good. Smith superb, backed up by bowling attack superior to England's. Root and Anderson competed well. Stokes missed. England's ODI team comprehensively won series 4-1.

2018 Mar-Apr. New Zealand away. New Zealand 1-0
Captain-Root. New Zealand deserved winners of series after dismissing England for 58 in 1st Test and battling to save 2nd Test. England's ODI team won close fought series 3-2

2018 May-Jun. Pakistan home. Series drawn 1-1
Captain-Root. Wisden sums up this series as 'Pakistan were superb in one Test and rubbish in the other. Ditto England'

2018 June. Scotland away. ODI. Scotland win.
Captain-Morgan. Superb performance by Scotland.

2018 June. Australia home. ODI England win 5-0
Captain-Morgan. England superb in all departments. Record 481-6 in 3rd ODI. Australia affected by the absence of Smith and Warner and Starc, Hazelwood and Cummins. Augers well for 2019 World Cup.

2018 Aug-Sep. India home. England 4-1
Captain-Root. England shade fortunate to win series by 4-1. Injuries to Bumrah affected India. Kohli brilliant. Good all-round performance by England. Cook farewell with century.

2018 Nov. Sri Lanka away. England 3-0
Captain-Root. Positive cricket and good all-round performance enabled England to win this series. English spinners performed better than those of Sri Lanka. ODI series won by England 3-1.
2019 Jan-Feb. West Indies away. West Indies 2-1
Captain-Root. Thoroughly deserved win for West Indies. Good leadership and all-round skill by Holder, capable bowling attack led by Roach. England disappointing. ODI Series shared 2-2.
2019 May-Jul. The World Cup. England and Wales
Captain-Morgan. **England win the World Cup.** After 44 years England succeeded under superb captaincy of Eoin Morgan. Classic Final decided by Super Over to defeat New Zealand, led by excellent Kane Williamson. Under the captaincy of Williamson and previously McCullum, New Zealand have played the game in the right spirit, highly competitive yet fair and generous. England now the only country to win the World Cups at Soccer, Rugby and now cricket.
2019 July. Ireland home. England 1-0.
Captain-Root. Ireland bowled England out for 85 in 1st innings. Lead by 122. England 303 in 2nd innings, then dismiss Ireland for 38 in 2nd innings (Broad 4-19, Woakes 6-17)
2019 Aug-Sep. Australia home. Series drawn 2-2
Captain-Root. Brilliant and exciting series. Smith outstanding for Australia (774 runs in 4 Tests) Stokes outstanding for England (Staggering century at Headingley to win game from desperate position.
2019 Nov-Dec. New Zealand away. New Zealand 1-0
Captain-Root. Excellent New Zealand team deservedly won series. Root double hundred in 2nd Test.
2019 Dec-2020 Jan. South Africa away. England 3-1
Captain-Root. After losing 1st Test England won next three Tests very easily. Excellent performance by English team.

2020 July. West Indies home. England 2-1
Captain-Root. Excellent series behind closed doors as a result of Covid 19 crisis. Credit to Holder and Root for the good spirit in which the games were played.

2020 Aug. Pakistan home. England 1-0
Captain-Root. England won 1st Test thanks to superb partnership by Buttler and Stokes. Superb 267 by Crawley in 3rd Test plus Anderson's 600th wicket. Pakistan confirmed their emerging strength. Weather affected 2nd and 3rd Tests. Excellent spirit between both teams and splendid umpiring throughout.

2021 Jan. Sri Lanka away. England 2-0
Captain-Root. Excellent batting by Root and good bowling by Anderson ,Broad, Bess and Leach enabled England to series win.

2021 Feb. India away. India 3-1
Captain-Root. After winning 1st Test, thanks to another double-century by Root and good bowling by Anderson, Bess and Leach, England was outplayed in all departments by a fine Indian team.

2021 June. New Zealand home. New Zealand 1-0
Captain-Root. England was outplayed by a very fine New Zealand team. Superb debut by Conway with a double-century and excellent bowling and catching throughout.

2021 August-September. India home. India 2. England 1 Undecided 1.
Captain-Root. This was a magnificent series in which Root scored 564 runs and Anderson and Robinson bowled heroically for England. India had a superb team, strong in batting and an excellent bowling attack. The final Test was left undecided, with much speculation that India would have won the series. Remembering Headingley 1981 and 2019, then who can ever write off and England team.'

This concludes the men's Test matches up to the end of the India series in August-September 2021. The effects resulting from Covid 19 have been devastating for every country around the world, and great credit should be given to all the cricketing authorities associated with making it possible for Test Matches to take place around the World. Special thanks must also be given to every single player who gave their all to provide some substance of normality during these troubled times.

The skills on display from every member of the teams from West Indies, Pakistan, New Zealand, India and England have been superb. The excellence of the umpires has been endorsed time and time again by the review system and it is perhaps fair to say that the umpires were right in their decisions considerably more than the requests for reviews! What was most pleasing, was the spirit in which the cricket was played. There was little if any dissension as to umpiring decisions, and the evidence of unnecessary and personal sledging was minimal. Competition was fierce yet properly exerted. What a joy it was to see Jimmy Anderson take his 600th Test wicket, remembering that day in Cape Town on 22nd February 2003 when this young man shot to fame by dismissing four top Pakistan batsmen in taking 4–29 against Pakistan to enable England to win their opening game of the 2003 World Cup. His class was shown then and has remained a constant threat to the top batsmen in the world ever since. Anderson's skill has been recognised by players around the world, perhaps none more so than the tribute paid by the great Australian opening bowler, Glen McGrath who was so full of praise when he genuinely stated that "Anderson's skill level was higher than anything he could achieve". Not bad for the lad from Burnley. He looked world-class on 22nd February

2003 and has remained so up to September 2021. A truly brilliant career.

Over the past 15 years we have seen so many fluctuations with the performances of the English cricket team. From the highs of regaining the Ashes in 2005 and the magnificent defence of the Ashes in 2010–2011 to the white-washing by Australia in 2006–2007 and 2013–2014 and the 4–0 defeat in 2017–2018, we have seen England reach the pinnacle of being the best Test team in the world. We have seen India and South Africa reach the status of being the best team in the World and England has been hammered in certain series and then bounced back to win the following series comprehensively.

England has been blessed with many fine captains over this time. Vaughan, Strauss, Cook and now Root have excelled as both players and batsmen. They have been so well supported by batsmen of the skill of Pietersen, Bell, Trescothick and Collingwood and the indefatigable Flintoff. The bowling of Flintoff, Harmison, Hoggard, Swann and Panesar has been superb and the wicket keeping of Jones, Prior and Read has been excellent. Since the early part of 2014 we have seen the brilliance of Ben Stokes emerge as batsman, bowler and fielder. As a cricketing nation going back we have been blessed with all-rounders that can be compared with any in world cricket; the brilliance of Ben Stokes, the fierce determination of the lion-hearted Freddie Flintoff, the single-mindedness of Ian, now Lord Botham, the stubbornness of Trevor Bailey and going back into the 1920–1930s, the stout-hearted Maurice Tate who managed to take 38 wickets in Australia on the Ashes tour of 1924–1925, including the bowling of the equivalent of one hundred 6-ball overs in three of the Tests.

More recently, we have seen the emergence of some

excellent young cricketers of the likes of Burns, Sibley, Pope and Crawley on the batting side and from the bowling side we have seen the emergence Robinson and Archer, capable of bowling at 90 mph and the Curran brothers and Bess and Leach, all of whom will improve the more and more they play. These young players are all supported by the continued excellence of Anderson and Broad with over 1100 wickets between then and Woakes and Buttler with Bairstow and Wood in the wings.

Although the focus of this book has been on the longer form of the game, the confidence provided by England winning the 2019 World Cup has been considerable. With the young talent mentioned above English cricket could be entering an era of further success. Australia will always be a challenge, either home or away. India, with their batting strength and on their own wickets will always be difficult to beat. South Africa are going through a period of re-building after their magnificent period of excellence with the likes of Smith, Amla, Kallis, de Villiers, Steyn, Morkel and Philander all having retired. New Zealand will always fight way above their weight and there are such encouraging signs from West Indies and Pakistan with their excellent bowling attacks and improving batting. India has been excellent at home with their superb batting led by Kohli, and excellent seam bowling from Bumrah and Shami. It is perhaps fair to say that their spin bowling is not as strong as the days of Harbhajan and Kumble, although Ashwin and Axar Patel bowled so beautifully in the 2021 series in India.

With so many excellent cricketers around the World, just itching to reveal more of their wonderful talent cricket supporters all over the World have a treat in store once we get through this awful Covid 19 virus situation.

CHAPTER 21

Cricket after Covid 19

Cricket will not be the same as it was before the outbreak of the virus. The need for change has been focused as perhaps never before. The basic fact is that funding of cricket in the UK is going to be severely reduced from the levels of recent years. It is also fair to comment that without funding from the ECB (English and Wales Cricket Board), the majority of the first class and minor counties would not function.

The counties have been spoiled for many years by not having to rely upon their members and admission charges to keep themselves financially sound. Sponsorship is now a large source of revenue for every county and with the economic downturn this will be reduced substantially.

This will mean that counties will have to consider very carefully how they spend their income. One certainty is that the large cost of paying overseas cricketers high salaries will have to be substantially reduced. One positive effect of limiting the number of overseas cricketers is that this will encourage more aspiring young cricketers from the UK to try their hand in the professional game.

Counties will also need to carefully consider their staffing requirements. It seems that most counties have positions on their payrolls such as: Head Coach, Assistant Head Coach,

Academy Coach, Performance Analyst, Physiotherapist, Strength and Conditioning Coach and Assistant Coach. I would suggest that the majority of these positions have been as a result of the funding available and not as a necessity to improve the playing standards or the fitness of the players.

Cricket over the coming years will see a significant reduction in the number of overseas players and support staff. We will be reverting to the position in the twenty-year period after 1945 when counties were run by a secretary and the cricket run by the captain.

International cricket will also be faced with financial difficulties as a result of the Covid 19 pandemic. In 2017 the ECB signed a new media rights deal valued at £1.1billion to cover the years between 2020 and 2024. This deal will be used to fund a broad range of initiatives across the sport at all levels, including a guaranteed and unprecedented £475million to fund the county network — First-Class Counties, National Counties and County Boards. It is hoped that with the possibility of a reduced Test cricket programme over the foreseeable future this stream of income will not be adversely affected. The ECB is doing an excellent job in promoting cricket at all levels, including women, disability and the men's game. The gradual decline of cricket being played at secondary schools, other than at public schools, has required the ECB to take the initiative to ensure that our national summer game remains open to youngsters from all backgrounds, male and female, colour and creed.

To see the English cricket team and the English crowds celebrating the performances of cricketers of the class of Adil Rashid, Moeen Ali and Jofra Archer is such a delight in this racially conscious world in which we live. These fine cricketers and gentlemen have been accepted as being part of the English cricket team, as much as many fine cricketers of colour from previous generations, including Ranjitsinhji, Duleepsinhji, the Nawab of Pataudi, Basil D'Oliveira, Norman Cowans, Devon Malcolm, Roland and Mark Butcher and Phillip DeFreitas. Whilst each of these fine cricketers has been subjected to racial abuse from a few stupid individuals they have all conducted themselves with great dignity. Cricketers of all colours and creeds have been accepted within the Lancashire Leagues for many years with little if any racial abuse from spectators or opponents. It would perhaps be a very brave man to racially abuse some of the great West Indian fast bowlers, such as Wesley Hall, Charlie Griffith or Roy Gilchrist. A cricket ball travelling at 90 mph and weighing some five and a half ounces can do a lot of harm!

The county cricket played over three or four days is certainly in for a challenging time over the years ahead. It seems fair to say that the spectator at these county matches, either First Class or Minor Counties are generally aged and brought up in the tradition of "proper cricket". The numbers have reduced dramatically over the years, and even at grounds such as Lords, The Oval, Trent Bridge, Old Trafford and Edgbaston the paying public would never be sufficient to support the running of these clubs. Other Test playing grounds such as Durham, Cardiff and Southampton would struggle even more.

The traditionalists have to take their 'heads out of the sand' and accept the shorter formats of this wonderful game. The skills required in 20/20 and 50 over ODIs are equally important as those needed to do well at the longer games. These shorter versions are becoming more and more important in keeping the general public interested in this wonderful game. The Indian Premier League (IPL) and the Australian Big Bash have been tremendously successfully and enjoyable watching for cricket lovers around the World. There seems little doubt that The Hundred competition planned for 2020 will be successful when it does manage to get off the ground, hopefully in 2021.

To see cricketers of the skills of Bumrah, Rashid Khan, Ben Stokes, Shane Watson, David Warner, Jofra Archer and Jos Butler adjusting their talents for Test matches to One Day Internationals to 20/20 matches is quite wonderful. The skill required to hit a yorker from Bumrah, bowling at 90mph to the boundary or Jofra Archer bowling a slower ball at 50mph compared to his usual 85–90mph is immense. The leading bowler in 20/20 cricket over the past couple of years has been Rashid Khan, a young man from Afghanistan who by constant practice has turned himself into the top bowler and sought after by many of the top 20/20 teams from around the World. His skills have already made him a millionaire. Top cricketers such as Chris Gayle, Dwayne Bravo and Shane Watson are content to use their skills in 20/20 cricket as opposed to representing their countries in the longer forms of the game.

With excellent crowds watching the IPL and the Australia Big Bash, 20/20 cricket is here to stay. The popularity will catch on in the UK. The crowds enjoy the shorter game, as it can be played at times convenient for families, is more exciting and fast-moving and enjoyed by players with specialist skills. With the introduction of The Hundred it will be interesting to see how players will adjust their allegiances away from their counties or states towards their city bases? The teams, based on franchises are as follows:

Birmingham Phoenix (Edgbaston)
London Spirit (Lord's)
Manchester Originals (Emirates Old Trafford)
Northern Superchargers (Emerald Headingley)
Oval Invincibles (Kia Oval)
Southern Brave (Ageas Bowl)
Trent Rockets (Trent Bridge)
Welsh Fire (Sophia Gardens)

The Ladies cricket teams will also take part in The Hundred. The men's competition is poised to provide some exciting cricket with top stars from around the world joined by local players from the English counties. We are in for an absolute treat when the competition gets under way, hopefully in 2021. The teams taking part will initially include the following players:

Trent Rockets. Joe Root (England), Rashid Khan (Overseas), D'Arcy Short (Overseas), Lewis Gregory, Alex Hales (Local Icon), Nathan Coulter-Nile (Overseas), Harry Gurney (Local Icon), Steven Mullaney, Matthew Carter, Luke Wood, Tom Moores, Dawid Malan, Ben Cox, Luke Fletcher and Luke Wright.

Southern Brave. Jofra Archer (England), Andre Russell (Overseas), David Warner (Overseas), Liam Dawson, James Vince (Local Icon), Shadab Khan (Overseas), Chris Jordan (Local Icon), Tymal Mills, Ross Whiteley, Delray Rawlins, Ollie Pope, George Garton, Alex Davies, Max Waller and Craig Overton.

Northern Superchargers. Ben Stokes (England), Aaron Finch (Overseas), Mujeeb Ur Rahman (Overseas), Chris Lynn (Overseas), Adil Rashid (Local Icon), Adam Lyth, David Willey (Local Icon), Richard Gleeson, Ben Foakes, Tom

Kohler-Cadmore, David Wiese, Nathan Rimmington, Brydon Carse, Ed Barnard and John Simpson.

Welsh Fire. Jonny Bairstow (England), Mitchell Starc (Overseas), Steve Smith (Overseas), Colin Ingram (Local Icon), Tom Banton (Local Icon), Ben Duckett, Ravi Rampaul, Simon Harmer, Qais Ahmed (Overseas), Liam Plunkett, Ryan ten Doeschate, David Payne, Ryan Higgins, Danny Briggs and Leus du Plooy.

Oval Invincibles. Sam Curran (England), Sunil Narine (Overseas), Jason Roy (Local Icon), Sam Billings, Sandeep Lamichhane (Overseas), Rilee Rossouw, Tom Curran (Local Icon), Reece Topley, Hardus Viljoen, Fabian Allen (Overseas), Alex Blake, Will Jacks, Chris Wood, Nathan Sowter and Laurie Evans.

Manchester Originals. Jos Buttler (England), Imran Tahir (Overseas), Dane Vilas, Phil Salt, Tom Abell, Matt Parkinson (Local Icon), Saqib Mahmood (Local Icon), Daniel Christian (Overseas), Wayne Madsen, Wayne Parnell, Mitchell Santner (Overseas), Joe Clarke, Marchant de Lange, Ed Pollock and Eddie Byrom.

London Spirit. Rory Burns (England), Glenn Maxwell (Overseas), Eoin Morgan (Local Icon), Mohammad Nabi (Overseas), Mohammad Amir (Overseas), Roelof van der Merwe, Mark Wood, Joe Denly, Dan Lawrence (Local Icon), Mason Crane, Kyle Abbott, Adam Rossington, Zak Crawley, Jade Dernbach and Luis Reece.

Birmingham Phoenix. Chris Woakes (England), Liam Livingstone, Moeen Ali (Local Icon), Kane Williamson (Overseas), Ravi Bopara, Benny Howell, Tom Helm, Shaheen Afridi (overseas), Pat Brown (local icon), Adam Hose, Cameron Delport, Henry Brookes, Adam Zampa (Overseas),

Riki Wessels and Chris Cooke.

The make-up of the men's teams above will make for an exciting and unique competition. The women's competitions will include the exceptionally talented international stars such as:

Australia skipper Meg Lanning will join **Welsh Fire**. South Africa's Lizelle Lee heads to **Manchester Originals**. England's Tammy Beaumont will join her international captain Heather Knight at **London Spirit**. The pair last played together at Lord's when England lifted the ICC Women's World Cup in 2017. It's **Birmingham Phoenix** for hard-hitting New Zealand all-rounder Sophie Devine. Devine's Kiwi compatriot Suzie Bates is now officially a **Southern Brave** player. South London's **Oval Invincibles** welcome South Africa captain Dane van Niekerk. England duo Nat Sciver and Katherine Brunt, who were **Trent Rockets** first two picks on October 3, will have young Australia spinner Sophie Molineux joining them. Alyssa Healy — who smashed a record-breaking 148 against the West Indies — is heading to **Northern Superchargers.**

Cricket supporters of all backgrounds and preferences have enjoyed the spectacle of seeing stars from around the World competing against local born English cricketers. With excellent crowds the interest in cricket has been rejuvenated.

What of the future of Test cricket? The Ashes series between England and Australia will always be keenly contested, wherever the games are played. England's Test matches at home will also be well supported against any of the Test playing countries. England, when they play away will be well supported by the "Barmy Army. Test matches between South Africa and Australia and India against Pakistan will always be keenly contested. Perhaps it is reasonable to say that 5-day Test matches will continue to be supported by traditionalists wherever cricket is played but the real future of cricket as a spectator sport is in the 20/20 game and the 50-overs ODIs.

The longer, 3–4-day cricket around the world, will continue to be played before ever-reducing crowds and will always require substantial subsidizing from the income gained by television fees generated from the shorter versions of the game. It is hoped that the authorities in control of cricket within the UK will continue to recognise the importance of county teams below the first-class county structure. So many brilliant cricketers have cut their teeth in playing 'minor county' cricket, and it would be a crying shame to see the 3-day game being further reduced. Players of the ilk of Bill Edrich, John Edrich, Peter Parfitt, Clive Radley and Olly Stone have all learned their basic skills playing for Norfolk prior to joining First-class counties leading to international selection. Good club cricketers need to have the opportunity to represent their own counties as an encouragement to play at a higher level.

Perhaps the most famous and best cricketer that ever graced "Minor County" cricket was Sydney Barnes who played for Staffordshire between 1904–1914 and from 1924–1935. He took 1432 wickets for Staffordshire at less than 9 runs per wicket. He took 189 wickets in 27 Test matches played solely against Australia and South Africa at 16.43 runs per wicket. In the four-Test series against South Africa in 1913–1914 he took 49 wickets at 10.93 runs per wicket. In the Bradford League playing for Saltaire he took a total of 904 wickets at 5.26 runs per wicket. These are phenomenal figures in all levels of cricket.

Herbert Sutcliffe and George Hirst, both true greats of the game agreed that "Sydney Barnes was the greatest bowler there has ever been and what's more the greatest bowler there ever will be". They may have reflected upon this statement had they seen Shane Warne, Fred Trueman, Denis Lillee, Glen McGrath and Jimmy Anderson bowl in later years.

The great Australian batsman Clem Hill told Neville Cardus that, on a perfect wicket, "Barnes could swing the new ball in and out "very late", could spin from the ground, pitch on the leg stump and miss the off". He bowled at a pace that varied between medium and fast medium.

Sydney Barnes played little first-class cricket, apart from Test matches. He played limited matches for Lancashire and Warwickshire, but because of being paid more for playing League cricket he saw his future away from the county cricket circuit. The fact that he was able to move from League to Minor Counties straight into the England XI was evidence of this man's ability.

Minor Counties cricket, or 'National Counties' as it is now called, should always be considered important as being a means of encouraging younger cricketers who do not intend to pursue a full-time career in the game, yet still wish to play cricket at the highest level available. The Minor Counties Championship was formed in 1895 with Norfolk being one of the original counties involved. Norfolk County Cricket Club had been set up in 1827, when it was considered to be 'second only to the Marylebone Club' and was re-constituted in 1881.

It should also be recalled that the last county to be admitted into the First-Class Championship was Durham in 1992, since then they have won the Championship on three occasions, and have been able to provide cricketers of the highest skill with Ben Stokes, Steve Harmison, Paul Collingwood and Mark Wood springing to mind. Durham Cricket Club was formed in 1882 and it took a great amount of effort, dedication and financial input to make it the club it is today, and with a ground accepted for Test matches.

Other Minor Counties clubs located in areas surrounded by large populations, such as Staffordshire or Northumberland, given the right stimulus with suitable financial backing may well seek to become First Class counties. The existing Minor Counties will always struggle to get too involved with day/night 20/20 or one-day limited over cricket, simply as a result of funding for lighting systems suitable for such games. Great care needs to be given to the future of Minor Counties cricket. It has been said by a certain ex-England captain that "Minor Counties cricket is a waste of time and resources". This attitude throws away 125 years of tradition in assisting our national game to develop whereby good players are able to graduate from school to club to county to international level. To do away with Minor Counties cricket could be seen as similar as the thought to abolish the lower levels of the Football Leagues. Jamie Vardy the England striker and star of Leicester City Football Club was able to advance his career from Stockbridge Park Steels to Northern Premier League team FC Halifax then to Conference Premier League Fleetwood Town and then to Leicester City enabling them to win the Premier League in 2015-2016. He has been able to score goals at every level. Young cricketers need to see the way ahead for improving their skills and advance to a higher level of attainment.

It is so very encouraging to read in 'The Cricketer-

Summer 2020' that the ECB has recently appointed Richard Logan, an ex-professional seamer, to the position of Operations Manager of the National Counties Cricket Association.

The generous support from the ECB to the current first-class counties has enabled the hiring of cricketers from overseas, and this practice needs to be questioned as to a means of encouraging young players from this country to take up the game.

Turning briefly to club cricket, it is noticeable that teams in the 2nd tier of their county club organisations are able to hire overseas players. Sponsorship is welcomed but with the downturn in the economy as a result of Covid 19 will mean that less money will be available for expensive and unnecessary overseas professionals. The egos of certain sponsors for their teams to win everything will be sorely tested. It is hoped that with less money in the game over the coming years, traditional values associated with cricket will return, with players accepting Umpire's decisions, no sledging intended to destruct the batsman's state of mind and dare I say 'players prepared to walk other than when they run out of petrol!'

The game of cricket has changed over many years, yet there is no need to lower the values enmeshed into the game. Whether it be Test matches, ODIs or 20/20 matches values still matter. Excessive appealing is cheating as is a batsman standing his ground when he knows that he has hit the ball. Adam Gilchrist's action of walking will be far more appreciated than a batsman scoring a century when he knows that he was caught but given not out. The game of Golf has its own rules and respected by the vast majority of players who are prepared to draw attention to their own infringements of the rules. The sportsmanship shown by Jack Nicklaus in conceding a metre-long putt to Tony Jacklin to half the Ryder Cup in 1969 will be far more remembered than his string of victories in majors over the years.

Cricket will survive this Covid 19 crisis as it has survived the two world wars and on-going conflicts around the world. It has been so refreshing to see Sri Lanka win the World Cup, to see Bangladesh beginning to compete at the highest level, to see Afghanistan emerging as a Test nation. Despite the horrendous situation in Zimbabwe, they can still produce cricketers of high skill. Within the British Isles we see Ireland and Scotland producing teams capable of beating England in ODIs.

Whilst funding levels will change over the coming years, sensible measures are being put in place to introduce new formats, such as The Hundred, the Big Bash and the IPL to promote the game to millions. Test cricket will need to change with better floodlighting, different coloured balls and improved over rates. Traditionalists will have to change their approach and appreciation of the modern 20/20 and ODI cricket. County cricket will simply not survive without the shorter game and cricket enthusiasts will appreciate the skills displayed in the shorter game. The recent 20/20 series against Pakistan and Australia have been wonderful for the game and long may the shorter version remain. The past fifty years has seen the introduction of the World Cup, initially a 60 over per side competition, reduced to 50 over per side. The first World Cup/Tournament was won by India in South Africa in 2007.

This wonderful game has changed so much over the years, yet with good management and governance will survive and improve. Players will adapt their techniques but the basic tenets of the game of hitting the ball and bowling the right delivery will always prevail.

Hampton Court Green 1836 The Ashes 2005 What will this wonderful game look like in 2100?